MW00328521

MAXIMUM
IMPACT

———

Maxim's Quiet Rise as Silicon Valley's
Most Prolific Analog Chip Maker

ED,
I REALLY ENJOYED AUTHORING THIS BOOK. THE
STORIES WILL LET YOU EXPERIENCE THE CULTURE
YOU ARE ACQUIRING. IT'S A FUN READ!
WISH YOU THE BEST...

TUNG

Published in the United States – First edition, May 2019
ISBN: 978-1-7338580-3-8

Author: Tunç Doluca
Writer: Kevin Paterson
Copy Editor: Beth Bruno
Cover: Anurup Ghosh
Inside Book Design: Olivier Darbonville

Published by Doluca Publishing

www.MaximumImpactBook.com

. . . for purchasing *Maximum Impact*.

Please write a REVIEW of this book on
Amazon. We need your feedback.

Your review will help spread awareness of
this impactful story.

DEDICATION

This book is dedicated to the tireless
employees of Maxim, past and present.
They made it all happen. So did their
families that gave strong support during
the countless hours spent building a
great company. In addition, this book is
dedicated to future employees who will
carry the company to new heights.

In honor of Maxim's founding CEO,
all profits from this book will be donated
to Jack Gifford's favorite charity,
East Palo Alto Tennis & Tutoring in
East Palo Alto, California.

THANKS

I would like to sincerely thank all the founders and employees of Maxim for their direct contributions to this book. Though we could have interviewed many more current and former employees for interesting stories during the building of Maxim, we had to draw the line somewhere as stories of Maxim and its ventures are boundless.

In addition to those interviewed, many more colleagues made valuable contributions to Maxim in the early years, the likes of Chuck Thurber, Pirooz Parvarandeh, Dave Timm, Charlie Allen, Len Sherman, Roger Fuller, and Robert Sheer, to name a few. I did not leave out anyone on purpose, but only because I could only pick a handful.

It would not be possible to capture the full extent of passion, effort, ideas, innovation, and pure genius that has built Maxim. However, I know that today a unique semiconductor company stands as an ongoing testament to Maxim's people and their significant contributions.

ENDORSEMENTS

———————

"Maximum Impact provides a fascinating behind-the-scenes view into the creation of one of the most successful technology companies in history. Tunç Doluca captures the brash, courageous and often outrageous character of the founders of the early semiconductor industry. Anyone interested in learning how today's technology companies were created and what it takes to become successful in the innovation age should read this book."

MATTHEW MASSENGILL, *Chairman of the Board, Western Digital Corporation*

"Maximum Impact is the story of a truly great Silicon Valley company and the visionary leader who made an enormous impact on the semiconductor industry during his storied career."

MATT MURPHY, *President & CEO, Marvell Semiconductor*

"I look at Jack and Maxim as premier examples of what the semiconductor industry is really all about. I encourage anyone who is interested in how to start and run a successful company, to read this great book."

RAY ZINN, *Co-founder, Chairman, CEO and President, Micrel Semiconductor*

"*Maximum Impact* captures a snapshot of the 'characters of Silicon Valley.' Jack Gifford was a model of knowledge, skills and abilities with a few quirks to go along! He and his team are some of the legendary Greats in the Valley."

RICK HILL, *Chairman of the Board, Marvell Technology Group*

"I have watched many electronics companies come and go. Maxim Integrated is one I have watched for a long time. *Maximum Impact* is a great story that puts Silicon Valley's rise into context and provides an inside look at Maxim's growth and many challenges."

WILLIAM WONG, *Senior Technology Editor, Electronic Design*

"This is my kind of book—it shows the highs and the lows, successes and stresses of Maxim in that highly competitive semiconductor business. It's all about the people who made it happen. Doluca has done a superb job of bringing readers the adventures of the early founders and creative designers in a very competitive world. We learn much about Jack Gifford, semiconductor veteran and first CEO of Maxim, the man who brought huge growth and return to shareholders and made Maxim the envy of most Silicon Valley semiconductor giants.

This book is for anyone interested in how a fledgling company pushes through its growing pains, endures challenges, and celebrates its people."

STEVE TARANOVICH, *Senior Technical Editor, EDN Network, Analog and Power*

FOREWORD

by Bill Sullivan

———————

The Maxim story traces the steps of one of the most successful companies in the semiconductor analog marketplace.

When Tunç inquired about my interest in writing the foreword for this book about Maxim, I immediately said, "Yes." The story of Maxim and its charismatic founder, Jack Gifford, had to be shared. As a CEO in Silicon Valley for many years, and as a Maxim board director since December of 2015, I had become both familiar and greatly impressed by the company history.

This is a story of a brilliant founding CEO who wrote a business plan on two and a half pages, raised $5-million in the early 1980s and assembled a team of world-class designers to implement the plan, almost flawlessly. It's also the tale of an incredibly demanding founder, who implemented many unconventional management practices (some that may be frowned on today)—all in pursuit of its now-legendary business success and ingenuity. The creation of Maxim is a story of incredible drive, focus and desire to win.

My first direct encounter with Maxim was in the early 1990s while I was R&D manager of HP's Optical Communication Division. We wanted the Maxim designers to develop analog chips for a fiber optic transceiver that would transmit and receive data at a fraction of the cost of the existing solution. Maxim's quote exceeded our design cost objectives, and when I asked the Maxim's vice president, Bill Levin, why the quote was so high, he launched into a lengthy introduction to "return on engineer design time" (RODT).

I was fascinated that Maxim measured the economic return of every design hour in the company. I thought HP measured everything, but this was beyond anything I had ever heard. It was then that I began to recognize that Maxim possessed a unique view of how to successfully measure and deploy engineering resources. To this day, Maxim is still the most financially disciplined and focused company I have ever known.

Maximum Impact provides compelling insights into many of the powerful business keys that helped create the phenomenal success embodied by Maxim over the years. The author will take you on an exhilarating journey through the tumultuous early days of Silicon Valley. You'll enjoy this story through the eyes of a captivating founding CEO and his companions, as they help create transformational technology.

Bill Sullivan

Chairman of the Board of Maxim Integrated since 2015

*Also, former CEO of Agilent Technologies

CONTENTS

Snapshots of Maxim's founding years

PART 3: GROWTH

PART 4: LEGACY

PART ONE

CONCEPTION

INTRODUCTION
TO A LEGEND

"This is the tale of the most successful semiconductor company you've never heard of. Formerly run by a charismatic CEO you've never seen on TV, it makes unglamorous products you'd never consider requesting by name, unlike that other chipmaker. Meet [Jack] John F. Gifford, a gruff and plainspoken semiconductor veteran who has built Maxim Integrated Products into one of Silicon Valley's most profitable makers of analog integrated circuits. How good is Maxim? A $1,000 investment in the Sunnyvale, California company's 1988 initial public offering would be worth $93,120 today, a 9,212 percent increase. A similar investment in Intel, by contrast, would be worth $24,650, and in Advanced Micro Devices, just $3,770."

ADAM LASHINSKY, APRIL 30TH, 2001[1]

M any in Silicon Valley and beyond may dispute this *Fortune* magazine article's title dubbing Maxim Integrated as "The Valley's Best Chipmaker."[2] However, no one who knows this analog integrated circuit (IC) maker's achievements would question its place among the tech companies that have made a great industry impact.

As proof of the company's ranking alongside the most successful tech companies, its late CEO—blunt, straight-talking Jack Gifford—said in a 2001 interview: "We have returned . . . to our shareholders forty-nine percent per year growth for the last fourteen years. No other company in the history of the world's done that. Year after year. Forty-nine percent per year! If you had bought the company stock in 1989, then you'd have gotten a forty-nine percent increase per year. Per year. So . . . we're a legend."[3]

Punch the numbers into your compound interest calculator, and you'll see that this 14-year profit adds up to a 266-times increase. Maxim's record speaks for itself. With the help of its wildly successful MAX232 product, the company recorded its first profits in 1987, only three years after its founding, and has continued its profit streak every year since going public in 1988. Its annual revenue hit $500-million in the 1998 fiscal year and rocketed to $2.47-billion in 2011.

A company's early and later success can be measured in many ways—revenue, profit, growth, market cap, renown, or even influence. However, in this technological era, evidenced by a dramatically burgeoning Silicon Valley, ingenuity has become the measure above all others. And it's here that Maxim Integrated, especially during its first 10 to 15 years, has stood head and shoulders above its tech rivals. In its heyday, Maxim was an ingenuity machine, pumping out hundreds of new products every year. In the early 2000s, it introduced a record 500+ new products in a single year—that is two new products on average every business day! Yes, such immense creativity and execution are unheard of. And today, the company is still quietly prolific, having amassed and now marketing roughly 10,000 products in its analog and mixed signal stable. At its founding, Maxim took the road less sexy and carved a niche by innovating and making these types of chips, rather than entering the other side of the circuit market, the newly booming digital chip market.

Maxim's team of engineering innovators, always its most prized asset, has not just produced a historic number of tech inventions. They have enabled the company to create consistent record growth and extensive global impact. Today, its integrated circuits are hidden in the bowels of tens of thousands of different product types and likely tens of billions of products worldwide. From smartphones, laptops, and tablets to most electronic devices in the industrial, healthcare, communications, data center, and automotive sectors, Maxim has made its mark. Yes, that mark has often been quiet and hidden, not one that shouts to the world like the names Apple or Intel, but it's certainly one made with great impact.

However, my goal in this book is not just to highlight the great success of Maxim. More importantly, I want to tell the inspirational rags-to-riches story of a present-day semiconductor legend, as Jack would call it, and unpack the wealth of success keys the story reveals. This book is not intended to comprehensively document the era's tech industry, nor the environment we call Silicon Valley. Nor is it intended to necessarily endorse or condone every behavior of the leadership team and company since the norms today are quite different than they were 25 plus years ago. Rather, I want to take you on a wild ride—with its charismatic CEO (the Maxim story's main character), its crew of genius founders, and its employees—filled with the fun and history-making adventures that many say have made the company a quiet legend in the tech universe. And, if it seems like I've made some pretty big claims so far, it's because I want to celebrate the generation of Maxim founders who came before me by unveiling their often unpromoted achievements.

As the current CEO, who in 2007 succeeded the renowned Jack Gifford, I have closely watched Maxim's remarkable rise in the tech world. I joined the founding team in 1984, just after the company's start in 1983. Since that time, I learned from and was trained by the best in the business. During my tenure at Maxim, I often participated in or listened with fascination to the extraordinary founders' war stories of conquest, competition, and prolific ingenuity. Maxim had an astounding rise after its formation. The hard-driving culture of the CEO, founders, and early employees made this possible.

In 2009, many in the technology world, especially we at Maxim, were deeply impacted by the shocking news that the company's founder and long-time CEO, Jack Gifford, had suddenly passed away. The world may know him as one of the "founding fathers" of the analog chip industry, but Silicon Valley and the wider tech biosphere know him for his most important legacy: Maxim Integrated, or just Maxim, as it is often referred to in The Valley. Jack built a company from the ground up to $2-billion in sales—a specialized integrated circuit innovator with an unparalleled string of ingenious products that include many thousands of cutting-edge microchip inventions. These accomplishments also provided income for tens of thousands of employees and their families over the years.

Yes, Jack was a tough manager who perfected the art of tough love. Many are the unique and legendary water cooler stories shared about him at tech companies in recent decades; and most are completely true. But very few individuals can claim to have left such a significant mark on so many during their lives as Jack did.

This story needs to be told for the benefit of a new generation of employees, entrepreneurs, and company leaders. Though this book tells the tale of a great semiconductor company, its founding CEO and his larger-than-life personality has inevitably taken center stage within many of these pages. The adventures of Jack and Maxim's other founders also embody business lessons and a legacy that should be memorialized for the sake of those who carry the torch of progress forward.

When I proposed to Jack, in 2006, the commissioning of a book about the amazing rise of the company, he summarily rejected my proposal. "Only leaders with big egos write such books," he stated in true, brusque Gifford fashion.

However, recently, I realized that three of the original founders, including Jack, have now, unfortunately, passed away. During the writing of this book we also lost Fred Beck, arguably the founders' founder for Maxim. That phrase, as applied to Fred Beck, will make sense as you read on. I felt like the story was destined to fade, along with memories, and soon to be forgotten beneath the sands of time. This would be a shame.

The company and its founders had to be honored. So, I decided to interview those still with us who have experienced and observed the Maxim journey. All those quoted were interviewed for this book, unless other sources are quoted and referenced. In this book, I tell the story of the company and its powerful impact on the industry. And to give you a window into the colorful characters that created this epic tale, I will retell, with the best recollections of all involved, the stories of the formative days of technology and Maxim. I'll also widely quote Jack Gifford, giving you a taste of his flamboyant and no-nonsense personality. In Chapter 28, for the sake of a more unbiased and detached perspective, longtime Maxim board director and one of the original investors in Maxim, Jim Bergman, tells the more recent story of the company's transition to the *New Era*, under my leadership.

However, the focus of this book is mainly on the adventures of the early founders of Maxim. Without them and their fearless foresight, the company would not have made its mark on tech history. This is their extraordinary story.

Tunç Doluca
CEO, Maxim Integrated

2019

01

HUMBLE
BEGINNINGS

"Sometimes the world benefits when we can't do what we think we'd like to do. Such is the case with Jack Gifford, who created a business foundation and environment that fostered major technological advances, particularly in analog and power electronics. His many achievements have even led him to be known as one of the 'founding fathers' of the analog industry."

DORRIS KILBANE[1]

L ike many high achievers, Jack Gifford started out in humble surroundings, growing up around the L.A. docks in a blue-collar home. His orphaned father, Frank Gifford, grew up in a steel mill town in Homestead, Pennsylvania, leaving at the age of 14 to find his fortune in the oil fields of Oklahoma, Ohio, Montana, Texas, and California. During those early years, Frank made money entertaining the oil field workers by prize fighting. He also played professional baseball.

"He was actually good enough that the Pittsburgh Pirates signed [him], and he played a year in the major leagues," said Gifford of his father in a 2002 interview.[2] "By the time he got to California, he was about 37 years old and his playing days and fighting days were pretty much coming to an end."[3] In California, his father met the youngest sister of one of his oil field friends, and he married her in 1938. He landed a job "digging ditches" for Mobile Oil in Los Angeles.

According to Gifford, his mother's family left the extreme drought, poverty, and dust storms of the Dust Bowl years in Oklahoma and surrounding states during the Great Depression. His parents, he said, were "pretty grass roots people."[4] Jack Gifford was born in 1941, grew up in Los Angeles, and eventually attended Banning High School, in the rough harbor neighborhood. Years later, his father worked his way up to a supervisory position at the oil refinery.

After completing high school, Jack did his father proud, attending the University of California, Los Angeles (UCLA), on a full baseball scholarship. During his sophomore year, in 1960, he married his high school sweetheart, Rhodine. He was 19 and she was 18. The newlyweds quickly moved to a one-bedroom apartment in the Westwood area. Jack's scholarship of $95 a month barely paid the rent, so to help pay the bills, Rhodine went to work at a wheelchair company in Santa Monica. Soon, the Giffords' first baby arrived, and they needed to hire a babysitter to help during the day.

Jack was passionate about baseball and dreamed of playing professionally. However, as he said, he would need to succeed in his college endeavors first. "Attending UCLA was a tremendous culture shock for me coming from the docks."[5] Though he was not prepared for the academic challenges of the university, Jack's tough, fighting, family background had cultivated in him the tenacity he would need to overcome those challenges.

During his first weeks at UCLA, says Rhodine, he became quite overwhelmed by the rigor, as compared to what he was used to in high school. So, he went outside and sat down under a tree to "get himself together and make up his mind that he was going to get through school," she says. There he resolved that "he was going to get through college, because he knew that was important to being successful." Knowing that his father had not had the chance to graduate from high school, Gifford was determined to honor his father and take advantage of his opportunity. It was at this pivotal time that Gifford's competitive nature, fostered by playing sports, kicked into overdrive. He exuded an intense drive and passion for success, says Rhodine, a 100 percent commitment to everything he put his mind to. "He was a type A personality. He was very competitive… always wanted to win, but not at the cost of hurting anybody. It was just his own personal desire to win and achieve."

However, Jack never dreamed of the kind of remarkable business success he would later experience in the tech world. "We did not grow up with a lifestyle that enabled either one of us to even imagine that he would start a company or be CEO of a company," says Rhodine. "It was not even in our dreams. When we were first married . . . our first goal was for him to graduate from college and get a job. Our second goal was to buy a home."

It was during those challenging but joyful years at UCLA that Gifford was forced to decide between his aspiration to play pro baseball and his greater desire for a family. He loved playing baseball during those college days, she said, and even received a career offer from the same major league team his father played for, the Pittsburgh Pirates. However, in those days, professional baseball wasn't as lucrative as it is today, and economically, it just wouldn't work, if he was to raise and support his young family.

That's when Jack developed a new passion for electronics and made the pivotal decision to pursue a career in engineering instead, a decision that would not only benefit him and his family but would ultimately impact the world. He graduated from UCLA in 1963 with a Bachelor of Science in Electrical Engineering (BSEE) and was soon recruited into the "major leagues" of Silicon Valley. There Gifford would providentially meet the other star players he would team up with to enter a new high-stakes business World Series in the budding technology industry.

THE FAIRCHILD
REFORMATION

"I made my mind up that they were going to have trouble getting rid of me, and… began building a very competent analog organization at Fairchild, which ended up becoming the most competent in the world."

JACK GIFFORD[1]

After graduating from UCLA, Gifford would experience his next great challenge and culture shock by entering the electronics industry, and later, Silicon Valley. "It was a tremendously vibrant, fast-moving business," he said in a *Silicon Genesis* interview. "So, my background was probably very good for the business we ended up in. I had a competitive background from athletics."[2] He immediately started his career at the age of 22 as an entry-level design engineer, working for a startup company, Electronic Specialties, in the Los Angeles area.

While there, according to Jack's wife Rhodine, Don Valentine and Jerry Sanders, now legendary Silicon Valley executives who were working in sales at Fairchild Semiconductor at the time, made a business call. Coincidentally, during that visit, the two men met the young Jack Gifford in a meeting, and something about him caught their attention.

A few months later, Fairchild contacted Gifford for an interview. He was very excited about this big break, said Rhodine, as he equated Fairchild in those days to the famed New York Yankees baseball franchise. During that fortuitous meeting, Fairchild Semiconductor drafted Gifford, at the age of 24, from his "farm team" into the "big leagues."

Apparently, Valentine, sales head at Fairchild, and Sanders, a company salesman, and later, CEO of Advanced Micro Devices (AMD), had waited some time to arrange that interview, while they reorganized their sales force to give Gifford the position and an account they had already chosen for him. Despite his previous design engineer role, the company insisted on starting him out as a salesman, calling on Hughes Aircraft. In this position, Gifford began to learn and hone the skills that would allow him to later create sales and marketing strategies to launch several cutting-edge tech companies.

He worked for a year "with the most talented, aggressive, sales organization the world has ever seen... and ended up in the lower management levels of Fairchild in 1965."[3] The fast paced semiconductor industry, says Rhodine, was "a real eye opener for both of us. That was our first exposure to working really long hours in a more than Monday through Friday job." However, she says, it was at Fairchild that the Giffords realized that Jack had stumbled into the next gold rush industry, and that "maybe we would not have to worry about finances or money" ever again.

Fairchild Semiconductor dominated its industry at the time and would soon become a creative dynamo that would build the foundation for the modern-day tech revolution. The company was formed by the notorious "traitorous eight," a group of eight employees from Shockley Semiconductor Laboratory who left to found Fairchild in 1957. The previous year, according to Wikipedia, William Shockley had "recruited a group of young PhD graduates" with the goal of developing new semiconductor devices.[4] "While Shockley had received a Nobel Prize in Physics and was an experienced researcher and teacher, his management of the group was authoritarian and unpopular."[5] When the research focus didn't prove fruitful, and the team's demands for Shockley to be replaced were rejected, the eight tech pioneers—Julius Blank, Victor Grinich, Jean Hoerni, Eugene Kleiner, Jay Last, Gordon Moore, Robert Noyce, and Sheldon Roberts—left to start their own company. "Shockley described their leaving as a 'betrayal.'"[6]

In September 1957, after the group reached a business agreement with Sherman Fairchild—American businessman, investor, inventor, and founder of over 70 companies—they pioneered Fairchild Semiconductor. The new company quickly carved out its niche as a leader of the semiconductor industry. Members of the "traitorous eight" were between 26 and 33 years of age, and six of them held a Ph.D. "While Hoerni was an experienced scientist, only Noyce was involved in semiconductor research, and only Grinich had experience in electronics."[7]

"In 1960 it became an incubator of Silicon Valley, and was directly or indirectly involved in the creation of dozens of corporations such as AMD and Intel. These many spin-off companies came to be known as 'Fairchildren.'"[8] Though this book is not intended to fully document these companies, nor the story of Silicon Valley's tech industry, hopefully, this wider history will give you a glimpse into the world within which Gifford and his Maxim colleagues arose.

Gifford's next big break came in 1965, a year after entering the "Wild Fairchild West." That story began hundreds of miles north, at Fairchild's Mountain View, California, location with soon-to-be renowned applications engineer, Bob Widlar. In his blog, *Analog Footsteps*, Todd Nelson describes Widlar's legendary introduction to Fairchild: "His interview with Fairchild Research and Development (R&D) manager Heinz Ruegg didn't go well," especially when Widlar told him what he thought about Fairchild's analog circuit engineers' work: 'What they are doing is bull---t.'"[9] Fortunately for Widlar and the world, the applications engineering division head, John Hulme, saw past his crusty exterior. From the interview and Widlar's previous work with Ball Brothers, John Hulme somehow recognized an engineering genius and hired him "despite objections from the first-round interviewers."[10]

Widlar, with the help of Dave Talbert and Hung-Chang's "theory of compensated devices," began designing the now-famed μA702, the industry's first true linear integrated circuit and first monolithic operational amplifier.[11] At Fairchild, said Gifford, he and Vic Grinich were two of the few employees that:

> *". . . had any real understanding of gain and phase relationships, and how amplifiers worked. We had a design background and Bob (Widlar) recognized that through dealing with me as a salesman. Then, as he and Dave Talbert developed the μA702, they bootlegged samples out to myself and Floyd Kvamme and asked us to see if customers were interested in it, as it was a very complicated circuit. We began to start explaining the circuit. As we sold this idea . . . there became a huge interest in the product."* [12]

Though Widlar was "very much a radical" and perhaps "not altogether stable," he secretly and determinedly began designing this amplifier and aggressively pursuing the connections that would make it successful.[13] Apparently, he and Talbert, both young and heavy drinkers, moonlighted outside of work hours developing the amplifier process that would "give them

35-volt breakdowns."[14] When Gifford and Kvamme started showing the circuit to the market, Gifford says, "The reaction was phenomenal" because it would reduce board sizes dramatically. "Most of the computing that was done in the defense industry in those days was done fundamentally with analog [as opposed to digital] computing, and so this thing was a huge advantage to reducing size and weight."[15]

Though Widlar had designed the circuit without any company sponsorship, when Fairchild's Tom Bay and Bob Noyce learned about the revolutionary invention, they told him they wanted to make a product line out of it. Then, as Gifford put it, Widlar, this junior applications engineer:

> "... just looked at 'em both... and he says 'The hell you are.' He's talking to Tom Bay and Bob Noyce, two of the most sophisticated, impressive people that I've ever met and he's telling 'em 'get screwed, you're not gonna do this.' The next day they asked, 'Why not?' And he said, 'Well, first of all, you guys don't know what you're talking about, you don't know what the circuit is, you don't know how it works. And, furthermore, no one in the company knows how it works and is used. I'm not gonna let you ruin my reputation.'"[16]

Bay and Noyce were furious and "would have killed him, but... it would have been like killing the golden goose," said Gifford.[17]

They eventually struck a deal with Widlar: If they found a product manager he agreed to, they could take the product to market; however, Widlar interviewed 15 accomplished product managers and rejected them all. Then, according to Gifford, Bay and Noyce, in frustration, asked the renegade engineer: "Well... who would you accept?"

"There's this kid called Gifford down in L.A . . . he knows amplifiers," answered Widlar.

"Gifford, who's Gifford?"[18]

Shortly thereafter, Gifford was flying to Sunnyvale, California for an interview. "It couldn't have lasted ten minutes," he said. "They call me the next day and they say, 'Well ... get your house for sale. You're going to be the Linear Circuit Product Manager. And, I went, wow!"[19] As history records it, in 1965, at the age of 26, Gifford became the industry's first linear (analog) integrated circuit product manager, he says, with a nice, "big office ... the first office I'd ever had in my life."[20]

When Gifford arrived to view his new digs, a welcoming duo of senior managers walked in and asked, "Well ... how do you like this office?"

"Oh, this is nice," replied Gifford.

"Well, don't get used to it. You're going to be out of here in ninety days," they remarked as they walked out laughing.[21]

Gifford soon discovered that the hiring managers had brought in "the kid" to appease Widlar and get the μA702 product announced. Then they planned to send him back to his original post. However, as a rookie manager, says Gifford, "I made my mind up that they were going to have trouble getting rid of me, and ... began building a very competent analog organization at Fairchild, which ended up becoming the most competent in the world."[22]

Analog chips, as opposed to digital chips—the other sector of the circuit market—process signals that represent gradations of real-world phenomena such as sound, speed, pressure, and temperature. Digital circuits, the most well-known of the two types of chips, can only differentiate between "on" and "off" signals, manipulating or storing data as the numeral 1 or 0. Mixed signal circuit boards combine analog and digital chips.

During that first year as manager, Gifford worked carefully with the eccentric and temperamental engineer. "A major one of my responsibilities was babysitting Bob Widlar. And he would almost talk to nobody ... [besides me] if I could get him in the right mood," said Gifford. "He was still secretive as hell."[23]

However, during his short career, Widlar invented the basic building blocks of analog integrated circuits (ICs), including the first mass-produced operational amplifier ICs (both the μA702, and μA709), the first integrated voltage regulator ICs (μA723), and many other revolutionary products. Each of his circuits included, states Wikipedia, "at least one feature which was far ahead of the crowd" and became a "product champion" in its class.[24] They made his employers, Fairchild Semiconductor, and later, National Semiconductor, the leaders in linear integrated circuits.[25]

By November 1965, Widlar and Talbert realized that Fairchild would not cut them in on the windfall profits they were making as a result of their designs. So, they accepted offers to join National Semiconductor in Santa Clara, California. Widlar would only write one line on his Fairchild exit interview form: "I want to be RICH!" He quickly accepted 20,000 stock option shares from National valued at $5 each. He told Hulme, his division head at Fairchild, that the only thing that could keep him with them was "one million tax-free by whatever way you choose."[26]

A few years later, already a "legendary chip designer" at the age of 33, Widlar voluntarily retired into a hideout in Mexico, becoming Silicon Valley's "most celebrated dropout."[27] Four years later he returned to National Semiconductor as a contractor. Widlar lived the life of an alcoholic genius, who went on all-night-long bar binges.[28] According to Jack Gifford, Widlar liked to harass and fight others when drunk but regularly overestimated his own abilities in such confrontations. On one occasion he was "absolutely clocked" by the offended Mike Scott, a future CEO of Apple Inc.[29] Charlie Sporck, former CEO of National Semiconductor, retells another incident: During a European roadshow Widlar got drunk and publicly refused to speak to the audience unless he got more gin. Sporck says, "We had no choice. We had to get his glass filled up. And then he went on with the lecture." But, "he was just so damn smart . . . even drunk he could just wow these people."[30] People would cross the country "just to listen to him lecture on circuit design . . . and he would do it half smashed most of the time. But he really popularized the use of analog circuits in microchips."[31] If it weren't for Widlar's persuasive, bold, aggressive personality, said Gifford, the industry would not have grown as it did. "So, he not only designed the circuits; he made them acceptable." Widlar was "more than a genius," said Gifford. "He was insane" and "the meanest, toughest son-of-a-b--ch you've ever seen."[32] But he was the right person at that time in history for helping launch the burgeoning analog industry.

"Widlar's eccentric, outspoken personality and his bohemian lifestyle made him the *enfant terrible* of Silicon Valley. He is remembered in legends, myths, and anecdotes that are largely true."[33] According to Bo Lojek, author of *History of Semiconductor Engineering*, he was "more an artist than an engineer."[34]

Besides his fortuitous encounter with Widlar, and during those early days at Fairchild, Gifford also met another talented engineer by the name of Dave Fullagar. This young Brit would play a pivotal role on the Fairchild team, and in Maxim, the company Gifford would later found. Before his path converged with Gifford's, Fullagar had his own unique and humble origins on the moors of North England, half a world away from Gifford's rough L.A. beginnings. "Until I was 12 years old, we lived . . . in a house with no electricity, so a crystal set was my only option," says Fullagar in an interview for the blog *Analog Footsteps*.[35] "In 1954, I read an article entitled 'How to build a radio in a flashlight.' It used something called a transistor—a Mullard OC71. I went down to the local radio store to buy one. 'Never 'eard of a transistor, boy. Don't know naught about that,' said the proprietor in a broad Yorkshire accent."[36]

Fullagar later landed his first job with Ferranti, a leading UK defense contractor, in Edinburgh, Scotland. In a book interview, he described the nature of that position: "I worked on a terrain-following radar for a bomber that was supposed to fly to the Soviet Union at treetop height. They used to fly the engineers over the highlands of Scotland at 300 feet to validate the radar's terrain-following ability. It was a good incentive to get the design right." Later, in the 1960s, he took a position with an American company, Transitron, in Massachusetts. After realizing that Transitron was in decline, Fullagar moved to Fairchild in early 1966.

"My assigned task when I joined Fairchild R&D in 1966 was to design the successor to the μA709," says Fullagar.[37] "However, the device was tricky to stabilize. There was no short-circuit protection, and it would latch-up and self-destruct in nanoseconds." Soon after he proposed the internally compensated μA741 to the Linear R&D Group managers, in 1967, he found himself sitting in the office of Gordon Moore, Director of Research and Development (R&D) at the time, and eventual CEO of Intel. "He asked me if I'd mind moving to Mountain View because that would expedite the introduction of the part," says Fullagar. "It was exciting. It was just a creative period when Fairchild was absolutely king of the heap. And thanks to Jean Hoerni's planar process, it had the best processing in the industry, the highest performance transistors, and a very successful logic family."[38] Fullagar continues:

> *"(Widlar) and Talbert formed this incredible duo, and with almost no official sponsorship from Fairchild, created a linear family, the 702, 709, 710 and 711. Those products went on to form the basis for the Fairchild linear products, and I think all of us in the design community pay homage to that effort because it was so incredible. By 1968 there were a host of second-generation products under development. Fairchild seemed to rule the world with National really being the only competition in sight."[39]*

The contributions of Fullagar, Widlar, and Talbert—along with a team of brilliant engineers [about eight in total]—turbo boosted Fairchild's position in the fledgling tech industry. "Within a period of a couple of years," said

Gifford, "we owned 80 percent of the market."[40] Soon after Widlar and Talbert left for National Semiconductor, Gifford was again promoted and began running the entire analog R&D department. This role would give this young visionary the experience and connections that would set the stage for a new era in his career, and in Silicon Valley . . . but not before some upheaval at Fairchild.

03

RENEGADES & GENUISES

"Jean Hoerni made the two most significant contributions in our entire industry, including the integrated circuit. The planar process... was just one of those beautiful inventions, you know, that rivals the light bulb."

JACK GIFFORD [1]

During his Fairchild days, and before the series of shock waves that gave birth to the "Fairchildren," Gifford made fortuitous connections with several early tech industry renegades and geniuses. This was the Wild West tech world, where regular competitive shootouts took place, where victories were won, and where defeats, such as the Shockley implosion described earlier, littered the corporate landscape.

Gifford's personality seemed a perfect match for this high-stakes Silicon Valley environment. As Jim Bergman, venture capitalist and eventual Maxim board director, said: "In the early '60s . . . it was really a dog-eat-dog kind of business. People were pretty tough . . . aggressive, in-your-face, let's-get-it-done" type personalities. Consequently, Gifford's "take-no-prisoners" nature was a "suitable style," and the greatest X-factor in his success at Fairchild and the wider world of Silicon Valley.

Not only did The Valley's engineers and entrepreneurs work hard in those days; they also played hard. Gifford recruited a team of full-throttle young engineers for his Fairchild linear analog group, including Mike Markkula and Mike Scott, both of whom became Apple's CEO at different times, and others. Fullagar, who was on that team, said, "We were all in our mid-twenties at the time, and used to socialize together at the Wagon Wheel bar and other places after work... just a bunch of kids having a good time." These young men became known for their hard-drinking pub crawls.

That after-work tendency for the guys to let off steam sometimes even permeated their work hours. As Rhodine recalls: "I remember every summer, Fairchild would have these trips for the salesmen and the management. They would go to Mexico, Hawaii, Puerto Rico, or the Bahamas." Because she and Jack had hardly ever taken a flight or family vacation before, she sometimes felt envious. After seeing the pictures and hearing the stories, she says, she got the impression "they were more fun, party trips" even though the guys "would tell me they were business meetings."

She recalls that once during a trip to Acapulco, Mexico, her husband and his co-worker, Jim Martin, had an accident with one of the jeeps they all would drive around. Martin was rushed to the hospital, where Gifford pushed him around in a wheelchair. Coming out of the elevator wearing flip-flops, he sliced his toe open. They both ended up getting stitches and tetanus shots. "It was definitely not all work," says Rhodine.

During regular work hours, there's no evidence that the party hijinks took place in Gifford's department. However, on occasion, they certainly did elsewhere in the company. John East, former CEO of Actel, in an *Electronics Weekly* blog, describes the following incident that happened during his early time at Fairchild:

> *"I had been at Fairchild about three months and showed up for work the day before Christmas expecting a normal work day. The operators, all women in those days, started showing up with food. A big potluck was set up right at the beginning of the 7 a.m. shift. Technicians and engineers started showing up with things to drink. It looked like punch. It wasn't. By noon everyone was a mess. I didn't know what I was supposed to do about it. So . . . I did nothing. There were hardly any wafers sorted that day, which was a lucky thing. We would only have messed them up."*[2]

However, he says, human resources soon got wind of the incident and prohibited such future shindigs at work. Still, that didn't stop them from continuing off-campus.

On this wild, high-stakes journey to Fairchild and beyond, Gifford providentially met and became friends with other Silicon Valley renegades like Fred Beck, an IC sales and distribution pioneer. Beck grew up in Santa Monica, California and worked his way up the industry ranks to become COO of Avnet, one of the world's largest distributors of electronic components and major supplier of Hughes Aircraft. In that role in Southern California he developed a strong business relationship with Jerry Sanders, western area sales manager for Fairchild at the time. When Sanders was seriously considering hiring Gifford for a sales position calling on Hughes Aircraft, Beck said he got involved. "Jerry asked me to casually interview Jack while he worked for Electronic Specialties," to confirm that he was a good candidate for the Fairchild position. "He didn't know it was an interview at that stage. We had lunch together—that was my first exposure to Jack—and I liked him very much."

Gifford was ultimately hired by Sanders, and soon he would also become good friends with Beck. Little did the young salesman know that this initial chemistry over lunch, and the extensive time he would spend with the Avnet COO in the Los Angeles area, would be pivotal to the much later launch of Maxim Integrated. "We spent a lot of personal time together," said Beck. "I had a sailboat, and we did a lot of sailing."

It's likely that the two men's friendship was forged by their common difficult and competitive backgrounds. "Through the first 15 years of my life," said Beck, "my parents were financially destitute... we lived in a salvaged 27-foot trailer located on my uncle's lot (free rent and a leaky trailer)." However, Beck had the opportunity to attend Brentwood Grammar School, at the time a school of the very wealthy from Bel Air and Brentwood. "It gave me great confidence," he said, when he discovered it was easy "competing academically and athletically with the kids whose chauffeurs brought them to school." After college, Beck joined Hughes Aircraft, where he worked for Howard Hughes, the renowned American film tycoon, business magnate, and record-setting pilot. "From time to time," said Beck, "Hughes actually came into the company office. While there, I read an article on the invention of the transistor. I was intrigued, did some research, and became a believer that the transistor was the future of the world." After deciding that he needed to be in the electronic components business, Beck accepted a position with Airborne Electronics, later bought by Avnet. It was years later, after he had worked his way up to the position of COO, that Beck assisted in Gifford's hiring journey to Fairchild. Later, though Beck was offered the presidency of Avnet three times, he said, "It was of no interest to me."

Beck and Gifford saw less of each other when Gifford outgrew his sales position and moved to Fairchild's Mountain View location. However, they continued to maintain the relationship and, years later, formed a Silicon Valley power business team.

As a new analog product line manager, Gifford said he proved his detractors wrong. "They didn't fire me," he said, despite their laughing threats his first day on the job.[3] He eventually became manager of the entire analog division and hired some very talented engineers along the way. "We had about eight or nine of us, and we, at one time, had 80 percent of the market," said Gifford. "The design talent at Fairchild was unbelievable, with Bob Widlar, Dave Fullagar, Jim Giles, Darryl Lieux, and Dave Talbert as a process developer."[4]

At Fairchild, Gifford also rubbed shoulders with the "traitorous eight"— the original founders of the company—and, as previously mentioned, was tasked with overseeing the mercurial Widlar, along with Talbert, his partner in innovation. Later, as CEO of Maxim, Gifford often honored the revolutionary role of Widlar, and Jean Hoerni, IC circuit innovator and former Fairchild CEO. He even set up a company, on-campus monument to memorialize the two men for their cutting-edge work.

Hoerni, who earned two Ph.D. degrees in physics, was recruited by William Shockley to conduct complex theoretical calculations of diffusion rates. However, as one of the "traitorous eight" that left Shockley Labs, he went on to co-found Fairchild Semiconductor, where he devised the "planar process" in 1959. This ingenious process is considered to have made integrated circuits possible and to have formed the foundation for the tech era.

"In my opinion," said Gifford, "Jean Hoerni . . . made the two most significant contributions in our entire industry, including the integrated circuit. [Without] the planar process, we wouldn't be here."[5] Even though ICs have gone through many transformations, he says, this innovation "is still, today, unchanged as a process. It's remarkable . . . it was just one of those beautiful inventions, you know, that rivals the light bulb."[6] In addition, said Gifford, without Hoerni's invention of "the gold-doping of the transistor, we wouldn't have the computer industry today because . . . the other transistors prior to gold doping weren't fast enough."[7] The doping process diffused gold into the base and collector regions, reducing circuit storage times. As a result, he said, today we have multibillion-dollar companies making . . . high speed computers and buying millions and millions of these transistors."[8]

In the early days of the electronics industry, transistors were built in layers in a mesa structure with etched-out sides to disconnect them from each other. The mesa consisted of different layers with connections between them and was notoriously unreliable because all the edges were exposed. The groundbreaking planar invention flattened transistors, dramatically increasing reliability. The circuits' layers were isolated by oxides, which don't wear out and don't let interference pass through. Ultimately, the planar process prepared the way for the dependable mass production of semiconductor devices, while greatly increasing labor productivity.

"We all have a lot to thank Hoerni for," says Fullagar, "because his process is what got the whole semiconductor industry going. He didn't get as much recognition as Gordon Moore or the people at Intel, partly because he was kind of the heads-down-scientist kind of person."

Unfortunately, a serious conflict at the company destroyed the team spirit and eventually led to Hoerni's departure. The tension was triggered by Sherman Fairchild's early exercising of his right to purchase shares of the members of the "traitorous eight." Related and unrelated conflict and infighting ensued. This led to the early 1961 departures of Hoerni and Jay Last, both original founders for Amelco, where Hoerni would become vice president. Weeks later, Kleiner and Roberts joined them. Blank, Grinich, Moore, and Noyce stayed with Fairchild for a while longer. The original "traitorous eight" founders had split into two groups of four.

A few years after these departures, in early 1965, management problems worsened, and a gradual company implosion began to take place. Fairchild had been considered the undisputed leader of the semiconductor industry in the early '60s. However, by 1965, when Widlar and Talbot made for the exit, followed by other key employees, it became apparent that the company's dominance was no longer certain.

The loss of Widlar and Talbot, creators of integrated operational amplifiers and other key components, was a huge blow for the company. As Fullagar says:

> *"Widlar built six significant products in succession without consulting management. When he'd done building them, he dumped them on marketing's desk and said, 'This is an op amp, this is a comparator, this is a regulator, go and sell them.' He did it with the help of a process guy called Dave Talbot. And, Jack Gifford did a good job of marketing, bringing the sales-marketing genius to their inventions. Jack also had a strong team of people working for him at that job. So, the Talbot-Widlar combination, partnered with Gifford's sales and business savvy, was, in my mind, the father of the analog industry."*

Many of these circuit concepts still remain in production today. Though Widlar created this technology at Fairchild, he took his knowledge and creativity to National Semiconductor in 1965, and later to Linear Technology, as co-founder.

Fortunately for Fairchild, shortly after the Widlar-Talbot departures, Gifford started to manage the entire analog operation and helped temporarily halt the corporate crumble. Only days after the company's Widlar loss, new hire Fullagar arrived to help fill the departing engineers' shoes and suspend the brain drain. In mid-1966, Fullagar came to the rescue, said Gifford, shortly after the company "shut . . . half the world down."[9] As the story goes, the μA709 operational amplifier IC was only yielding one good die per silicon wafer. That was "a disastrously low yield," says Fullagar, paralyzing the company's ability to meet demand and shutting down customers' production lines. As Bob Widlar, the 709 designer, had just left, Fullagar was tasked with analyzing the circuit to discover the reason for the low yield. Though the electrical design checked out fine, he eventually traced the yield problem to a manufacturing process change.

Without Fullagar's next contribution to Fairchild and the entire semiconductor industry—the μA741 circuit—said Gifford, Fairchild "probably wouldn't have survived as an analog company" during that challenging time.[10] Although this first mass-produced IC op-amp, said Fullagar, was a remarkable product, "it did have a number of idiosyncrasies that made it quite difficult to use." Widlar had already designed "a successor product at National, and Fairchild needed to compete. The μA741›s primary claim to fame was that it required no additional components." Fullagar included a compensation capacitor on the chip, making it "extremely easy to use." This design epiphany, he says: ". . . satisfied customer demand, since the 741 became a best seller for Fairchild and is still being manufactured today, some 50 years later, although not by Fairchild. I believe that's the longest production run of any IC, analog or digital." The chip contributed the lion's share of analog sales at the time.

Despite these successes and the temporary reprieve in Fairchild's decline, in February 1967, five top managers followed the previous company exodus after they had a sharp disagreement with Noyce. Then, according to Wikipedia, "Noyce started litigation with shareholders and effectively removed himself from the operational management."[11] By July 1967, the company had become unprofitable and lost its "leading position in the market to Texas Instruments."[12] According to Wikipedia:

"In March 1968, Moore and Noyce decided to leave Fairchild and again, as nine years prior, turned to Arthur Rock. In the summer of 1968, they founded NM Electronics.[13] Blank, Grinich, Kleiner, Last, Hoerni, and Roberts set aside the past disagreements and financially supported the company of Moore and Noyce.[14] A year later, N-M Electronics bought the trade name rights from the hotel chain Intelco and took the name of Intel."

Finally, Grinich and Blank, the last of the eight, left Fairchild in 1968 and 1969. Grinich later cofounded and ran several RFID tag development companies, while Blank founded Xicor, a financial company funding innovative startups, later sold for $529-million.[15]

Also, during that closing era of Fairchild dominance, the unraveling climaxed when Fullagar, along with three other key employees, joined Hoerni, by then at Intersil; four employees departed to start PMI; and Gifford left with three others to form Advanced Micro Devices (AMD). Other tech companies, Cermatek, Signetics, Motorola, and Intel, also benefited from the wealth of Fairchild's mass exodus of talent.

The final birth of the many Silicon Valley "Fairchildren" was complete. Most significant to the story, and to that of the analog circuit industry, Jack Gifford was about to launch his first startup, inspired by his idea that a pure analog company could make a significant mark on the tech world.

04

AMD INSPIRATION & FALLOUT

"Jack, we can't live with this guy.
This guy's crazy..."

Jack Gifford[1]

"The tech industry seems to breed larger-than-life people, like Jerry Sanders, the guy Jack Gifford recruited to come and run AMD. Jerry was flamboyant. He had long silver hair and a big Bentley car in Silicon Valley that picked him up every day at the airport, because he lived in Bel Air. So, he'd have a Bentley in Los Angeles and one in Silicon Valley, and he flew up every morning on a Southwest flight (it wasn't the cheap airline at the time) . . . to run the company." That, according to Kip Hagopian, venture capitalist and co-founder of Brentwood Associates.

Little did Gifford know, when he left Fairchild to launch an analog chip startup, that he would soon cross paths with this renowned business figure, Jerry Sanders. Since those early days, Sanders' reputation as a flamboyant Silicon Valley character has flourished. He is known to collect both homes and cars, with residences in Bel Air, Russian Hill in San Francisco, Aspen, and a beach house in Southern California, in addition to about 12 cars in his ensemble, including two Bentleys, a BMW sports utility vehicle, and two Mercedes Benzes.[2] In a 2001 *SFGate* article, Sanders says this about his swashbuckling lifestyle:

"I like living in nice houses. I like driving nice cars. I like wearing nice clothes. I like eating good food. I like getting good seats at the theater. I like to have a good seat at the ballet. I'm blessed. I've worked hard. I've earned my money... I'm an American dream kind of guy. But I'm not what my cars are. My view is that content is king, and I think if I have any celebrity, it's because of what I say and what I do, because they're meaningful and they resonate with people."[3]

However, Sanders' life had not always been one of champagne and caviar:

"... after a beating when he was 18 that nearly killed him, after being fired from a job he loved when he was 33, after starting his own high-tech company and running it with panache and vigor for 32 years, and after more than a decade of unrelenting struggle against industry giant Intel—Sanders is still battling."[4]

Now, let's look back at one of Sanders' earlier battles, the co-founding of AMD in 1968, while still licking wounds from his firing from Motorola. First, counter the common on-the-street understanding that the idea for

AMD and its actual founding was initiated by Sanders; the real story is quite different.

The strategic inspiration that a pure analog semiconductor company could make waves in the new digital-dominated semiconductor world first occurred to Gifford at Fairchild. According to his self-description, he was a 26-year-old kid at Fairchild Semiconductor, as the first director of Analog Products, with 300 people working for him. Though most of the tech world saw digital chips as the wave of the future, Gifford had the visionary foresight to see a huge business and profit opportunity.

Rhodine Gifford describes the initial inspiration's startup days: "One day Jack came home from work, and said, 'I've got this idea for a company.' So, actually, AMD started in our living room. I used to sit at the top of the stairs and listen to the meetings as four or five of the founders strategized about the launch, about finding funding, and later, about possibly bringing on a new co-founder with more prominence and experience in the industry."

Initially, the startup team pooled their resources into a joint "pot of money" to withdraw salaries from. Then, after seeking financing for six months, the startup team realized they would need veteran help. They were repeatedly turned down by potential backers who seemed only willing to lend funds to someone with more experience.

Gifford said his Wall Street friend, Bruce Waterfall, attempted to broker the deal with "ten or fifteen people" before telling him, "Well, Jack, it's got two big problems. One, they don't know what the hell you're talking about. They don't understand this stuff at all. And, secondly, they don't know who the hell you are. I mean . . . you've never done anything before. You're 26 years old."[5]

A few weeks later, after Motorola fired Jerry Sanders, Jack decided to drop in on his former Fairchild colleague, then living in Southern California. "Rhodine, let's go down to Malibu and see Jerry," he announced to his wife.

"[Let's] see if I can talk him into getting involved with us. So, we go down there and these guys rented this place on the beach and he's . . . got no money at all. I don't even know how he's paying for it . . . [but] he's just completely despondent. I'm all excited and tell him what I want to do and . . . that we really want him to get involved . . . Finally, he says, "No, I've had it. I'm going to get into the record business."[6]

However, the ever-persistent Gifford, after giving Sanders the night to sleep on it, decided to "give it one more shot in the morning." Suddenly, Gifford came upon a winning negotiating strategy:

"Jerry, listen. I know what you want to do. I know you want to go into this Hollywood stuff, but I promise you that we can do this thing. We can go out. We get the twenty million in sales . . . you can take that money and go back and do this [start a record company]."

"You really think so?"

"Yeah. You give me two years and we can get this done, and then you can go do that."

"All right . . . but I get to be the president."

"Sure, you can be president."

"And . . . I want a digital part of this."

"Fine."[7]

So, at the cost of the presidency and the purely analog company he so desired, Gifford tied up an agreement to launch AMD in partnership with Sanders. In a later interview, Sanders gives his take on the agreement:

"First, a young man named Jack Gifford . . . had an idea to start a company to make linear integrated circuits. And that was interesting

to me, but frankly linear integrated circuits in my view were a niche
opportunity, and although the analog world will always be with us,
because that's what the real world is, I just didn't see that as an exciting
thing. Whereas I was more interested in the digital world where you
could build more and more complex things."8

Soon after the AMD agreement, the two headstrong business leaders were
boarding a plane on their funding road show. Gifford describes it this way:

"If you could imagine Jerry and I together trying to make a
presentation. I mean, we were interrupting each other . . . It had to be
the funniest thing you ever saw. With our egos and both of us trying to
sell this thing. So, then on top of that, it had no invention. It was just a
second source company."9

Unfortunately, when potential financers inquired about Sanders, said
Gifford, they discovered that many business leaders in the tech world "hated
him." Ironically, their startup ship would have sunk "if it weren't for Jim Martin
. . . who Jerry Sanders had fired at Fairchild," said Gifford. Apparently, Martin
had left to become involved with one of the world's largest fund management
businesses, Capital Group. Mysteriously, after the two men contacted Martin,
he agreed to approach his company about funding for the AMD venture. His
pitch was successful.

After eventually launching the company in 1969, the founding team of
about nine, said Gifford, soon found the work environment becoming
extremely tense:

"Jerry was just tyrannical, and there were only two guys who could
control him, myself and John Carey. Jerry would sit in his office and

plot things. We'd have these meetings at night, and then he would tell us what he thinks we ought to do. Well ... half of them were just hairbrained ideas. [We'd] just end up getting into these massive arguments ... that would last into the middle of the night."[10]

Eventually, said Gifford, within the first year of operation, the other founders approached him, saying, "Jack, we can't live with this guy. This guy's crazy ... we don't want him as the president. We just don't like this environment." After they appealed to Gifford to find a replacement for Sanders, he agreed to make a few calls. He decided to appeal to Don Valentine, the former Fairchild manager who first hired and mentored him. At the time, Valentine was working for Capital Group. On the phone, Gifford described AMD, the vision, and the challenges with the current president. After inquiring whether Valentine would become the new president, there was a long silence on the phone, then ... "You fu--ing gotta be crazy. I got no interest in that," came the response, followed by a "click" as he hung up.[11]

That AMD season of his life, said Gifford, "was agonizing ... I mean ... the mental stress. That was just one of the worst two years of my life."[12] After the abrupt end to the Valentine conversation, Gifford convinced the team that Jerry could make a good president if they would just give him another chance. However, about a month later, on a working Saturday, the situation imploded. "Jerry comes down to my office and he's got some idea and ... we get into an argument about it, and he says something very attacking [and] threatening. And I just got mad," said Gifford.[13]

That's when the s--t hit the fan. "I just grabbed ... [and] threw him in the chair...," said Gifford. "'Listen, you son of a b---h, ... a month ago everybody in this company came to me to get rid of you. And, if you don't change your ways, you're going to be out of here.'" Stunned by the confrontation, Sanders talked to him for two hours, agreeing that "I gotta change," and discussing what that change would look like.[14]

However, it seemed Sanders was "just petrified" that Gifford was "interested in his job… which I [had] no interest in" and within two weeks approached the board for support. He then "sets them against me," said Gifford, before going to every one of the team members to say, "if you support Jack Gifford, then I'm going to fire you, too." So, Gifford concluded, "That's the story. He fired me."[15]

This abrupt crash landing to Gifford's relationship with Sanders was inevitable, says Fullagar. "Jack had a huge ego. Jerry Sanders had a huge ego. They couldn't survive in the same company for long."

Thus, another season in the life of Silicon Valley pioneer and disruptor, Jack Gifford, came to an abrupt ending. He would soon take a sharp detour through the dirty soil of another California industry before pursuing, again, his vision of an analog company.

SILICON
SABBATICAL

"Jack had his fingers in other endeavors besides just Maxim.
He always had a bunch of ideas, and a bunch of things going on."

ROB GEORGES, MAXIM VICE PRESIDENT OF
CENTRAL ENGINEERING

A fter a successful albeit a roller coaster ride through the volatile tech
world of Silicon Valley, no one would be surprised if a business mogul
decided to take a sabbatical. However, when Gifford decided to "get out of the
business," pick up a shovel and drive a tractor, many of his peers were greatly
surprised. The Giffords had never held "dreams of farming," says Rhodine,
but at that time, in 1971, Jack no longer wanted anything to do with the
tech industry.

Unlike some business people who look for the perfect opportunity, as a highly-driven entrepreneur Gifford tended to just look for the next good opportunity. He seemed to possess the uncanny knack of recognizing the potential in ventures that came his way. "Jack had his fingers in other endeavors . . . he always had a bunch of ideas, and a bunch of things going on," says Rob Georges, 30-year Maxim veteran and Vice President of Central Engineering.

Even before his agricultural undertaking, Gifford "got involved with a tire balancing company out of Australia," says Fullagar. "They were the first people to market a digital tire balancing system. He managed to sell that company to Sun Electric, a large supplier of automotive equipment to repair stations." Though two Australians started the company, says Fullagar, it was "Jack who wrapped it up into a company and had the contacts in the U.S. to market and sell it."

Next, when some friends who had been original investors in AMD mentioned a pear ranch that was available for a good deal, Gifford jumped at it. Soon he was running a successful 300-acre pear ranch, near Sacramento, California, which he would eventually expand.

During harvest season, Gifford lived in a trailer on the farm. Rhodine, along with their three daughters, would drive up from the Bay Area for the day to visit and bring him lunch or dinner. "We would always joke that he was like a snail carrying his house on his back," she says, because he would relocate the trailer to the part of the ranch they were harvesting at the time. "We never quite knew where Dad was going to be."

"Unfortunately," says Rhodine, "summers were not all that much fun, because Gifford would be working throughout the girls' vacations. The harvests were always in the summer, and it was hot and buggy up there. Plus, we didn't have a house." However, she says she was relieved to learn that her husband had no plans to move the family there permanently. Perhaps, in the back of his mind, he considered it a new, exciting, but only temporary challenge.

One year, all the pear farmers in the region had a bumper crop, greatly depressing prices. So, Gifford decided to truck down bins of pears to sell at the corner of El Camino Real and Highway 85 in Sunnyvale/Mountain View area. A farm employee sold the pears, and the Gifford girls helped with sorting and bagging. Retailing the pears on the side of the road allowed them to cut out the middleman and offer the fruit below market value, at a price of 10 cents per pound. "We sold out. People thought they were great Bartlett pears."

Gifford's entrepreneurial spirit soon kicked in again, and he decided to expand the pear operation by adding 1,500 acres of tomatoes. The tomato harvesting machine had been invented and introduced to the market just a few years before, in the late 1960s, by two scientists from UC Davis in California. However, Gifford decided the mechanization of the tomato harvest needed some improvements. He recruited Ed Sliger, a Silicon Valley engineer, to help him solve a farming problem. According to Rhodine, a system had not yet been perfected for lowering the tomatoes from the picking machine into trucks without bruising or losing them. After creating a new company called Positrol, and with Sliger's help, Gifford created a conveyer system that solved this serious industry challenge. Later, according to Rhodine, he sold the technology to a picking machine company.

One of Rhodine's most vivid memories is that of riding on one of the huge tomato harvesting machines with her husband. It felt like riding on a boat. "You're getting shaken and rocked the whole day. I'm very susceptible to motion sickness, so it was not fun. It was always hot and humid, because there were a lot of rice fields in the area. And the mosquitoes were huge . . . like birds!"

Within the first year or two of Gifford's back-to-earth lifestyle, Silicon Valley came calling again with a new opportunity. Jean Hoerni, who had founded the semiconductor company, Intersil, after leaving Fairchild, tracked

Gifford down to ask him to oversee the analog IC division. Hoerni sweetened the pot, says Fullagar, by promising to help Gifford raise money to start his own company later. Eventually, the two men struck a deal that allowed Gifford to consult on a part-time basis, while continuing to farm.

At the time, Gifford was already discussing with some business friends the idea of starting a product conditioning company called Zatetics. "I was really emotionally committed to doing that, and I completely believed in it," said Gifford. "I know it would have worked, [but] . . . I couldn't raise the money."[1] Though Hoerni said he would help Gifford with Zatetics, he says, the CEO "was just really stringing me along. He didn't want me to do that."[2] However, won over by Hoerni's offer, his stature in the industry, and the opportunity to help pioneer cutting-edge analog technology, Gifford agreed to work three days a week at Intersil while continuing to farm.

Hoerni's engineering and business leadership feats made their mark on history, said Gifford. But despite his accomplishments in both areas, he was highly underappreciated. In the tech world, he was often judged as an amazing inventor with poor management skills. "However," said Gifford, "here's a guy that started five companies. Never . . . did it with his own money and never failed, and yet he had this knock on him because he was . . . a very shy person. [But] he's one of the best managers I've ever been around."[3]

Though Gifford started part-time at Intersil, he was soon persuaded to go 'all in' by another of Hoerni's ingenious creations. Even as a CEO, said Gifford, ". . . here he is inventing things. He built the first CMOS micro-controllers [and] CMOS analog watch circuits."[4] The complementary metal-oxide-semiconductor (CMOS) process is widely used today for making integrated circuits. "Intersil should have owned the universe, you know."[5] One of the company's investors pressured Hoerni to focus on taking the company public, and on the digital semiconductor side of the business. He thought the analog division and inventions were a distraction.[6]

So, before making his decision, Hoerni asked Gifford to look at the technology and give his opinion. According to Gifford, besides his impressive analog technology with low-voltage CMOS, Hoerni was also developing custom circuits. After looking over the circuits, Gifford said, "Jean, listen . . . you can do what they want, and it will be fine, but . . . you got a great business here."

To which Hoerni responded, "Well, would you run that for me?"[7]

Clearly impressed by the circuits, Gifford quickly agreed. After five years of farming, he left his agricultural endeavors to oversee the analog division of Intersil, assuming the full-time position as director of analog marketing. At Intersil, as tech history records it, he was instrumental in developing the revolutionary "low power CMOS for analog applications, which became one of the largest analog IC markets in the world."[8]

06

INTERSIL DISRUPTIONS & GROOMING

"I was disruptive, and yet I was running the most profitable operation . . . I'd been fired once before so I was used to getting fired."

JACK GIFFORD [1]

After exchanging his farmer-Jack coveralls for a full-time suit and tie in 1973, Gifford returned to Silicon Valley and began fervently building and marketing the Intersil analog division around the prolific ingenuity of Hoerni and the company's other brilliant engineers. However, Gifford had already earned the reputation of a disruptor in the tech world. He soon began making waves again, challenging the status quo, demolishing old structures, and building new ones. As usual, casualties were sustained in the dustup . . .

all, on hindsight, in preparation for the eventual launch of Maxim, Jack and his colleagues' greatest creation.

At Intersil, Gifford developed new strategic connections and again rekindled his relationships with Beck and Fullagar. Though Gifford and Fullagar had gone their separate ways after leaving Fairchild, Jack to AMD in 1968 and Fullagar to Intersil in 1969, the two had kept in touch over the years before joining forces again around analog innovation at Intersil. Dave Fullagar says he became the "first IC designer working for Jean Hoerni."

As he was quoted in an *Electronics News* article:

> *"I think Intersil lured me, but it wasn't financial. I didn't really know what a stock option was and couldn't have distinguished between an IPO and a UFO. Intersil offered a chance to create my own analog-design group with a clean slate and to work with Dr. Hoerni, one of the true giants of the semiconductor industry."*[2]

However, says Fullagar, he soon discovered one serious flaw at Intersil: "It was frustrating to be designing products that I felt weren't selling because of inept marketing."[3] Dave adds later: "Their marketing was so terrible that I went to Jean Hoerni and said, 'You've got to get somebody in here who's good at marketing . . . I know Jack Gifford and he'd be a good fit.'" Soon after this conversation, Jack joined the Intersil team. For a while, Fullagar worked as Director of Analog Engineering, alongside Gifford, who was Director of Analog Marketing.

During the early 70s, Intersil endured some rocky years, plagued by bad management and suffering through a stock market crash. Jean Hoerni left the company to pursue other endeavors, and management began to implement a strategy to groom the company for sale. They recruited Jim Riley, previously CEO at Signetics, said Gifford, who "promptly . . . began to ruin the company."[4] Then, said Jack, management brought in Marshall Cox, "another guy who shouldn't have been given the job . . . [and] had no ability to run an integrated circuit company. He had no background and experience."[5]

Also, according to Gifford, poor management had allowed serious ethical problems to erode the company. "It was my nature . . . [to be] very vocal and very negative about the . . . cronyism [at Intersil.] It wasn't a meritorious environment," said Gifford. "He [Marshall] had a bunch of friends in the sales organization . . . It was a corrupt company . . . there were kickbacks and people being bribed. I mean, reps were having to pay to keep their lines. And it was a mess."[6] Because his division was so successful, said Jack, others paid attention to his thoughts about the company corruption and other issues. "I was never outspoken to the extent that I went above Marshall Cox or to the Board . . . but I would tell people what I thought if someone asked me."

As a result, Cox told Fred Adler, the chairman of the board, that Jack was "a very disruptive influence at Intersil and should be fired."[7]

"I was disruptive," Gifford said, "and yet I was running the most profitable operation. I'd been fired once before, so I was used to getting fired. I got fired by Jerry Sanders and the Board at AMD. So, one day I get this call from Fred Adler to meet him in the conference room."

Adler says, "Jack, I understand that you're . . . very disruptive to the company. You're causing a lot of problems." Next, Adler gets up to go to the restroom, and says, "When I return, I want you to tell me why I shouldn't fire you, because I intend to."[8]

Angered by Adler's words, Gifford stormed out of the conference room and made a bee-line for his car. "I couldn't believe it. I was just, just irate and thought, *To hell with it. I don't need him or this job.*"

However, when Jack got to the parking lot, Adler came running out to talk to him, calling for him to explain himself.

"F--k you . . . you don't deserve an explanation," replied Gifford, before jumping into his car and driving home.[9]

Shortly afterwards, Jack got a call from Roger Smullen, his immediate supervisor, to find out what happened. Smullen convinced Gifford not to resign before sitting down with Adler to explain why he was creating a disruption. After listening to Jack's explanation of the company cronyism he was calling out, amazingly he gave Gifford more stock options and promised he would change things. Two months later, Adler fired Cox.[10]

Though Gifford courageously challenged the corrupt company status quo and triggered the beginning of a cleanup, his actions also stirred up another hornet's nest. Because he had an indirect role in the firing of the Intersil CEO, Cox, Jack soon found himself on the "hit list" of Don Hoefler, the editor of *Microelectronics News*, a Silicon Valley newsletter and gossip tabloid. Unbeknownst to Gifford, Hoefler had a close relationship with Cox and took offense to Jack's part in the shakeup. Apparently, Cox told Hoefler that Gifford had committed dishonorable acts at Intersil, then betrayed him and "got him fired." That's why, said Jack, Hoefler "attacked me viciously for years."[11]

Years later, after moving on to another opportunity, Gifford decided he'd had enough of the false accusations and sued Hoefler for libel and slander. Legally, it was very difficult to win such cases, unless the accuser could prove the other party lied intentionally. In a later interview with Rob Walker, of Silicon Genesis, Jack said his attorney, fortunately, was able to pressure Hoefler to admit, on the stand, to purposely making up his false stories. "Yeah, I lied about him because that son of a b---h did this to Marshall Cox," blurted out Hoefler. As a consequence of this startling admission, the court ruled that the defendant would have to pay substantial damages and allow Gifford to write in the newsletter under Hoefler's byline. For months, Jack wrote articles dismantling all the previous lies. During this settlement process, Hoefler died. Referring to the stress of the legal battle and resolution, Gifford concluded: "Actually, I think I killed him . . . is the bottom line."[12]

During his tenure at Intersil in those years, because of the many false accusations in circulation, Jack's reputation in the tech world took a hit. Yet, he ignored the infamy outside of Intersil for a while and kept building the analog world within. At the same time, Gifford's 'inhouse' renown began to grow, in preparation for a greater role.

Outside of the office, says Fullagar, he, Jack, and the other young tech pioneers at Intersil socialized at the local watering hole, The Wagon Wheel. "At the time, I didn't see any of the hard-driving potential CEO material in Jack; we were just a bunch of kids having a good time," observes Fullagar. But other company brass were taking notes.

Amid its management woes, Intersil would also be struck another huge blow, this time from a ferocious bear market, which savaged Silicon Valley from January 1973 to December 1974, a crash considered one of the worst global stock market downturns in modern history. It came as a result of the convergence of a perfect storm of factors: the collapse of the Bretton Woods monetary system, the 1973 oil crisis, the Nixon political scandal in the US, and the dollar devaluation, all of which led to a major 1970s recession.

Then, in late 1973, during these US and tech-world traumas, says Fullagar, "I took a 12-month leave of absence to go sailing to the South Pacific, followed by two years setting up a technical presence in Europe for Intersil." While on his South Seas sailing adventure, the market began to crater. "When I left, Intersil stock was $22 a share. I got to Acapulco in May of 1974 and called Jack to ask, 'How's the stock doing?' He said, 'Oh, it's nine and a half. It couldn't possibly go any lower.' Then, says Dave, "I sailed across the Pacific to Tahiti and [saw in] the *Wall Street Journal* . . . it was one and three-eighths [1^{3/8}$]. At that point, I knew my sailing trip was over, so I went back to work."

Besides the fact that his personal stock savings took a major hit, he knew that it would be "all hands on deck" back at Intersil to keep the semiconductor ship afloat.

Soon Fullagar moved to Europe for two years to help build company presence and market share overseas, outside of the carnage of Silicon Valley. When he returned from the UK in 1976, Fullagar once again managed the IC design group under Gifford, then in his mid-30s and running the analog division.

That same year, Adler recruited Orion Hoch to help the company recover. Hoch, CEO of Advanced Memory Systems (AMS) at the time, merged Intersil and AMS, and became CEO of the joint venture. According to Fullagar, "Ori was a very mature, very sophisticated manager. And he, I think, from day one, had in mind polishing the company up and selling it. I give him credit for lifting the stock from $1^{3/8}$."[13] Intersil was eventually resurrected and, by the early 80s, sold for $35 a share.

In the late 1970s, Gifford became Senior Vice President reporting to CEO Ori Hoch, and Fullagar assumed the VP of R&D role, managing about 75 engineers. However, Fullagar took on his new position, not quite knowing what he was in for. "Jack told me that running the engineering group would only take 10 minutes a week and wouldn't interfere with my ability to do my own design work. Ha ha ... somehow, I fell for it. That was the end of my life as a hands-on engineer!"[14]

Managing the group was pretty much a full-time job, but it became a thriving division that produced many successful products, including the 7106 digital voltmeter chip and a whole range of industrial timers, counters, switches, and display products.[15] During that prolific engineering season, several exceptional designers began to rise above the rest, including Dick Wilenken, who lived in Yreka, California. He would later join the Maxim team as their virtuoso, off-campus hermit engineer. In addition, at Intersil, Dave Bingham and Lee Evans, both very creative engineers, were designing many products, including chopper amplifiers and DVM chips, using the new cutting-edge CMOS process.

Fortunately, Hoch, who had honed his CEO skills at the helm of Litton and AMS, began righting the ship. According to Gifford, "He was a very . . . [merit-]based person. [In the midst of] the chaos and the anarchy going on there, he sorted out who was making a difference and who wasn't."[16]

In the summer of 1981, Hoch promoted 40-year-old Jack, who became his successor as CEO of Intersil. "That was my first CEO job," said Gifford. "We were doing very well . . . I had built this thing up to a $130-million-dollar company, just very highly profitable."[17] According to Rhodine, Jack credited Ori Hoch for believing in him, mentoring him, and opening the door for him to take over as CEO.

However, just prior to Intersil's senior captain handing the ship over to Gifford, a big technology player took notice of the newly thriving Intersil and came calling. And that ignited an even greater disruption in the Silicon Valley universe.

07

BUYOUT & BLOWOUT

"Jack, you were the best guy I ever fired!"

JACK WELCH, AS QUOTED [1]

The night view seemed to hold the audience spellbound as they gazed at the innumerable lights that twinkled across Silicon Valley as far as the eyes could see. Sitting in the restaurant atop the Pruneyard Towers in Campbell, California, the Intersil management team listened with wonder to the speaker's words, as he waved his arm across the scene below. "Eighty percent of it is ours!" With that grand gesture and great claim, General Electric (GE) executive, Jim Baker, referred to the company's share of the incandescent light bulb business. This was the scene, Fullagar says, that played out at the acquisition dinner after GE staked out its claim on Intersil.

It was the early 1980s, shortly after the recession and energy crisis had dominated the headlines and crushed the U.S. economy. GE, one of the corporate Goliaths of the world, had caught wind of a technology created by the small, highly creative semiconductor company. This conglomerate, as one of the largest makers of motors and light bulbs in the world, needed a solution to its own energy problem. It soon was knocking on the door of this relatively insignificant David of Silicon Valley, the newly groomed Ori Hoch venture.

Just prior to the Intersil acquisition, says Fullagar, GE had decided it needed in-house semiconductor manufacturing for two key business plans. Within the Industrial Products Sector, Don Grierson, an ambitious young GE executive, was promoting "The Factory of the Future" concept, requiring both a semiconductor capability and CAD expertise. Simultaneously, Jack Welch, overseeing the company's Consumer Products Sector, saw great value in an emerging technology being developed at Intersil—a high voltage DMOS FET (Field Effect Transistor). Unlike bipolar transistors, FETs required almost no input current to control the load. This highly efficient component potentially offered GE greater dominance in the appliance/motor market, and in the lighting sector, as it shifted its focus onto marketing its new, compact fluorescent bulb.

A few weeks after the prestigious GE-hosted acquisition dinner, says Fullagar, a delegation from the light bulb division showed up at Intersil, "including a gentleman who had a briefcase chained to his wrist!" The secured case contained a prototype of their latest, top-secret, invention—a new generation of the fluorescent light bulb. "One of its key components was a high voltage FET, a technology that Intersil was developing." Two engineers that Gifford had recruited from Hewlett Packard in 1979 had started to develop the FET product using a DMOS structure.

The FET technology wouldn't just benefit lighting products. GE decided, said Gifford, "if they controlled the speed of motors . . . [all of their washing machines and refrigerators] would have this huge power savings" and also improve their monopoly in that business.[2] "We were doing quite well. I'd taken Intersil from four million a year up to a hundred and thirty million . . . I was like the General Manager of it . . . and I had gotten us into a DMOS [FET] business."[3] The new process at Intersil seemed like the missing piece of the puzzle. To Intersil management at the time, FET was a tiny piece of their business and not an exciting technology either. However, to GE, these high voltage devices were gold.

Nonetheless, GE's agreement to purchase Intersil's technological treasure would prove challenging. As word got out about the company's FET product, said Gifford, "our name comes up on the [GE] radar. And, all of a sudden, now, we are a target . . . this had no economic value at all hardly to Intersil. They come flying down on us [and] offer the board five times the market" to purchase the company.[4] (*See the historical footnote at the end of this chapter for the conclusion to GE's technological pursuit.)

Though Hoch had groomed Intersil for such an opportunity, after he, Adler, and the board discussed the sale with GE brass, said Gifford, "they realized that I needed to go along with this."[5] But securing the support of Gifford, now Vice President and second in command, would not come easily. "I don't want to sell it. I don't want to work for GE. I don't want to be part of a big company," stated Gifford adamantly. According to him, most people at Intersil didn't want to work for GE. They feared that their creative, entrepreneurial edge would be blunted by the mammoth corporate systems. "I can make this a billion-dollar company. I knew what to do next," Gifford proclaimed.[6] However, that's not the direction the board wanted to go.

Hoping to persuade Gifford and other senior management at Intersil, says Fullagar, the board arranged for a meeting in Hawaii to discuss details of the acquisition. However, Jack and others in the 'resistance' movement had another idea. Gifford formed a team to "undo the purchase" or "not let it go through," says Fullagar.

> *"He made us dress up in our best suits. We were in sweaty Hawaii temperatures, dressed to the eyeballs trying to persuade the board" not to follow through on the deal. "I got assigned Pete Bancroff's wife, who was a real attractive lady from Serbia . . . and I was supposed to take her aside and say, 'We don't want to do the acquisition.'"*

However, even after the anti-buyout team's efforts, the board would not budge. The deal was too sweet. "GE was buying the company for $35 a share. Only six or seven years before it was 1^{3/8}$," says Fullagar. Realizing that they needed Jack Gifford on their side, especially since Hoch was grooming him to take over as CEO, the board arranged a dinner between Jack Welch, soon to be CEO of GE, and Jack Gifford, along with Fullagar, his close partner in the resistance movement.

Soon, Gifford and Fullagar were driving in Jack's new, black Lincoln Continental, which Dave considered a "monstrosity," on the way to San Francisco for their fateful dinner meeting with Welch and other executives. Gifford recalls his first impressions of his counterpart. "Nice guy. I like the guy," said Gifford of Welch. During the dinner meeting, "both of us get about half drunk. Maybe all drunk . . . we get along great, and finally, I tell him all of the reasons why it won't work."[7] Gifford explained the concern of most people at Intersil that the big institution culture of GE would swallow up the entrepreneurial and independent nature of their company. He also described the stock option incentive system within Intersil that drove their competitive and inventive culture. Then, according to Gifford, this conversation followed:

"Jack, I understand," replied Welch. "If you don't want to sell it to us, I'll call the dogs off . . . But, I tell you what. I promise you that if you sell it to us, I will set you up as an independent subsidiary of GE. [And] you can have . . . all your stock options. You guys will work just like you are now, and nothing will change."[8]

"You can't do that!" exclaimed Gifford with surprise.

"Yeah, I can," countered Welch. "We've only got one other independent subsidiary. It's Utah International. But I'll set you up just like that."

"Hey, let's go home. We'll wake up in the morning. If you still feel the same way, call me. We'll talk about it."

At ten o'clock the next morning, Jack answered the ringing phone. "Well, what do you think? Do you want to do it?" inquired the now familiar voice of Welch on the other end.

"If you can do it, I can't object to it if you can keep everything like it is," answered Gifford. "Stock options and it's done."[9]

Within months, in early 1982, everything would be set up the way the two men agreed, just after Gifford became CEO of Intersil and shortly before Welch took the CEO reins at GE. Ori Hoch, mission accomplished, left Intersil for greener pastures, and Gifford continued his turbulent tenure at the helm of the scrappy semiconductor company. The two CEOs also quickly became good friends. For some time, said Gifford, he was GE's golden boy. Welch admired the flexible business and entrepreneurial bent of Intersil, said Gifford, and "drug me around everywhere he went . . . using us as a model for how he wanted the rest of GE to be."[10]

"In fact . . . they'd have these cocktail parties on the weekends in Boca Raton, Florida," continued Gifford, "and there'd be 200 of these general managers. I'm running a hundred-million-dollar operation; some of these guys are running . . . four-billion-dollar operations."[11] Welch would take Gifford around the room while introducing him to the other executives and raving about Jack's accomplishments at Intersil. Soon, however, said Gifford, "I became a real target for all these guys." After about six months of this, he started to hear from his other general managers. 'Hey, this isn't fair . . . I've worked for GE all my life. I don't have stock.' And he had a mutiny on his hands."[12]

Amid the rumblings during the merger transition, things at Intersil began to change dramatically. Within two months, says Fullagar, "The guys with the green eye shades moved in" and placed Intersil in the industrial products division under intense scrutiny from the traditional, rigid management. To make matters worse, the division manager and Gifford "did not hit it off." Baker and other GE managers wanted to keep Intersil on the same salary structure as their people in Poughkeepsie, New York. They didn't understand the higher cost of living, and that "house prices are three times as much," explained Fullagar.

In addition to the challenges around salary structure, Intersil slowly began to be squeezed into the big business GE mold, according to Steve Combs, managing director of technology of Intersil at the time. "GE was such a structured company. I could walk into one of the VPs offices and count the ceiling tiles and number of buttons on his phone and tell you how much he made and what his title was." Their status structure perks extended throughout the company, especially to corporate executives.

"At the VP level," says Combs, "you had a dedicated powder blue Lincoln limousine, and you had an aide. Then, at the executive VP level, you had the same limousine, three aides, and an aircraft. We used to call it the drag effect. So, whenever the VP would travel somewhere, he'd have these three guys. One guy would make arrangements, the other guy would carry bags, and the third guy, I don't know . . . Then, at the next level up, you had the corporate jet, limo, and five aides."

Eventually, this big company structure began to engulf Intersil within the industrial products division and to erode its effectiveness. Then, besides the financial disagreements over salary structure, Jack's priority in the acquisition agreement, namely the stock options, became a ticking time bomb. "I know there was a lot of unhappiness within GE that we were getting this privileged treatment with the phantom stock," said Combs. Every now and then, according to Gifford, Welch would voice his discontent with the agreement: ". . . those stock options are causing me a problem, you know. Do you really need those? Can't we do something?" To which Gifford responded, "Jack, that was the deal. I don't need them, but Intersil needs them . . . By the way, that was your idea."

Then, "I know, I know," Welch would grumble.[13]

In addition, Gifford's immediate supervisor, Jim Baker, continued to pressure him to give up the options, while Jack persisted in his fight for fair compensation for Intersil employees. There are two versions of the explosive events that would follow.

According to Gifford, the dispute came to a head about a year later at a company party. "I'm standing around talking to ten or fifteen of these guys and Jack [Welch] comes across the room, and he's got 10 or 15 guys following him. So, he's already had a couple of drinks, and he comes swaggering into my group . . . No sooner do the greetings stop and he says, "Why the f--k do you guys have to have those stock options?" Then, apparently, Welch continues to rage for a while before asking, "Well, what do you think?" By this time, fuming at the verbal assault, Gifford responded with, "F--- you!" before turning around and walking out.[14] The second version of the story, told by other former Intersil employees, involved a conflict between Gifford and Jim Baker, not Welch. Both accounts are likely true. Either way, news of the clash rippled through the company, shocking many who learned of the Intersil CEO's blunt denunciation of his superior.

About ten days later, according to Gifford, he got the fateful call from

Welch, asking him to come over to GE headquarters:

"Well, I gotta talk to you," says Welch.

"What are you gonna do?" replies Gifford.

"I gotta fire you."

"Well, why don't you just fire me? Maybe I shouldn't have done it, but you, you caused it."

"I know, but I gotta fire you."[15]

The eventual parting of the ways came in an unexpectedly shocking form, said Beck. Late one cold winter night, just before Christmas, Jim Dykes, Director of Semiconductor Operations, called Gifford, still working at the office. Beck continued:

> *"Dykes said it was Christmas time, he was in the area, and he just wanted to stop by and see Jack for a few minutes. Jack waited, and Jim showed up. He brought with him termination papers and a security team that abruptly and obnoxiously removed Jack and his belongings within the hour. Jack called me the next morning to tell me what happened. It was an outrageous act and incensed many of us. It was the beginning of the end."*

Paradoxically, despite the firing and the abrupt parting of ways, Gifford and Welch remained friends and continued to respect each other's accomplishments. According to Fullagar, the men really liked each other and were very similar types of people. "They were both hard driving and aggressive. They didn't come from wealthy backgrounds," he says. Sometimes, says Combs, "Jack Welch would come into the room and senior people would present what they wanted to do for the next year. He would either say, 'go,' or 'no go.'" But not before an interrogation. "In five questions Welch could have somebody, who thought they came in with a good plan, tied off from the rocks and floating at sea. I've seen vice presidents of GE go out of the room crying after Welch shredded them. Jack [Gifford] has done the same, obviously."

During that Christmas of 1982, Gifford left Intersil to move on to his ultimate entrepreneurial assignment, but he continued to receive Christmas cards from Welch. "Jack showed me those cards. He was quite proud of them," says Fullagar. Many years later, he says, Welch sent Gifford a copy of his autobiographical business book, *Jack: Straight from the Gut,* inscribed with the following: "Jack, you were the best guy I ever fired! Jack."[16] (Note: it's unlikely that Welch chose the unceremonious form of Gifford's termination by Dykes.)

After Gifford's departure, the Intersil division of GE continued to decline even faster. According to Rich Hood, then a company test development engineer before jumping ship to Maxim, Intersil people started out as "the darlings of the company." However, soon Baker was attempting to sabotage Intersil and prevent it from succeeding over other sectors under his supervision. Then, says Rich Hood, "They saddled us with some of their poorly designed factories . . . deadbeat operations . . . and there was no way we were gonna make a profit. Therefore, our phantom shares would be basically worthless."

The Intersil team began to experience the GE drag and the feeling of being squeezed into the corporate mold. At the same time, Dave Fullagar and the company designers were pursuing a new era of analog products, as the market made a fundamental transition. According to Combs, "It was moving from a bipolar process technology to a CMOS process technology, which resulted in lower power, higher performance circuits. That was really one of the key aspects of our success; we saw the tides were going to change." Intersil was a good company, says Fullagar; however, their team found it challenging pursuing such an entrepreneurial direction within the bowels of the giant that had swallowed it.

One of the greatest catalysts for an eventual mass exodus arose from tension between the digital and analog enterprises at the company. As Dave Fullagar says:

> *"Analog made all the money and the digital people spent it all, which is part of the origins of Maxim. And there was an exact parallel [frustration] going on at National . . . that was the genesis of Linear. Yes, of course, having GE step into Intersil initially appeared to be OK, but that didn't work out. I wasn't very happy, and other people weren't terribly happy. But Jack had only been gone since December, and we were sort of still thinking . . . 'Where's this thing going?' It was beginning to look like a dead end for us. I think, at that point, we thought Jack was probably quite happy playing tennis and retired. He said he made $10-million out of his tire balancing company. In his opinion, he didn't need to go back to work."*

Yet, at least one of Jack's comrades at Intersil was hoping he could persuade him to lead a team in a radical new venture. Fred Beck, then GE/Intersil Executive VP of Worldwide Sales, after observing some destructive dynamics at the company, started looking for the fire exit. Eventually, according to Beck, a fortuitous, inebriated conversation would reveal the true intentions of Ed Hood, Electronic Sector VP and second in command to Welch. Beck described the dramatic interaction that acted as a catalyst for the birth of Maxim Integrated:

> *"GE management had spent almost two weeks with us at Intersil. Hood had assigned himself to me, and they were busy picking our brains and trying to convince us theirs was the right way. The last night of the event we were having a banquet, and . . . the GE guys were huge*

drinkers, Hood in particular. He turned and said, 'Hey, Fred, tell me.
What are the three most serious problems?' Now, that was a stupid
question because they had just spent two weeks with us, going through
all the issues. 'That's a ridiculous question,' I said. 'You know the
answer. The first and most serious problem is the stock option program,
which I know you don't give a s--t about. And I know you're not going
to honor it.' He said, 'You're damn right, we're not.'"

With other Intersil staff listening in on the conversation, Beck continued to bait Hood into revealing, for the first time, his true intentions. In essence, said Beck, Hood was saying, "It's over, Intersil. It's our way or the highway." It seemed, says Fullagar, that Welch, as the new GE CEO, was so consumed with the massive reorganization—which involved the firing of hundreds of executives at GE and restructuring the company—that he no longer had the time to get involved with Intersil and the related conflicts.

The next day, after Hood's alcohol-enhanced conversation, Beck called Gifford with the proposal he had been pondering for some time. "Jack, look. Things are really going to unravel here, and we should really start a company. You would be the Pied Piper, and others from Intersil will follow you out."

Gifford was not yet on the same page, according to Beck. "I just don't want to do that. I'm retired. I'm loving life. I've had enough. I'm tired of the semiconductor industry. I'm doing some venture capital stuff, and that's all I want to do."

But Beck persisted with his appeal to Jack. "Everyone's ready to go," he said emphatically.

Finally, Gifford agreed to think about the idea for a couple of weeks.

Although, for many years, Jack had envisioned starting a purely analog circuit company, he says, it was the appeal from his former colleagues that finally convinced him to come out of retirement and resurrect the dream.

"Those guys came to me and said, 'Jack, you gotta do something, you know. Our careers . . . he's destroyed our career. And I was forced to do Maxim... I mean, I caused the problem, so . . .'"[17]

*Historical footnote (in Fullagar's words):

"After the acquisition, Intersil (i.e., Jack Gifford) reported to Don Grierson for a short time. To satisfy his CAD needs, Grierson acquired Calma Corporation in the same year as Intersil. Unfortunately, his Factory of the Future concept fizzled. I think once Jack Welch became CEO, he chopped Grierson's free-spending budget and we ended up reporting to Jim Baker (Grierson's boss). Ultimately, both Intersil and Calma were sold by GE for cents on the dollar.

The DMOS effort had a happier ending. Nathan Zommer, one of the two HP engineers referred to above, joined forces with an engineer from GE's Schenectady Research Laboratory and continued working on high voltage FET devices, which were fabricated by Intersil. Unfortunately, I don't know whether the fruits of their efforts ever ended up being used commercially in a light bulb or motor control system.

PART TWO

BIRTH

08

TACTICAL
LAUNCH

"[I wanted] to build… the best analog company

in the world that's owned by employees."

JACK GIFFORD [1]

E arly in 1983, at a coffee bar in Portola Valley, California, a trio of
founders—Dave Fullagar, Fred Beck, and Jack Gifford—met to discuss
the birthing of their new Silicon Valley startup. From this unlikely fueling
spot and launch pad, this core team moved into action, soon after Beck's
business proposal to Gifford and the appeal of other Intersil colleagues for
him to pioneer an analog company. Gifford quickly reached out to Fullagar to
see if he was interested in joining in.

"Oh, hell, yes," was his compatriot's immediate response.

Commenting about the company's launch, Georges says, "Fred was like an industry icon, co-founder of the company, and even really sort of conceived of Maxim before anybody. He had the germinating idea to start the place and knew he needed to pull in Dave Fullagar and Jack." The eventual success and impact of this new venture would far exceed each of these men's wildest imaginations.

As someone today considered to be one of the founding fathers of the analog microchip industry, Gifford clearly possessed the qualities that inspired the eventual 12 founders to follow him into the unknown. They saw in him a fearless confidence in all his business dealings and a readiness to confront the status quo and take the bold action necessary to make a startup succeed in cutthroat Silicon Valley. In addition, they recognized Jack's string of industry successes, the Midas touch that seemed to transform his endeavors into gold.

According to Beck:

"Jack was a star from the beginning. He knew where he wanted to go and was fearless, bright, and aggressive. It wasn't just Maxim. You could tell that Jack was a very determined guy. He was a very legitimate guy and very, very aggressive. Really a visionary. He saw things differently and he executed. He was enjoyable. He had his strengths and he had his weaknesses. [But] he was really a great guy."

However, more than Gifford's remarkable qualities and the veteran expertise of other founders who boarded the new analog ship, the launch team was inspired by the bold vision. As Gifford said in the 2002 *Silicon Genesis* interview, his idea was to build "the best analog company in the world that's owned by employees. The employees at Maxim owned, have owned, or will own seventy-eight percent of the company . . . All my life I'd been, you know, stepbrother to the digital thing," but this time he focused the new company solely on analog chips. "I am the best in the world at this. So . . . I was motivated to do this," he stated matter-of-factly.[2]

According to Steve Combs, one of the four founding company executives, Maxim began because the men saw a shift in analog. "We could see that GE was going to screw it up and people were going to scatter to the wind," says Combs. And so, Jack decided to gather an ace team of colleagues together before they found employment elsewhere. "Jack realized that people were not going to stick with the GE consortium," says Combs, "and that they were going to go to all these random companies around the Valley; [so] he was going to try to concentrate them."

One of the first orders of business was to find a suitable name for the scrappy semiconductor startup. According to Fullagar, Gifford wanted to avoid a triple-barrel name like Advanced Micro Devices (AMD), or Analog Devices Incorporated (ADI). He wanted a name that could not be shortened by acronyms or nicknames; one that could be printed and easily viewed on top of an integrated circuit package. Then one morning, says Rhodine, "Jack came into the kitchen and said, 'I've got the name—Maxim.' I said I thought it sounded really good." And thus, appropriately, amid the real-world sights, sounds, and smells of coffee and breakfast in the Gifford family kitchen, the semiconductor startup was christened. "Even though it's a French restaurant, it's a coffee, and it's a good boys' magazine," says Fullagar. "Maxim had the right feel to it."

The early founders knew one of the first great challenges was to avoid potential lawsuits during the transition period as they jumped ship from Intersil to Maxim. "We hired some attorneys," said Beck, and they said, 'Be very kind and don't irritate GE.' The team decided that Fullagar and Beck would resign first. They set up the ground rules, agreeing to "not do anything till then." Beck commented:

"I was the first to resign... I told Dykes that I was leaving, that we were going to start a company in competition with them, expecting them to walk me to the door. To the contrary, they refused to do that. They wanted to make sure we hadn't done anything, that the company hadn't started, and we hadn't taken any action . . . which we had not. So, we were legally clean and had not violated any rules. They asked me to stay for six months so they could reorganize. 'Don't say a word to anybody and carry on . . . ,' which was a pain in the ass for me to keep it [the future startup] confidential."

Though Beck temporarily followed their attorneys' advice to "do what they ask," he later told GE management, "I'm totally opposed to everything you're doing, so I can't represent you." Then, says Fred, "We finally agreed, and a couple weeks later, I was gone." During that same time period, says Combs, other founding team members also began preparing to leave the company:

"I remember when we left Intersil, it was very orchestrated. We all waited for our executive bonuses to get paid. Then, the next day, we made appointments with Jim Dykes, the GE Vice President who was running Intersil. Dave had a 10:00 a.m. appointment, I had an 11:00 a.m. appointment, Rich Hood had a 12:00 p.m. appointment and we all resigned the same day.

During that two or three-month period, as these founders and others disembarked from the sinking Intersil ship, the core team, led by Gifford, began to paint the detailed vision for Maxim. According to Combs:

"I think he [Gifford] saw that these people were going to leave and he had an opportunity to use them to build something . . . It wasn't like a

retirement home for designers. I mean, it was a tough environment. He was very demanding of everybody. So, I don't think it was benevolence or generosity that created Maxim. I think it was the idea that there's an opportunity that's not going to be pursued because Intersil is going to miss it."

Maxim founders emphasized, says Combs, "We are a pure play analog company. We're the only company of the big ones that was only doing analog. Texas Instruments was another big dog, but analog was five percent [of their sales]." While Analog Devices was close to a "pure play" company, he says, National Semiconductor only dedicated 10 percent of their company to analog. So, says Combs, potential Maxim recruits had a clear choice: "You could be a little fish in the National Semiconductor pond working on a business that's tertiary to the company's goals, or you could be the center of our company and be fundamental to our success."

In their visionary view of the semiconductor industry, Dave Fullagar and some of the designers realized that the analog market was making a "fundamental transition," says Combs. It was shifting from a bipolar process technology of past decades to a CMOS process technology, which produced lower power, higher performance circuits that would revolutionize the industry. "That was really one of the key aspects of our success . . . we saw the tides were going to change."

However, to start surfing this newly surging, big wave meant that the core team would need to first create a business plan to secure some venture capital. That's when they put together the now legendary, two-and-a-half-page business plan. The vision for this business plan, plus eight pages of résumés, was hammered out on some loose-leaf paper by Gifford, Beck and Fullagar during an early, under-the-radar, restaurant meeting. That providential meeting took place at *Chez Yvonne*, a local tech entrepreneur hangout in

Mountain View (long since passed away into Silicon Valley history). They debated, says Combs, whether this business plan was long enough, or whether it should be the typical, more sophisticated, business plan length of 20 to 50 pages. Jack eventually convinced the others that this shorter, high-level business view would stand out and catch the attention of venture capitalists, so they would actually decide to read it. Then, according to Combs, the résumés of the veteran, highly successful founders would do the rest. "Obviously, the plan didn't have a lot of detail. It had some calculations of what the market size would be and what the opportunity would be."

Chez Yvonne Restaurant in Mountain View, where founders created the legendary Maxim business plan.

In addition, says Fullagar, "The original business plan called for the speedy introduction of 14 second-source parts to generate quick cash flow, followed by proprietary parts." In the semiconductor industry, vendors commonly license one or more companies to manufacture and sell the same parts as second sources. Though the company needed to generate income quickly to keep it afloat during the opening battles that would ensue, according to Pirooz Parvarandeh, former Maxim Chief Technology Officer, "the company had in its DNA this notion that we don't want to be just a second source company. We want to be a company that creates valuable product differentiation."[3]

Consequently, after the tactical exits from Intersil, naming the company, and gathering the generals to plan for their fledgling foray into the tech world, it was now time to strategize for battle.

BUSINESS OUTLINE

Statement of Intent:
A major Data Acquisition Products company is proposed. If venture capital can be raised which satisfies the dual goals of providing sufficient working funds, while at the same time allowing the founders to retain attractive equity positions.

Objectives:
To become a pre-eminent Data Acquisition Products company in less than 5 years, using CMOS technology and innovative design as the basis for product leadership.

Market Characteristics & Opportunities:
Integrated-circuit-based Data Acquisition products were first introduced in 1968. The 1983 market size is estimated to be 1.04 billion dollars, growing to 2.2 billion dollars by 1986. Historically, Data Acquisition products have enjoyed the highest gross margins (50%) and FET's (120%) in the industry, while also experiencing growth rates comparable with microprocessors.

Companies competing for this business today fall into two categories: small companies whose integrated circuit technology is limited (and based mainly on 10 year old bipolar processes), and large, digitally-oriented semiconductor firms that lack applications knowledge and design resources in the data acquisition field. There is an outstanding opportunity for a dedicated company to become a major force in data acquisition during the next 5 years.

Companies currently in the Data Acquisition business include:

- Analog Devices
- Intersil
- Datel/Intersil
- Burr Brown
- Precision Monolithics
- Siliconix
- Teledyne
- National Semiconductor (Limited competing products)
- Motorola (Limited competing products)
- Texas Instruments (Limited competing products)

Plans:
The proposed company will be an engineering-intensive organization. Experienced, innovative circuit designers (the best in the industry) will use integrated circuit technology and CAD (computer aided design) tools to proliferate new products.

1

The first year design team will comprise 7 to 8 engineers, all of whom have extensive analog CMOS design experience (see under ' personnel'). Each engineer will initially develop 4 "industry standard" products, currently only available from one or two suppliers. Thirty such products have already been identified. They are minimum risk / maximum revenue producing devices, sufficiently mature that no design-in cycle is required. Market penetration of 15%-20% is all that is required to meet plan during the 12 months following announcement.

Following the first year, proprietary products will be emphasized. However, second-source devices will continue to form a significant part of the company's revenue base for the first three years. A profile of circuits generated per engineer, as well as a cumulative sales forecast, is shown in Appendix I.

The design team also has leadership experience in analog / data acquisition CMOS cell libraries. This capability will be offered for semi-custom design applications, similar to the digital gate array. Few other companies have this capability. Full custom will be offered to strategic customers, if the risk / reward equation is attractive.

Initially there will be no investment in expensive wafer fabrication facilities. The designs will be implemented in multi-sourced CMOS processes. Numerous foundries, capable of turning out high quality wafers at competitive prices, are available in both the United States and the Far East. When sales reach the point where an efficient wafer fab. facility can be loaded to 80% of capacity, a captive factory will be considered.

Offshore assembly will also be contracted to one or more of the numerous companies which provide this service.

CAD and MIS will be used extensively to increase design productivity, and provide superior manufacturing control and customer service.

Resources:
Phase 1 funding of $5M will be invested primarily (50%) in new product development and tooling. At the completion of this phase, 14 new products will have been announced, with 29 more in various stages of design. Phase II funding of $5M will be required to carry the company through to profitability in the 4th Qtr of year 2 (see Appendix II for details), by which time 30 products will have been announced.

Personnel:
All the founders have been in the integrated circuit

2

---

industry since its inception. Two have been company presidents, and five have been involved with successful startup ventures, including AMD, Intersil, Siliconix, and Intech. The design engineers are among the most innovative and productive in the world — all leaders in their respective fields of expertise. Of particular significance is the fact that all the pioneers of analog and mixed analog / digital CMOS are part of the founding group. The sales and marketing team has extensive distribution, field sales and data acquisition product marketing experience.

Performance:
The predominant performance goal is the efficient use of capital in the generation of new products. During the first 3 years, $8.9M is spent in R&D on new product development, compared with $10M of capital investment.

The following additional highlights are taken from the detailed plans in Appendices I & II:

- Sales of $80 Million in 4th year.
- Profitable in the 4th Qtr of 2nd year.
- FBT of 17% by 1st Qtr or 4th year.
- 30 Products announced in 2nd year, 40 in 3rd year.

3

Maxim's First Business Plan, April, 1983.
(Visit MaximumImpactBook.com to read the document.)

09
STRATEGY FOR
CONQUEST

"We weren't big talkers. We weren't big dreamers, but we were fearless, and we knew nothing could stop us."

Fred Beck

Sitting in a booth at the *Chez Yvonne* restaurant in Mountain View, California during one of their planning sessions, Gifford, Beck and Fullagar began strategizing for both survival and conquest. In other booths on either side of them they could overhear the hushed voices of other groups, also discussing strategy for their startups. "They're doing one too. Oh, they're doing one too," the Maxim team exclaimed to one another. "We didn't know who the people were," says Fullagar. "We could just hear them." This was a common scene at *Chez Yvonne* and other local gathering places for entrepreneurs during those early, frenzied, startup days in Silicon Valley when the tech world was exploding. A Lemelson Center article describes this high-paced environment surrounding the fledgling semiconductor startup team:

> *"...Pioneering microelectronics firms like Fairchild Semiconductor and Intel began transforming the region into a high-tech hotspot. In a 1983 Esquire article on Intel founder Robert Noyce, Tom Wolfe wrote, "Every year there was some place, the Wagon Wheel, Chez Yvonne, Rickey's, the Roundhouse, where members of this esoteric fraternity, the young men and women of the semiconductor industry, would head after work to have a drink and gossip and brag and trade war stories about phase jitters, phantom circuits, bubble memories and other mysteries of the trade."*[1]

It was during one of these February 1983 meetings, says Fullagar, that Gifford loudly proclaimed to the duo across from him: "You know, I'm just going to sort of watch over you guys. You guys are going to run the company."

Fullagar and Beck looked at each other incredulously, knowing that "Jack was completely incapable of taking a hands-off approach to anything," says Fullagar. "It never was going to be that way and it wasn't that way. Jack was sort of a micromanager and was very involved in everything."

As the men began hammering out the business plan, Fullagar was tasked with recording it and creating the eventual spreadsheet. This assignment was appropriate, he says, since he was one of the few people who could interpret Gifford's handwriting. "He just had this illegible scrawl, but I'd worked with him long enough that I could figure out what he was trying to say." Despite his writing issues, "Jack is great at doing back-of-the-envelope calculations and coming up pretty close to being right." After the meetings, Fullagar would edit and transfer the cryptic writing into a formal spreadsheet on his home computer.

"It's a shame," he says, "because we were too busy working to take photographs. I should have been documenting." Clearly, at the time, these founders didn't realize they were making history. They didn't have time for nostalgia or reflection. Notes Fullagar, "It was just [about] trying to survive. Just to make it and not go bankrupt or belly up. I mean, clearly in the early days, it was, you know, 'Can we pull this thing off?'"

Over the years, the veteran team had seen many vivid examples of companies going belly up, casualties of the Valley's extremely competitive environment. According to Fullagar:

> "First of all, nine out of ten startup companies in Silicon Valley fail.
> It isn't a given that you're going to succeed. When we started, it was
> a crapshoot. I recruited someone at the end of the Intersil days who'd
> been at seven startups and every one of them had failed. And it wasn't
> his fault; he was just an engineer. I have another friend who started a
> company based on a proprietary digital-analog converter technology,
> who couldn't make it work. The company just couldn't get enough sales
> to . . . pay the bills. I invested money in his company, and poof, it's all
> gone."

Despite the examples of startup casualties around them, says Fullagar, "Obviously, our dream was to be successful. But it was far from a given in the early days." At the same time, besides putting in the immense amount of work and commitment it would take, these friends wanted to have "a lot of fun along the way . . . and not for it to be a total grind."

Nevertheless, the Maxim team knew that they would need to be radically innovative, competitive, and risk-taking in their pursuit of success. Beck described their initial modus operandi:

"We never sat around and talked about how big or how good we could be. We never expected to be a massive company. In our own minds, we might have thought that, but that was never, ever a discussion. We just knew what we had to do, and we knew there was a need for us. We knew we would be as big as we wanted to be, but we never thought about how big that would be. It was just one day at a time. Let's just stay focused on what we need to get done. So, we weren't big talkers. We weren't big dreamers, but we were fearless and we knew nothing could stop us. There was a need . . . GE/Intersil was a mess, customers were hurting, and lots of talent was available. It was an amazing market opportunity."

Maxim was able to capitalize on a revolutionary change that was taking place in the analog market, shifting from bipolar to CMOS technology. The startup began hiring "industry leaders in analog CMOS circuit design, CMOS wafer process technology and analog test development," says Combs. "The number of talented engineers serving the analog market was relatively few and we had far more of them than anyone else." Also, Maxim boasted a pure specialization in analog ICs, while most other companies ran their analog division as just a small part of the whole semiconductor enterprise, thus diluting their analog focus.

As they laid the foundation of the company, says Combs, the founders knew they were creating something both entrepreneurial and groundbreaking.

"From the ground up, Maxim was revolutionary. It was unlike all the other companies . . . you didn't have to revamp or re-tweak everything. We had this advantage. We were starting from ground zero. It's like

when in World War II Japan gets flattened, they can go back and
they can now build things up in a way that's more sophisticated than
American industry—it [wasn't] just evolutionary growth, [it was]
revolutionary growth. . . . If you look at Intersil and all these other IC
companies . . . you couldn't just tweak one thing and have the output
change much. You had to change everything, the management culture,
the design culture, the process control culture . . . We did that in days
really. We had the opportunity to . . . start using the most modern
thinking and start all over developing our product."

Gifford and his comrades developed a specific plan for their market entrance and conquest, says Hagopian. The four main strategies in their arsenal involved: 1. Going fabless, which meant not spending millions buying a fabrication plant, but outsourcing the chip manufacturing, unlike most IC competitors, 2. Starting with producing and marketing second source products only to create cash flow right away and get the company on its feet, 3. Selling products through distributors and reps at first, rather than through hired company salespeople in order to keep costs down, and 4. Focusing on Industrial rather than consumer markets first. These strategies helped keep Maxim lean and mean during the early startup survival phase.

Over the years, says Hagopian, the strategies changed dramatically as the company became more established. But the startup phase tactics and eventual transitions were all "part of a grand strategy Jack had from the very beginning." This Maxim plan was designed to create a company that scaled quickly, so as to compete effectively against other analog semiconductor companies and excel above others in the same space.

This strategy specifically focused the company as one of "two kinds of startups," according to Dave Fullagar: the first was the completely innovative, change-the-world kind, and the other kind, like Maxim, seeks to "enter an existing market using proven technology, only do it better than the existing players." Startups that endeavor to be the former seek to revolutionize a certain field. For instance, he says:

"An MIT graduate who worked in my group at Maxim went back to college, got a degree in microbiology and founded a company with the goal of building a machine that would map all 3.2 billion base pairs in the human genome for under $100. This would revolutionize medicine but require significant breakthroughs in both semiconductor technology and microbiology. I visited him in his garage, a true Silicon Valley startup, in 2009. Nine years later the 200-person team, now owned by a large pharmaceutical company, is making great progress but has yet to market a product. Changing the world takes time and hundreds of millions of dollars!"

On the other hand, Maxim embodied a more common entrepreneurial spirit and sought to create better technology, starting with an initial offering of second-source products that boasted better reliability. "For our proprietary products, 'better' meant unique designs that satisfied a market niche not spotted by our competitors," explains Fullagar. "This is clearly a less risky approach than trying to change the world but is by no means risk-free." In fact, there are always more competitors pursuing this path, and to survive and thrive Maxim would need to be ruthlessly competitive implementing its cutting-edge strategy to succeed. Fullagar cites a recent example of a group of engineers that left Maxim to start a company with a business plan very similar to Maxim's, that didn't implement successfully. "They failed to gain any traction in the marketplace and went out of business after three or four years."

Maxim's team, in 1983, clearly had the secret sauce of veteran executives, immense confidence, top-notch engineers, and an aggressive entry strategy, among other "secret ingredients" we'll examine in subsequent chapters. Though the second-source products strategy was vital to helping the company develop momentum right out of the gate, Combs notes, they would eventually shift their attention toward the proprietary products. "It takes a product sometimes one to two years to get designed in. So, we had to pay for operations with the second-source products. Then we started adding proprietary products."

Second-source products already exist in the marketplace and are needed in existing equipment. To create these products, the team wouldn't need permission from the original company. However, if the other company had patents on those products, Maxim would need to negotiate those patents. The founders forecast, says Fullagar, that "once we had the second source product designed and fabricated, we were able to get immediate sales if we could persuade companies to use our product instead of the competitor's product." Generating positive cash flow is vital for the survival of a startup, he says. "If you have to go back to the venture capitalists for an unscheduled round of financing, you get taken to the cleaners."[2]

If they launched the company focusing on their own proprietary products, says Fullagar, there would be no immediate need for the products "because nobody had seen them before." Companies would first need to design the new product into their equipment before Maxim could create sales—a two-year process. "By that time, we'd be bankrupt," he says.

The founders' initial goal was to quickly create second-source products, then persuade manufacturers to use their analog circuits. As "nobody wants to do business with a startup if they've got a reliable source of supply from a bigger company," says Fullagar, "they would have to convince manufacturers by designing in greater reliability." They would do so by launching with Intersil products first, "because we knew them inside out." Vital to the plan was the speedy creation of 14 or more second-source products to create immediate cash flow before devoting much time and funding to proprietary circuits.

As a purely analog company, Maxim would bill itself as "the interface between the real world and digital world," transferring measurable environmental signals like temperature, light, pressure, and heat into digital signals. Once translated into digital signals, these values became usable by computers and other devices. Analog to digital and digital to analog converters became foundational to Maxim's product line.

After this analog strategy and business plan was hammered out, Gifford, Beck and Fullagar began the challenging pursuit of venture capital funds, the lifeblood that would sustain Maxim during its challenging fledgling days as the company learned to fly.

10

FUND RAISE AND COIN TOSS

"[Maxim was] one of the three best investments I led . . . in good company with Apple Computer and Teradata. [It was] also one of the best investments in Brentwood Associates' 38-year history."

KIP HAGOPIAN, CO-FOUNDER, BRENTWOOD ASSOCIATES

Pointing to the thick piles of business plans on his desk, Kip Hagopian, general partner of Brentwood Associates, addressed Beck, Fullagar, and Gifford, who were seated across from him in one of their first Maxim fundraising meetings. "I haven't read any of those," he said, according to Fullagar. "In fact, I've only read your plan because nobody ever had the nerve to ask me for 10 million dollars with four pages." So, what did Hagopian do? He invested, says Fullagar, of this foresightful venture capitalist.

That's how the trio's breakneck speed, fundraising thrust began. According to Fullagar, after leaving GE-Intersil, he, Beck, and Gifford quickly drafted the business plan and started raising the startup capital. They began implementing the 'Jack strategy' with venture capitalists, he says, a method reflective of Gifford's hard-nosed approach to all things business:

> "Jack was pretty savvy about this stuff. He knew a certain number
> of investment bankers, because he'd been through the process
> with AMD. His philosophy was, you go to these people and you
> make your pitch and if they're positive, you can work with them; if
> they're negative, don't let them say 'no.' Because once one guy says
> 'no,' they're a bunch of lemmings ... they'll all say 'no.'"

Before presenting their business plan to potential investors, and during Beck and Fullagar's transition from Intersil-GE, the founders had begun securing commitments to the startup from other potential founders. However, the trio carefully dissuaded their future comrades from resigning until they secured the financial fuel for the startup.

By March of 1983, the three men were on the road, presenting their business plan to potential investors, including two of Gifford's fellow alumni from the University of California, Los Angeles (UCLA), Kip Hagopian and Jim Bergman. The groundbreaking analog venture received one of many new injections of cash, to the three founders' surprise, when Hagopian announced that theirs was the only one of stacks of business plans he had actually read.

As personal connections of Gifford's, the desks of Bergman and Hagopian were a strategically natural starting place for the Maxim funding pursuit. Hagopian describes the background of that initial pitch meeting:

"Jack called me up one day in 1983 and wanted to know if he could

come in and talk about a company he was founding. The interesting
thing was that I really didn't know Jack, but he knew of me . . . Jack
came to me largely because I was from UCLA. I really didn't know him
at [college]. He was a year or two older than me . . . but we hit it off
. . . it was like we'd been old buddies. He always acted like he and I had
gone to college together. That was my reason for wanting to invest in
the company. And, obviously, we were very impressed with Jack [and
his pitch]. He was a cocky guy. He was aggressive, hyper-competitive.
A real character. He was one of those guys . . . they broke the mold after
they created Jack."

Hagopian, as co-founder of Brentwood Associates, spearheaded his firm's
involvement with Maxim as one of the lead investors. Twenty-seven years later,
as a veteran venture capitalist in a Maxim world sales conference presentation,
Hagopian describes his experience with the semiconductor company:

"[Maxim was] one of the three best investments I led . . . in good
company with Apple Computer and Teradata. [It was] also one of the
best investments in Brentwood Associates' 38-year history."

This startup, according to Hagopian, stood out as a sterling investment,
first, because of the "incredible team" with deep analog/mixed signal and
startup experience that exuded an intangible rapport from years of working
together. "They could hit the deck running. They'd worked together; they
knew each other; they liked each other; they respected each other. They were
experienced . . . but they weren't old," he says. In addition, the clearly laid
out plan caught the VC's attention. As mentioned in chapter 9, the strategy
included launching without a fabrication plant, starting with second source
products, selling through distributors/reps and focusing on industrial markets.

Over time, Hagopian says, Gifford's "grand plan" involved gradually migrating to proprietary products, recruiting a sales force, and starting its own fabrication facility. Based on his company's investment in Maxim and strong confidence in the company strategy, Hagopian became a board member of the startup, and eventually, Chairman of the board.

Even if he had received the short Maxim business plan without knowing Gifford, he speculates:

> *"I would have found out that those people were top-notch and have great track records. And I'd say, 'Yeah, come in and see me.' And, when they got there, I would say, "Now, why didn't you give a real business plan?" And, they'd say . . . 'F--k you. We know what we're doing. If you don't want to invest, go away!' That's how Jack was."*

Within three weeks, versus the usual three months, Hagopian and his company made an investment commitment. Nonetheless, he says, he and his team still did their research and thought through various issues, including market competition. "But we felt the market was growing fast enough that there was room to plug in and get a segment of it" if the plan was executed well. "The business model was fantastic—it was all about execution."

During the Maxim venture capital blitz, the core team also reached out to Gifford's other UCLA contact, Jim Bergman, of venture capital firm, DSV Associates. He and Gifford both grew up in Southern California and attended the same junior high and high school. Though Gifford was a year older, they played on baseball and football teams together growing up. Gifford attended UCLA on a baseball scholarship, while Bergman enrolled on a football scholarship.

Though the two men lost contact during those college years, with Gifford living in married student housing and Bergman living life as a "fraternity brat," they would eventually reconnect in the tech world. According to Bergman, their reacquaintance came while Gifford was working at Intersil, a company then taking an interest in acquiring Datel Systems. "I was a board member and investor in Datel. I reconnected with Jack, and I came out and visited him in his home."

Later, when Gifford and company came knocking, says Bergman, "Jack was kind enough to say, 'Would you guys like to invest?'" Knowing three of the other investors the Maxim team was working with, seeing the résumés of the startup founders, and hearing their persuasive pitch, Bergman eventually joined the investment team. As a partner in his solely tech-startup investment company, Bergman says he recognized a good opportunity when he saw one.

"They were smart people in a growing market, where there was a need for analog semiconductors. It was kind of specialized. It wasn't like Intel and the digital people—it had a little more art to it. The products tended to have smaller markets but longer lives . . . the life cycle of some of the products is 15, 20 years. [These products tend] not to have a lot of competition, so you can get good gross margins on them. So, it's quite a profitable business once you get into it."

In addition, says Bergman, the competitive environment at the time wasn't as strong as today. Besides the struggling Intersil, competitors included Analog Devices, Analogic, and Linear Technology. "Most of them were relatively young companies at that time. There was plenty of opportunity to break in."

After careful analysis of Maxim and the opportunity, Bergman's company invested. Ultimately, he became so impressed with the startup that later, in 1988, he also became a board member.

Other investors quickly came on board during the team's aggressive fundraising thrust. Securing the venture capital to kickstart the company "only took a month, which was pretty amazing," says Fullagar. Though the brief but impactful business plan and power pitch were effective, according to Combs, "the résumés are what sold the company, not the business plan. We could have said we were going to build office furniture and we would have got the money, because these guys knew us and believed in us."

Once in the door, the business plan laid out their funding goals, says Fullagar. "It projected the need for two rounds of financing of $5-million each. We believed this would be sufficient to get us into positive cash flow territory." Hagopian's Brentwood Associates, as well as Bessemer Venture Partners and Merrill Pickard, as the three lead investors, agreed to put in about $1-million each. Other private investors made up the difference. Bergman's company joined the investment team during the second round of funding.

During the first round, says Fullagar, the team arranged with VCs that if Maxim met its product goals, the second round of funding was guaranteed. "Of course, the danger in the startup is if you don't reach your goals, you don't have a very strong negotiating position. So, if you go back for money, they take another big chunk of the company." Many startups fail to meet their goals, he says, "and get screwed because they haven't performed."

For the Maxim team, based on this prearranged agreement, a year or two later when a new cash infusion was needed, the pressure was on. Not only were they working round the clock to push out all their designs, which eventually happened, but also the company bank account was running dry. "We were getting to that point," says Combs, where:

> *"Jack and I were having some long nights of wondering: 'Are we going to make payroll this week?' Man, that's a feeling like no other when you have these people that you really care about and they're working their hearts out, and you're not sure you have enough money in the bank to pay them next month."*

Originally, he says, they each bought founders shares for 10 cents. So, they wanted to keep the second round of funding as low as possible so as not to dilute the other owners. With this desire in mind, Combs says, the core team approached Bessemer Securities and Neill Brownstein.

"We wanted three bucks a share for the stock in the second round and Neill wanted to pay two bucks, and… Jack just couldn't close that negotiation. So, he said, 'OK, let's flip for it!' Jack hands me a half dollar. 'Combs, you flip it,' he says, 'and don't screw up!'"

With millions on the line, Gifford, ever the big risk-taker, put Combs in charge of its fate. Both Gifford and the president of Bessemer Securities, says Combs, were "larger than life kind of guys," willing to put it all on the line like that. "We flipped, and we won," says Combs.

That Midas-touch coin toss became one of the first of many good fortunes that came the way of the Maxim startup team over the life of the company.

Soon afterwards, Gifford, Beck, and Fullagar, and the other founding members waiting in the wings at Intersil, met at Gifford's house for a celebratory dinner. It is here that the informal launch took place, and the first snapshot of Maxim's pioneers was taken before it was 'all hands on deck.'

11

FRIENDS & FOUNDERS

"We liked each other. We worked as a team at Intersil,
and the idea of reassembling the old band was exciting."

STEVE COMBS

The Maxim launch celebration dinner took place in the affluent neighborhood of Woodside, California, at Jack and Rhodine Gifford's house. The home, surrounded by a large, wooded, and gated property, hosted this grand affair on Saturday, May 7, 1983, in the elegant dining room. It was in this room, surrounded by dark oak wainscoting, at a long refectory table, and over a pleasant dinner, says Fullagar, that Gifford gave a rousing speech in honor of the groundbreaking startup's founding. The "cadre of people" and friends around that table, says Georges, besides the renowned Gifford and Beck, included:

> *"... guys like Lee Evans, who was a really bright data converter designer; Dave Bingham, who was a power design guy, high level; my boss [Rich Hood], who was running test product engineering; and Dave Fullagar, who was one of the early inventors of the op amp—these are all pretty much giants in the industry, people that . . . had reputations and . . . [had] done really well and founded companies or designed super things."*

Many founders were also acclaimed, as were award-winning scientists, industry leading IC pioneers and engineers. (I've included, in brief, their extraordinary bio stories in the appendix at the back of the book. These stories were greatly instrumental in selling early investors on funding the startup.)

Following the founders' dinner, with 10 of 12 present, the esteemed, tech-industry experts retreated to the patio (see photo), where they enjoyed drinks and stimulating conversation. Here, they further strengthened their friendship and business camaraderie in preparation for the frontline business battle that would follow.

Also present at the dinner was intellectual property attorney, Jim Geriak, from Lyon & Lyon in Los Angeles, who had been helping guide the team through the resignation process, before and during their two-week notices. To avoid provoking legal problems, says Fullagar, Geriak had instructed each founder (all from Intersil except Sam Ochi) to not remove any documents from the company and to avoid signing anything at the time of resignation. "Intersil wanted us to sign an exit document, which included many non-compete clauses." Most companies, says Fullagar, attempt to present this document as part of the exit interview process, which some "naively sign."

The spring launch took place after the core trio's February through March writing of the business plan, fundraising, recruitment of the other 9 founders, search and rental of the first building, and setup of payroll. By Monday, May 9th, after the opening dinner, the team was initiating their opening business headquarters activity.

Significantly, Maxim founders emphasize that their launch and the company's success were not just built on talented people and a great business plan. The glue for all these foundational building blocks, says Combs, was friendship. "We liked each other. We worked as a team at Intersil, and the idea of reassembling the old band was exciting. Jack was well-connected and respected," he says.

These friendships, further strengthened by mutual respect and business camaraderie, began with the first three founders, who hammered out the business strategy together. According to Beck:

> *"I had a relationship with Jack on all levels, from friend to enemy, to business, to agreement to disagreement. You name it. Jack and I were very, very strong-minded and had our own views, but he was a very, very close friend, and he and I spent a lot of personal time together fishing and golfing, and you name it, as well as many fights in bars. It was a complete relationship."*

One of those "verbal" fights, said Beck, took place starting one evening at the former Barbarossa European Restaurant in Redwood City, California and lasted for hours, until 4 a.m. That "noisy and emotional conversation" even continued after the owners had left. "They knew us and were used to our debates. Eventually my wife climbed in the back window to break us up and get me home. There was considerable emotion and passion since every decision was 'live or die' in the beginning."

Though startup life at Maxim was hectic, says Fullagar, he and Jack had developed a close relationship during the Fairchild years. "From 1974 onward I worked for Jack, and we got along," he says in his understated, British manner. Looking back, he fondly remembers when Jack flew down to Puerto Vallarta, Mexico to join him for four days of his 10-month sailing adventure during a leave of absence. Years later, in 1997, says Fullagar, when he got married, Jack, Fred, and other Maxim colleagues attended the grand affair.

"Jack stood up to make a speech at my wedding and he choked up. Nobody had ever seen Jack speechless before. They were amazed. He was never at a loss for words. [Most people thought of Jack] as just a tough, hard-nosed, hard-driving, type-A kind of guy."

Almost all the key employees for Maxim came from GE, where they had built solid friendships and working relationships for years. "GE was really important to us in the beginning and became nothing as we went forward," said Beck. "The key employees at GE were just anxious to join Maxim."

Rich Hood was another long-standing colleague from GE/Intersil who had connected with Gifford years before the Maxim launch. He says he remembers interviewing at Intersil after graduating from college, sitting in Dave Fullagar's office, and seeing plaques on the wall memorializing various analog inventions, including the 741 op amp. He immediately recognized this IC as the building block of most analog designs he worked with in college. Then, according to Hood, "I just said, 'Oh man . . . I'll work as janitor. I wanna work for these guys. So, they gave me a job, and I always had great respect for the group of founders."

After working at Intersil for a year as a test development engineer, says Hood, his boss left. "I went to Jack and said I wanted his job, and Jack gave me the opportunity. He told me I had to go out and hire some people, senior engineers, and if I demonstrated that I could hire good people then he'd let me have it. And I did."

Hood recalls that many years later, months after Gifford left Intersil, "They finally got around to having a going away party for him." It was then that Jack, cautious about raising legal red flags with GE, would only wink, nod, and hint when asked about what he would be doing next. Though he and the other two main founders intended to hire many of their former colleagues, for a while they needed to keep it on the 'down-low.' After the farewell dinner, says Hood, "My wife went over to Jack and asked, 'What are you gonna do now?' And he just said something to her like, 'Stay tuned.'"

Weeks later, Hood would discover the breaking news after Jack invited him "to go get a hamburger . . . up in some little roadhouse above Woodside." Once he heard about the startup vision, he says, he knew "that Maxim was gonna get started and those guys were gonna be involved . . . I knew we'd be successful. There was just no way we weren't gonna be successful."

When Gifford finally asked Hood if he wanted to join their new venture, he quickly responded, "Yeah, absolutely!' Jack showed me the business plan, says Hood, and I was ready to jump out of my skin. 'Yes!'" Gifford quickly responded with, "How much money does it take you to live? I want you to tell me all your commitments, mortgages and car payments." Then, says Hood:

> "I prepared that for him and . . . that's how my salary was determined. Really, it wasn't even enough to get by. So, they felt sorry for me after about two or three months and gave me a raise, so that I could get off rice and beans. I mean we were lean and mean in those days . . . it was stock options and some salary. We were trying to stretch every dollar as much as we could."

During those financially tight, startup days, says Combs, "Designers were the sacred cattle. They were considered to be the rare resource" and the company profit center. In fact, according to Hood, at the time, "Only 200 people in the world" could design analog circuits. And, because Gifford wanted Maxim to be a "best-in-the-world" purely analog company, the founders held to rigid hiring criteria. Besides the four founding executives, among the founding dozen, there were five design engineers, two layout designers, and a director of test engineering.

Combs, the fourth founding executive, first met Gifford at a job interview for Intersil, after completing his engineering master's degree and doctorate at Stanford University, and some years of work at Hewlett Packard (HP). At HP he worked on advanced CMOS technology and managed a group on high voltage circuitry. "That's when a couple of guys at HP . . . [went] to work for Jack at Intersil. He asked them if there was anyone else over there that he should take a look at, and they said to talk to me." Soon afterwards, Combs was meeting with Gifford at the former Lost Mine Restaurant in Cupertino. "We had a couple of lunches together and the next thing you know, I was working at Intersil," where he ran the process technology research and development.

Soon, Combs was recreating some innovative technology from an Intersil clock chip, the company's biggest seller. After examining the chip design, he decided he could improve it and began redesigning the process technology and scaling down the IC size. "My first contribution was to quadruple the yield on their highest volume chip," says Combs, shortly before he began designing a new fab for the company. For the core team founders, Combs became an obvious choice for recruitment to Maxim as an executive.

One of the senior scientist engineers, Dick Wilenken, also first connected with other Maxim team members at Intersil years before, where he worked for Dave Fullagar. Wilenken is recognized today as the 'father of key analog switch and multiplexer technologies.' According to Fullagar, this eccentric engineer worked remotely and trained a local teacher to do layouts for his designs.

"He had a nervous disorder, so he left the Bay area and went to work up in Yreka in Northern California. Dick is a very unusual person. He's sort of a maverick. He went up to Yreka, and instead of building a house up there, he built three little cabins, one for eating, one for sleeping and one for working. We have a photograph of 'Maxim North,' which is the little cabin where he worked. He was a very productive engineer, but he believed in going back to basic principles for everything. So, he'd do multiplication or division [on paper] in a traditional way. Dick was a bachelor and Jean Taylor was married, but he paid her a good salary and it was a good arrangement all around."

Maxim North with maverick senior engineer, Dick Wilenken. Circa 1985.

Wilenken and Taylor were the only original founders not to attend the launch dinner at the Giffords'. However, for many years afterwards, this eccentric Maxim team produced some cutting-edge analog semiconductors while Wilenken worked from his Yreka cabin in the woods.

Though 11 founders joined Maxim as friends and work colleagues, one founder, Sam Ochi, attended the launch party as the only outsider. Ochi was hired for two main reasons: first, for legal reasons, the core team wanted to make sure the Maxim founding team was not entirely made up of former-Intersil employees; second, while working at Teledyne Semiconductor, Ochi had proven himself a talented second-source circuit designer.

The Intersil team had become familiar with his work second sourcing various Intersil products. According to Combs, Ochi was "really good at reverse engineering other people's ICs." Since the Maxim team planned on depending on second sourcing at first, they figured that Ochi's skills would be key to their initial success. "Jack found out about the work I was doing at Teledyne when we introduced a [family of chips] . . . called the ICL 7106," notes Ochi. As Director of Research and Development, his redesign of what he considered the leading chips at the time enabled Teledyne to compete well against Intersil. "In fact," he says, "in many respects, customers felt that our chips were better than Intersil chips." Ochi says that by optimizing their chip they achieved a "much lower noise process" and more stable internal reference than their competitor. "I think Intersil started paying more attention to what Teledyne was doing because we were taking business away," says Ochi.

When a headhunter called him saying, "Let's go to dinner with Jack," states Ochi, he only knew of the CEO from his notoriety within the gossip section of Don Hoefler's *Microelectronics News*, and from Jack's renowned founding of AMD. At the usual Maxim restaurant interview, Gifford, Fullagar and others seemed "favorably impressed," says Ochi, and offered him a position with the startup. "I knew that whatever Jack did, he had the Midas touch." Spotting a significant strategic opportunity for him, Ochi quickly accepted and soon left Teledyne to become one of Maxim's founding dozen.

The startup team, says Hood, "was an unbelievable group of talented people . . . there were no slackers. If people couldn't keep up with us . . . they typically just left. It felt like we were on a winning team in the playoffs." As the early funding was dependent on all 12 showing up, he says, they had "the blood brother conversation . . . 'all for one and one for all' kind of thing. We all took the pledge, we all showed up, and we all got started."

The names, employee numbers and titles of the Maxim founders present in this launch party group photo, from left to right (followed by those missing):
(Back Row) #2 - Dave Fullagar, Vice President, Research & Development; #7 – Roger Fuller, Senior Scientist; #5 – Dave Bingham, Senior Scientist; #8 – Steve Combs, Vice President, Operations; (Middle Row) #9 – Rich Hood, Director, Test Engineering; #4 - Lee Evans, Senior Scientist; (Front Row) #12 – Bev Fuller, Senior Layout Designer; #3 - Fred Beck, Vice President, Sales & Marketing; #10 – Sam Ochi, Senior Scientist; #1 - Jack Gifford, President & Chief Executive Officer; (Absent) #6 – Dick Wilenken, Senior Scientist; #11 – Jean Taylor, Senior Layout Designer

12

SETTING UP FORT

"Look, it's really important that the first 50 people we hire,
no one's mediocre. Because mediocre people hire more mediocre
people, so they don't look bad. We want to hire the best."

JACK GIFFORD, AS QUOTED BY STEVE COMBS

After the Maxim launch dinner, the team moved into their new facility the following Monday, and with great earnest began a recruiting and second-source design drive. All team members were tasked with helping find top talent, and the startup's executives began grueling interviews in search of new hires. These would be the fresh blood to help them beat their competition and outrun the cash flow clock that would soon threaten to scuttle their efforts. In the process, Gifford regularly implemented shock and awe interview techniques to test the mettle of potential candidates.

As a prime example of Jack's early recruiting strategies, eventual Managing Director of Maxim Europe, Tom Sparkman, describes his first taste of a Gifford interview. While working at Motorola, "the king of semi-conductor companies" at the time, says Sparkman, Beck invited him to interview. After meeting with Beck, he discovered he was one of the finalists among a dozen candidates for a sales position:

> "Fred says, 'Hey, you've done well. It's time for you to meet the CEO.' So ... [I'm thinking], how hard can this be, right? So, I go to the interview at Tao Tao, which was Fred's favorite Chinese place. Fred always ordered Chinese chicken salad. During the interview, [I could tell] ... Jack was an accomplished sales guy. He knew the right questions to ask. [After] 35, 40 minutes, Jack turns to Fred and says, 'Well, Fred, I think he's kind of a piece of s--t guy, but if you think you can do something with him, then it's fine with me if you hire him.' And, Jack literally stood up from the table and walked out. I'm devastated ... I told Fred, 'I'm so sorry. I screwed up. Sorry, I wasted your time ...'" [But Fred answered,] 'No, no. You did great. Oh my God, you should have seen what he did to the other guys. You were fantastic.' They hired me, and ... I went to work with them two days later."

After this first harrowing meeting with Gifford, says Sparkman, he took a 45 percent salary cut and began working with earnest at the startup. Yes, despite his stressful introduction to Maxim, like many other early company employees, Sparkman carefully considered his options and happily decided to take the leap to join the new semiconductor company.

You see, though he was considering three other job opportunities, the intangible sense of confidence and destiny in the founders outweighed all else on his pro-con list: "It was just a gut feel that said, 'No, this is the one that

I want to do.' I actually never believed Maxim would make me rich. I really didn't, at least before I joined. But I knew that these were guys that I could learn from, and that's probably why I joined."

He says he was greatly impressed with the credentials of his many interviewers and the visionary boldness of the company business plan. Whether it was Gifford, Fullagar, Combs, or Beck, he says, he could clearly tell, "These guys have what it takes; they've got "the gravitas.""They knew their stuff. And, Sparkman's post-interview conclusion of Gifford was, "My God, I mean … this amount of hubris doesn't come from you not having a string of successes." He says he knew from the start that he'd "probably never work harder in his life," but that he'd learn invaluable lessons from the best in the business.

It seemed like other recruits felt the same as Sparkman, despite often taking huge salary cuts. Yes, they may have been intrigued with the stock option benefits. However, many were not sure about the value of company shares because this type of remuneration was still fairly new to Silicon Valley, and because their value would be determined by how successful the company ultimately became. Yet, soon Maxim added many new recruits to its high-energy team.

From the beginning, says Combs, Maxim placed a huge premium on hiring the best. He says Gifford set the tone from the start, with the following hiring philosophy: "Look, it's really important that the first 50 people we hire, no one's mediocre. Because mediocre people hire more mediocre people, so they don't look bad. We want to hire the best." According to Combs, after the second or third round of design people hires, the team's many former colleagues …

"realized that Maxim… [had] some momentum, and they realized they were going nowhere at Intersil and wanted to come over. There are only

so many people that can design an analog circuit in the world, and our goal in the early days at Maxim was to collect as many of them as we could."

Those new hires would be vital to the company's eventual success.

Gifford was an excellent judge of people, says Hagopian. "He had a Maxim practice of extreme rigor in finding and evaluating people, then putting them through multiple interviews . . . he was always looking for the best people he could get." The constraints of tight startup funding actually helped screen out unqualified candidates. "One of the tests was: 'Would they take the low salary?'" he says. "The guys that had confidence in themselves knew they could do better by performing. Those were the guys we hired. And it served us really well. And people got rich."

In the beginning, said Beck, the Maxim team was very selective about the people they brought on board. In fact, all three of the core founders interviewed every one of the first 100 new hires. "And the folks we brought in, with a few exceptions, were outstanding. When you build a team like that, you just have a lot of confidence. You just know that . . . you're unstoppable."

During the recruiting push, says Hood, he was able to hire the person that gave him his first job at Intersil. "It was payback time . . . and it was fun. I hired a couple of other people who were leaving Intersil anyway, and of course the word got out. We were just getting started, but there was a lot of buzz in the industry about us, and so it was fairly easy for us to get some really good talent." Eventually, senior engineers from National, Fairchild, and Intersil were heading over to Maxim to interview for positions.

Neither the Giffords nor other founders anticipated in their "wildest dreams" the eventual impact of the company and the financial rewards associated with it, says Rhodine. However, the first office, in a former Bank of the West building in Sunnyvale, California, seemed an appropriate starting place for a company that needed to make cash quickly to survive and convince VCs that it was a good second-round investment. It was also during the Bank of the West startup days that—besides the good buzz in the industry—other signs of good fortune appeared. Fullagar tells this story:

"Very shortly after we opened for business in the bank building, I was trying to talk Dick Foddrill into joining us. I took him out to a nearby Chinese restaurant. I think he was quite nervous about joining such a fledgling company. But when he opened his fortune cookie, it said, 'You should accept the next job offer you receive.' I kid you not. I couldn't have orchestrated this! Anyway, Dick accepted the offer and worked for Maxim for at least 30 years. He was the layout designer for many of Dave Bingham's very successful circuits."

For the quickly growing startup at the bank building, life was frugal but fun at first, like a camping adventure in the wild with friends. "We had no furniture; we had no phones; we had nothing," says Fullagar, about their small, spartan, 1500-square-foot quarters. But, humorously, and perhaps as a serendipitous sign of Maxim's future, "We had people coming and trying to make deposits because they didn't realize it was no longer a bank. People would enter, head down, with their checkbook in hand, then look up and say, "Oh my God, what's happened?"

As the engineers were creating their hand-drawn electronic chip layouts (rubies) next to the deposit window, says Georges, people would drive up to make deposits. "The group used to joke that that's how they got their lunch money." Eventually, Rich Hood called his mother-in-law, who worked for Bank of the West, and someone came to open the box. "The thing was just full of envelopes—checks to be deposited—that had been in that deposit box for months."

To make phone calls in those days before cell phones, team members went next door to Coco's Restaurant to use the payphone. "We had to come to work with a big pocketful of dimes so we could recruit the rest of the people we needed," he says. It was three or four weeks before Maxim got phones. "It seemed like a long time when you had to stand in line to stick a dime into a telephone to make a phone call." However, after "recruiting like mad to get additional circuit design and layout people," the company began to make significant progress.

Like many startups, says Fullagar, when Maxim was small, all staff would work wherever necessary. If the team needed someone in the mailroom, people would quickly volunteer or be assigned. "You just did whatever needed to be done . . . nobody thought themselves too important" to do menial tasks. And someone like Fred Beck, the marketer with nothing yet to market, became involved with building, furniture, and other negotiations to keep the company afloat. That, until the engineers pushed out the designs needed.

Besides hiring new designers, Maxim also brought on many contractors during the ramp up period. "We were anxious to get the designs done, a major factor in getting products to market and getting cash flow," says Fullagar. One of the designers, Sam Ochi, the only non-Intersil engineer in the early days, was specifically hired to focus on second source products, based on his experience at Teledyne. "He [Jack] didn't really want any of us to be reinventing the wheel," says Ochi. Gifford's strategy, he says, was to find market leaders in various product types, then take the product apart, find out the weaknesses and design around them.

"That was the strategy that I used multiple times, and in fact, that's a strategy that I learned . . . when I was at Maxim, that you can take any number of chips out there, serving the same market space, and there's always something that the design engineers either overlooked, weren't paying attention [to], or didn't realize. You look at those things, you make the identifications, and you design a chip to compete directly with them."

In fact, says Ochi, the early Maxim datasheets and data books reflect this philosophy of competing by finding the flaws in the chips of other companies and fixing them. Repeatedly, these publications talk about "the Maxim advantage." The advantage specifications were always represented in bold print, he says, "so that the customer [could] . . . look at it right away, and say, 'Oh, yeah, I'd rather get the Maxim part, because it's better; it's more stable; it does this better.'" Jack's emphasis on these superior specs, says Ochi, is "what made Maxim successful in the beginning," and what continues to make it successful today.

The other key to early Maxim success, says Fullagar, came in the form of *The Peppermill Planning Sessions*. At these strategy and planning meetings, which took place at The Peppermill Restaurant in Sunnyvale, California, the team plotted their next new product offensive on the marketplace. "We realized that we couldn't have meetings at Maxim. They would get too interrupted because Jack would get called to the phone," he says. "Also, it was difficult to get people out of the work environment to think about new products and new ideas." In that weekly Tuesday morning meeting, starting at 8 a.m., five or six team members would brainstorm, including Fullagar, Gifford, Combs, applications engineer, Charlie Allen, and marketing specialist, Brian Gillings.

Though these meetings were instrumental in formulating or deciding on the ideas for many revolutionary products, says Fullagar, they also created another kind of disruption.

> *"The problem was that when Jack disagreed with us, sometimes [he'd raise] his voice louder and louder, and suddenly the four-letter words would start coming out. The management moved us farther and farther into the back corner of the restaurant. They never threw us out, but they tried to make sure that we didn't disturb . . . the rest of their clientele."*

These constructive disturbances among Maxim comrades during the bank building days acted as a type of boot camp in preparation for many skirmishes to come. Eventually, says Fullagar, "we got [used auction] furniture, and we got phones. After about six months, we outgrew the Bank of the West building." However, that wasn't before the little startup found itself on the front lines of an epic battle with its tech behemoth foes.

13

SUED

"Anyone important at GE would have loved to have been part of our team and was trying to find a way into our company. GE took objection to that. They threatened lawsuit after lawsuit."

FRED BECK

Although the Maxim team members did their best, in most cases, to tiptoe around GE-Intersil's legal radar, both before and after the launch, eventually they provoked the sleeping tech giant. GE presented the offense as relating to their proprietary analog resources. However, the core team at Maxim suspected that their hiring strategies were the real source of irritation. Beck described the aggressive company hiring actions their rival took exception to:

"Of course, we didn't think GE would ever sue us, . . . [though] we thought they would create some real problems for us. But we were

123

fearless. So, over a year or so, we hired [dozens] of people from GE. He [Jack] was completely fearless of what GE might do. We were surprised when they finally did sue us."

Fullagar remembers the legal threat differently. When four of Intersil's "most senior circuit designers, plus Hood and Combs, all resigned in the same week, we knew there was a *high probability* they would take legal action since we'd stolen the 'crown jewels.'" Consequently, he says, they made sure that "all the key people required to implement the business plan handed in their notices within a few days of each other." These swift, consecutive departures "didn't allow Intersil enough time to take legal action to prevent us from getting the complete team," explains Fullagar. The Maxim team was aware of the National Semiconductor suit 18 months earlier against Linear Technology, a similar startup that took about 10 key employees from National. Thus, after so many key staff left Intersil for Maxim, the startup team began wondering when the legal hammer would drop.

The eventual General Electric lawsuit, he says, wasn't really about Maxim's second source products, or its head hunting of Intersil's human resources, "although that was what really bugged them because we took many of their key people." And it really didn't take much to entice top hires to join Maxim. According to Beck, "Anyone important at GE would have loved to have been part of our team and was trying to find a way into our company. GE took objection to that. They threatened lawsuit after lawsuit." Gifford's fearless actions during that time stemmed partly from Maxim's early legal counsel, even before the resignations, that prevented anyone doing something foolish that would "give Intersil the basis for a meaningful lawsuit."

According to Combs, commenting about Maxim's legal restrictions during those startup days, "You couldn't actively recruit. I remember going to Rich Hood's going away party, and I said, 'Hey, it's been great working with you. I hope we can stay in contact.' His right eye kept twitching, and he says, 'Oh, I'm sure we'll be in contact.'" As a naïve recent college grad, Combs says he kept wondering, "What's wrong with this guy?"

In the end, despite Maxim's hiring of many Intersil employees, the only legal leg GE had to stand on was the accusation that Maxim was stealing most of the process to build their early products. At the time, says Fullagar, Maxim engineers were using a metal gate CMOS process, which many in the industry considered antique:

> *"It was ridiculous to sue us for something being proprietary when everybody else was using the same process, and many people had discontinued using that process many years before. They were able to mount a legal distraction for us, which was quite expensive because we had to defend ourselves against what amounted to bulls--t."*

GE took the legal 'proprietary process' tack, he says, because they couldn't make a case out of the second-source products Maxim was creating.

> *"The law says that you're entitled to earn a living with your skills. What you can't do is steal proprietary information and move it to another company. We had to make sure that nobody was taking anything from Intersil—no documentation, no mag tapes, as we called them—which defined the product. We had to have a paper trail showing that we had engineered these products from the ground up even though they were second source products."*

Also, though the Maxim designers were making some product improvements, the second source product designs needed to be nearly identical functionally. In addition, says Fullagar:

"We weren't the only people second sourcing these products. One of the more popular products, which was a digital voltmeter display product, had already been second sourced by Teledyne. They would have been hard pressed to sue us on that basis. So, they latched on to the process idea . . . One of the engineers at Intersil, who later joined Maxim, said he was completely embarrassed to be suing us on this [basis], but it was his job to do it."

All the Maxim officers and some of the engineers were served with legal papers at their homes. According to Fullagar, the documents outlined GE's threats to "go after everything we owned, in addition to shutting down Maxim—the usual stuff in these situations." Clearly, he says, "It was a revenge suit" designed to tie up a great deal of time and money. Mounting a full-scale defense against GE included recruiting a large legal team, Lyon & Lyon, and renting most of the top floor of the Red Lion Hotel in San Jose. From this legal "headquarters," Maxim team members readied themselves for their depositions and final defense.

Despite the ominous legal clouds, Gifford was extremely confident. Hood describes how the CEO informed him of the legal threats:

"I can still remember I was working on an old Volkswagen, and Jack called and said, 'Hey, Rich, they're gonna give you a subpoena here any minute. Don't get upset. It's coming, you're covered.' [The Lawsuit] . . . was pretty intimidating to read . . . pretty scary. I'm glad he called me ahead of time to make sure I was prepared for it."

The expensive legal conflict, says Fullagar, was "do or die" as they knew their promising startup would "get shut down" if they didn't fight to win. After a six-month battle, the two companies settled out of court. "Lyon & Lyon were paid partly with stock in the form of options or warrants to minimize cash drain," says Fullagar, "a practice Kip Hagopian later described in a board meeting as 'Optionola.'"

The outcome "was nothing that really hurt us," he says, and GE was unsuccessful in stopping Maxim from producing any products. According to Todd Nelson, in *Analog Footsteps*, after GE's alleged infringement of trade secrets, the companies settled after . . .

> *"Maxim agreed to let GE/Intersil pick 10 of Maxim's chips during the ensuing five years to manufacture and market on a royalty-free basis. In return, GE granted Maxim rights to certain product know-how, trade secrets and patent rights. I'm told one of the alleged thefts involved the charge pump that went into the MAX232."*

Although Maxim toed the line on the 10 royalty-free chips, somehow in subsequent years Intersil employees still found their way over to the growing startup. It seems that many Intersil employees were quite eager to leave the sinking ship. Years later, in 1988, GE sold Intersil to Harris Semiconductor for pennies on the dollar.

Humorously, says Georges, by suing for the rights to Maxim's first 10 products, GE was giving its legal enemy a backhanded vote of confidence. "By definition they were saying, 'I think these guys are going to succeed and we want the rights to manufacture those products.' I mean, that's like a stamp of approval," he asserts. This moral win for Maxim gave the relieved team a second wind, leaving them to fight another day.

14

GEARING UP
FOR BATTLE

"The [Maxim] Failure Rate . . . is absolutely ridiculous. We were
confident we knew how to make better CMOS analog parts.
But nine failures in a billion hours? That's ridiculous."

EARLY MAXIM AD COPY CRAFTED BY JACK GIFFORD

During the first few months and years of Maxim's mobilization, starting in the bank building for the first 10 months and continuing at its second Sunnyvale headquarters on Pastoria Avenue, the team and its management began to gear up for competitive combat. Clearly, other analog companies had already gained a head start over Maxim. However, the aggressive startup possessed one seemingly paradoxical advantage in the competitive Silicon Valley marketplace, according to Combs. The company was starting out from ground zero, with nothing.

As previously mentioned, the team's position after its battles with and escape from Intersil can be compared to that of Japan or Germany after the destructiveness of World War II had obliterated their infrastructure and manufacturing. In Germany's case, while occupied, France and the USSR gutted what was left of their industry to build their own industries. When Germany finally re-industrialized, it had to acquire all new machinery, while the USSR and France were saddled with outdated German machinery, since most companies are unwilling to invest in new equipment when their existing machinery still operates. Japan, on the other hand, was never as industrialized as the West. Like Germany, it benefitted dramatically from new, large manufacturing investments as it rebuilt. Neither country had to deal with entrenched industries bogged down by old equipment, outdated systems, and non-competitive mindsets.

Likewise, Maxim's ground-zero beginnings inspired strong entrepreneurial mindsets and actions that would soon propel them ahead competitively. "Maxim was revolutionary. It was unlike all the other companies, so we didn't have to revamp or re-tweak everything. We started [fresh] from day one," states Combs. The team couldn't just tweak the old; they had to create the brand new or think in out of the box ways just to survive. Also, whether it was purchasing used furniture, making calls from coffee shop pay phones, or paying people with company shares, Maxim learned to improvise. Two examples of this type of creative thinking, in both small and large ways, are the development of Maxim's extreme quality standards and even how it obtained its first company car.

One day, during the startup phase, the Giffords attended a charity auction at Woodside Priory School in Portola Valley. Their friends, whose son attended the school, had invited the couple, likely having heard about Jack's extremely generous and risk-taking tendencies. When the auctioneer started bidding on the big auction item, a car, Jack quickly jumped in. According to Rhodine, she objected strongly, saying, "We don't need or want another car." However, he continued bidding, saying, "I know, but Maxim could use it." Rhodine describes the grand conclusion of this competition. "The bidding continued, with Jack thinking he would just get the price up for the school. Well, the next thing I heard was 'SOLD' and the auctioneer pointed to Jack!" Then, according to Combs, since Gifford had no need for this vehicle, he announced to the team: "Well, that's our new company car." At the time, explains Combs, the Toyota four-wheel drive wagon, was "perfect for running parts" between the two Maxim buildings. "The early days were pretty wild," he concludes.

The first company car, a 1983 Toyota Tercel.

Those "pretty wild" days are vividly illustrated even more by the team's competitive, big thinking around its product quality. According to Combs, "Maxim was a quality supplier from day one." The management team "realized that to survive during it's second-source product-creation stage, it [quality] would have to be one of our big focuses," he says. Extreme quality, far superior to the competition, explains Fullagar, "was especially important for the second source parts because that was our lever to gain acceptance with the customer. Otherwise, why would a company like HP give business to an unknown startup when they could buy from an established company like Intersil or Analog Devices?"

That's when the core team brainstormed the radical concept, unheard of at the time in the IC industry, of '100 percent burn-in.' According to Fullagar, this process involved placing all analog parts into ovens at 150 degrees centigrade, "under actual operating conditions for 24 hours prior to sale." This trial by fire approach, he says, "weeded out suspect parts and enabled us to make the claims we did." What were these claims? Take a look at this excerpted wording from an early Maxim ad:

> *"The failure rate of our CMOS analog parts is absolutely ridiculous!**
> *Would you believe a mere 9 failures per billion hours?*
> *In commercial parts?*
> *No. You probably wouldn't.*
> *Frankly, even Maxim was a little surprised.*
> *We were confident we knew how to make better CMOS analog parts. But nine failures in a billion hours?*
> *That's ridiculous.*
> *It means our second-source analog circuits are at least ten times more reliable than those made by the original manufacturers. Or almost twice as reliable as most digital parts made in Japan.*
> *Better yet, we're not just talking about a few isolated parts. Our complete line of A to D converters, operational amplifiers, counters/ display drivers, power supply circuits, timers and filters is that good.*
> **In fact, it's so ridiculous that we had the 'Big Eight' accounting firm, Coopers & Lybrand, audit and certify our product reliability data."*

The burn-in process, which empowered such grand statements, states

Fullagar, greatly spurred the startup's market launch: "The process eliminates most of the early failures. It is like buying a Ford right off the factory floor compared with one that had been tested for 500 miles to get all the bugs out."

The second secret ingredient in the recipe for this winning chip reliability was that of pre-screening silicon wafers, the material used for creating semiconductors. Management gave one staff engineer, Robert Scheer, the specialized responsibility of evaluating incoming wafers and looking for characteristics that would cause them to fail. As a result, according to Fullagar, Maxim established "very strict incoming criteria for wafers" they bought from foundries. The two-step, screen-burn system, created the near-unbelievably low chip failure rates.

Maxim's analog competitors, says Fullagar, "did not publish their failure rates, to the best of my knowledge, with good reason!" So, startup team members helped other companies out. They bought the key competitor's products, tested them, and published the results with side-by-side comparisons against Maxim's products. "Their failure rates were several times ours," sometimes 10 to 30 times.

The company quality claims allowed it to even compete in the very quality-rigorous Japanese market. "One of the things we were most proud of is that many companies entering the Japanese market had to do a secondary quality screen. We didn't . . . because our quality was good enough," declares Combs. The Coopers Lybrand certification of Maxim's quality claims provided the final stamp of approval that launched the startup's new second source products into the market.

In addition to this strategy of quality superiority in its competitive battle, Maxim continued to recruit and mobilize its special ops troops, especially its engineers. These chip designers, says Combs, "were the precious commodity at the company, and you wanted to just keep them isolated from all the noise and let them do their thing." He says that managers attempted to create a "crystal palace" environment for designers that allowed them to focus exclusively on creating cutting edge analog chips to take on the competition. "We had a layer interfacing them to Jack, [the] product line managers and business managers. So, Jack would rail on the business managers, and then they would go back and try get the designers to perform." This process was eventually modified to create business units and vice presidents.

Fullagar, as Vice President of Design Engineering, protected his engineers from meetings and other distractions so they could spend 100 percent of their time doing design work. In addition, Jack moved heaven and earth to provide them everything they needed for peak performance, including cutting edge simulation tools, and feedback from customers, outside sales reps and contacts. According to Ochi, Gifford created an environment so that designers "didn't have to think of anything except to rack their brains, coming up with new designs or chips or better ways of doing this or that."

Senior engineers at Maxim, like Dave Fullagar, Dave Bingham, Lee Evans, Terry Martin, and Charlie Allen, and the many new recruits set to work creating ingenious analog circuits. And engineers like Steve Combs and Robert Scheer began getting new process technologies running at foundries. This team, says Hood, were "very, very talented . . . at figuring out what kind of products we could build and then pulling it off." The Maxim team, starting at 12, then growing quickly to hundreds, operated for many years "very much like a family," according to Georges. "The patriarch was, for sure, Jack. He ran everything. He was in charge. You knew who Dad was and you knew you better behave."

Using very stringent hiring criteria, says Georges, the team would interview to find both technical excellence and cultural fit. The culture (discussed in a later chapter about the 13 Principles) encompassed values like extreme honesty and frankness, as well as the open sharing of success keys to help mentor others.

As with many startups, launching with big vision and a small team meant that most employees wore "many hats," says Georges. "I designed facilities [and even] bought compressors that I knew nothing about. So, I had to research . . . I was kind of a jack of all trades." This startup culture, with loosely defined job boundaries, helped raise company success because team members went beyond their narrow jobs "to just make it happen." Years later, job boundaries started narrowing, creating problems with "handoff and communication" states Georges:

> *"It's what makes a big company less efficient than a small company. In a startup, everybody understands that they do everything. They just go do it. In a big company, your computer needs fixing, you call IT, they come and fix it. It may be delayed. At Maxim, in the early years, if a tester went down, I fixed it. My computer broke, I fixed it. There is nobody to call. There's no IT. There's no HR. Managers were their own HR managers [and] wrote their own offer letters."*

During the first few startup years, says Georges, Gifford decided he only wanted to hire staff with at least 10 years of experience. However, in some cases, the Maxim ship's captain made course corrections on this policy. "My former boss, Rich Hood, talked him into hiring me because he wanted to get me over there. I was the young guy for sure." Georges started at Maxim in his mid-20s, as a test engineer, a month after the launch.

He says that, like other Intersil employees, he was ready for a new opportunity and could see the analog division of GE on the decline. During those Wild West days, the tech world was upsetting the status quo, breaking all the rules. In fact, he says, the lifestyle of tech workers was so wild, it was rumored that "hookers would drive up in RVs . . . right before lunchtime. You'd see guys going in and out, and then at 3 o'clock in the afternoon they'd drive off. It was crazy times back then." And, for most engineers, the world was their oyster, offering abundant opportunity. Consequently, Georges was able to be selective, turning down an Intersil offer to work in Singapore, providentially making him available when the Maxim opportunity arose.

The Maxim team also made a hiring exception for me in my young engineering days while I was working at Intersil. Within the first two years of my time at Intersil, the person who originally recruited me from college, Ziya Boyacigiller, left to become one of the top engineers at Maxim. So, I called him to ask: "What's going on, Ziya? I thought we were going to go to a startup together, and you left."

He replied, "Well, I actually think we can't hire anybody from Intersil because GE sued Maxim for hiring people away. So, Tunç, you just sit tight. Do whatever you need to do, and when things change, we'll let you know."

Even as a junior engineer I saw that Intersil was deteriorating very rapidly. The core of the company was gone, and it seemed as if the analog operation was being devalued. I was a rookie in the trenches who didn't understand strategy, just thinking: *Give me a project and let me finish and deliver it to you.* The final straw for me came after working on a product for a year. When we finally took the chip to the lab, nothing worked. In most cases, at this stage, if you've done everything right, the part will wiggle and function. I realized that something outside of my control was seriously wrong. I'd already simulated the circuit and done all kinds of work to verify it was going to work. Realizing that something was awry with the process, I went to talk to the process manager. I remember returning to my office, after clearly hearing an "I don't care" attitude, and thinking, *I've gotta get out of here.*

When I called the Maxim team again, in the fall of 1984, they told me the court case was almost settled. "OK, just make me an offer," I said. Though Jack wanted more experienced engineers only, Fullagar and Boyacigiller went to the mat for me, vouching that I would produce. Soon afterwards, they made me an offer of stock options and even a bump in salary. Weeks later, I was working for Maxim as the youngest engineer on the design team. I'm grateful they took a chance on me and gave me the environment to thrive and, incredibly, go on to become CEO, which is a story for another chapter.

Besides the Maxim team's creative strategies and ace team-building efforts, it would need to gear up with the analog weaponry to win. Fred Beck, the team's marketing and negotiating general, reached out to suppliers, and soon, says Hood, "Several significant companies wanted to sell us equipment." Beck, the ever "unbelievable negotiator" began accepting multiple bids and writing extremely tough acceptance criteria. Core team members required "three bids for everything . . . even pens and pencils," says Hood. They "would pit people against each other, and there would always be a 'bad guy' in the corner office that would throw us out and say, 'No, that's not good enough.'" Fred Beck, he says, would have vendors "begging for mercy, and dropping their prices, and making commitments that were over their head to get equipment in the door." These suppliers "knew that we were gonna be a successful company, and they wanted to get in on the ground floor . . . thinking that if they did, then they'd lock in our business." Nonetheless, for years to come, the aggressive startup continued to use multiple, competing sources of equipment.

The Maxim crew ended up buying test equipment from Fairchild Semiconductor, and they managed to dramatically delay payment. "I had several million dollars' worth of test equipment . . . We didn't pay for [it] for a year or two because they could never meet our acceptance criteria," states Hood. "It was very unique to do that . . . most companies just buy the stuff and try to make it work. We actually had performance criteria that were very meticulous, way above what the industry normally required."

A near disastrous equipment challenge arose, says Georges, shortly after the company moved to its second headquarters location. The test group contracted for the installation of a semiconductor test floor, with a Halon system. This

137

system involved the release of a gas that would evacuate oxygen from the room and kill the blaze if there was ever a fire. "The problem is that we had not built a fireproof wall between our test floor and the rest of the offices. So, when the fire inspector came in, he was ready to arrest my boss, because if the system had deployed it would have pushed the fire out into [the area] where all the people sat and basically killed everybody. That wasn't a real big success to start with. We were learning as we went."

Like the rest of the startup team, says Georges, the test group worked long hours and weekends. However, the test facility provided for cool and entertaining overtime activity. The raised, air-conditioned test floor circulated air through the systems, the vents, and back under the floor. On the weekends, he says, "We had a TV hidden in the corner to watch football games while we were working and an ice chest [filled with beer] under the floor. We had put a TV antenna on the roof, so we were all set for working weekends." After their 50-60 hours each week, adds Georges, the test team would take home their IBM PCs (with 10 Megabyte hard drives) and connect to very slow 1,200 baud modems, while continuing to write code through the night. "A lot of hours, yeah, [but] it was kind of a fun time of getting new products out and working the weekends and nights."

A culture of shared risk provided great motivation for the team during those early years of fighting in the trenches to survive.

"When we started, [even] operators on the test floor had stock options. Everybody had ownership in the company, and so everybody cared about how to make this company succeed. Everybody understood, hey, if we don't perform, we're not going to get paid for it."

Despite the many rewards, says Georges, the long hours and startup battles began taking their toll. By 1985, Maxim had started selling about 25 products, and he decided to leave for another opportunity in Colorado. "I wanted a slower lifestyle, but then I realized it was boring . . . and I missed the action . . . so I rejoined in 1987." He remains today as one of the company veterans. After re-enlisting, Georges joined the growing Maxim team to continue supporting the entrepreneurial strategy of Gifford and the core team as they began to expand their international marketplace reach.

15

OVERSEAS CONQUESTS

*"We knew that if we started in the U.S. we would be consumed
. . . and therefore we would never get to the international markets
. . . We decided, to prevent that from happening, we would force
ourselves to go internationally. The U.S. would take care of itself."*

FRED BECK

Pursuing an unusual strategy, the Maxim team decided to first launch its
product marketing and distributorship campaigns overseas. It was a few
years after Maxim's aggressive launch into Germany and Japan that Tom
Sparkman, then Northwest Director of Sales, walked into Fred Beck's office:

> *"You know, Fred, I hear there's a job in Germany. [Director of Sales]"*
> *"Yeah, yeah. There is."*
> *"Well, I want the job."*

"Oh, okay. Well, how much do you know about the German market?"

"I don't know anything."

"Well, do you speak German?"

"No, not a word. Gesundheit?"

"Well, have you ever been to Germany?"

"No. Never even been."

"Get the f--k out of my office."

Despite the unceremonious eviction from Beck's office, Sparkman persisted. "I would show up every day and . . . [say], 'Fred. I heard there's a job in Germany.' And, we'd go through this little dance." However, one day, Sparkman was taken aback by Beck's response:

"Tom, what are you doing here?"

"Well, Fred it's three o'clock. It's time for our Germany conversation."

"Well, what are you doing here? Tom, our plane leaves in two hours. You got to go home and pack."

"That's a true story," avows Sparkman. "Literally, I went home, threw s--t in my suitcase, and we were on a plane two hours later."

Sparkman's colorful story not only illustrates the aggressive Maxim approach in those startup days, but also its risk-taking, sometimes spontaneous style in pursuing its goals. (More about Sparkman's Germany adventures later.) At the same time, though out of the box, the company strategies were usually founded on a clear rationale.

According to Beck, Maxim focused first on Europe, then followed with Japan/Asia before attempting to enter the U.S. market, because the team was convinced this was the best route to ensure long-term company success and growth:

"We knew that if we started in the U.S. we would be consumed
... [by the domestic market] and therefore we would never get to the
international markets. Or ... [those markets] would come very late and
... would be very weak. We decided, to prevent that from happening,
we would force ourselves to go internationally. The U.S. would take care
of itself. [This strategy] really paid off. The international market was
so tough to get into because of the constraints and requirements, and
the U.S. was much easier. It all happened according to our plan, and it
turned out well, obviously."

"Breaking into Japan," said Beck, "was painful . . . but we got there." The country was "absolutely opposed" to doing business with other nations and placed great restrictions on American suppliers. "Nowhere in the world was it more difficult" to set up the company than in Japan, said Beck. However, the Maxim team had one great asset in the country: Yoshi Fujisawa of Internix, a contact they had developed while working at GE-Intersil. "We had very close personal relationships. But he was very tied into GE. He provided great guidance in finding people to help us, but he had to protect his situation because GE was threatening us by now." GE was also threatening all their distributors and sales reps with termination if they worked with Maxim. In addition, said Beck, this Japanese contact believed he was being monitored closely and needed to take precautions.

"So, Yoshi would come to town. We'd have meetings with him, but we
would drive around in the limousine because he was so afraid of being
seen in a restaurant or a hotel with us. We would just drive around for
hours ... setting up our operation, having Yoshi introduce us to people
that could help us in Japan. He served us in the form of an advisor, so
that he was not in violation of any relationships that he had with GE."

Later, Maxim set up a joint company with Yoshi, which he became involved in. Not only did Yoshi provide invaluable help to Maxim Japan, he "was also a wonderful individual," Beck asserted. However, the Japanese bureaucracy was like "old water drip torture," he said. "They gave total favoritism to their local suppliers, no matter how bad their local suppliers were. They didn't want interference from international markets." However, he said, "The beauty of Japan was [that] once you got in, they wouldn't let you get out. They really worked with you to grow the relationship."

Some would argue that in a hyper-quality-conscious Japan, the Maxim nine-failures-per-billion certified standard was sure to open doors. However, said Beck, though this quality "didn't hurt us, I would say it didn't really help us [at first]. Japan didn't want us there and so they didn't buy into our quality. Part of their routine was to discredit your quality. So, no matter how good we were, it wasn't good enough. That was part of the game they played." Sometimes, Japanese companies would "just fabricate things to keep us out and disqualify us."

Though existing relationships and growing new relationships were the biggest factor to Maxim's success in Japan, once the startup began producing unique proprietary products, the doors began to open wider. "Once our really good products became world renowned . . . then they had to go like, 'well maybe we have to qualify this damn supplier,' as much as they didn't want to." Then, as Maxim continued to perform, said Beck, "you could, little by little, tear down the barriers. It was all political. It was brutal."

Although Japan's protectionist culture existed for digital semiconductors, their low domestic analog capability allowed Maxim to find a niche in the island nation, according to Fullagar. The startup eventually broke in, first with its second source products, which were assisted by their high reliability. Then Maxim achieved far wider acceptance with its cutting-edge new products. Eventually, says Fullagar, Hitachi and other big companies recognized

Maxim's "had to have" products. Those semiconductors included the MAX232 and the MAX690, which "provided solutions to specific market needs not available from anyone else." (More about Maxim's innovative products in a later chapter.)

The initial market resistance in Japan confirmed the Maxim decision to enter Europe, specifically Germany, first. This country, says Fullagar, "represented a market that was about the right size for our early production capability" so the company wasn't overwhelmed by demand or stigmatized by untimely shipping. Also, as in the case of Japan, Maxim team members had developed a good relationship in Germany during their Intersil days. Germany's lower protectionist barriers made it an obvious choice for a primary product campaign.

Maxim's German representative, Günther Wuttke of Spezial Electronics, played a vital role in Maxim's history, dropping Intersil in favor of Maxim, like Yoshi later did too. Not only did Wuttke take this great risk on an "unproven line" of products, notes Fullagar, but he also "often purchased more parts than he needed to help meet our quarterly sales projections." This switch of allegiances to Maxim was a major coup for the startup, since its sales force was entirely rep based for the first five years. Both Internix in Japan and Spezial in Germany were well-established reps in their respective countries, says Fullagar, and "were instrumental in achieving penetration of those markets for us." Wuttke's quick decision to start distributing Maxim products rather than Intersil's, says Sparkman, was inspired by his loyalty to Gifford. "He terminated millions of dollars' worth of business . . . with GE, to follow Jack to Maxim."

However, Sparkman's initial Germany opportunity arose not just from a need to establish a stronger direct local presence, but it also came from the need to put out some fires at the Wuttke office that threatened to sink Maxim. So, after Sparkman's preliminary scouting trip in Germany and Europe with

Beck, which included the "emptying of the minibar" in Paris, he returned to the U.S., where he found himself knocking on his boss's door again:

"Wow . . . that was really fun. I still think I want the job," said Sparkman.

"What do you mean?" replied Beck. "Tom, you start in two weeks. Your first meeting is February 9th in Germany."

Within two weeks, Sparkman had packed up his house, said his goodbyes, and departed for the land of beer and BMWs. At the time, Wuttke's distributorship was selling about two million dollars worth of products in Germany. Maxim had already set up a shell company, Maxim GmbH (Maxim, Inc.), with about three outside sales people and two inside sales people, largely run by Spezial.

When Sparkman arrived at the Maxim office in Munich in March 1991, he discovered the office had been completely abandoned, leaving behind an empty building without a soul in sight. "There are no cell phones, and there's no Internet. And I don't speak German." He eventually found out that some weeks earlier, as a prank, Wuttke had fired all the sales staff and office manager. "This is the s--t that Günther pulled. This is the relationship that Jack and Günther had. They just would f--k with each other any chance they got."

Swiftly, Sparkman and Peter Cornelius, a German-speaking U.S. Maxim employee who flew in to assist him, got to work, unraveling the extreme chaos at Maxim Germany. Though a technical assistant, Cornelius soon found himself acting as receptionist, answering the phone, then ringing off the hook. "Siemens would call and Bosch would call," he says, asking, 'Hey, we have an order and why are our products not here?'" Unable to find order numbers, the two men would have suppliers fax over their order backlog.

Sparkman soon realized that Wuttke had also taken all the orders but wasn't fulfilling any of them. In addition, he says, "We couldn't ship anything. We never had any product. I mean, you bargained with a customer. You got an order for 1,000 pieces, and you said, 'Would you take 50? And, then I'll send you 50 in a week, and 25 after that.'" After many months, they were able to catch up a $400,000 product delivery backlog, hire staff, and rebuild the office.

Wuttke, says Sparkman, thought his orchestrated stunt "was hilarious" and continued to "do everything he could to screw you" during those first months in Germany. They eventually uncovered another motivation behind the office chaos. Apparently Wuttke was upset at Jack's decision to establish a direct office setup in Germany, as it would initially erode his profit margin. "Günther was making 25 to 30 percent profit on every single order. But the stuff that would go direct, Maxim got all the profit," explained Sparkman. So, through his distributorship, Wuttke began undercutting the direct Maxim prices, no matter the cost to him. However, as Maxim Germany grew, Wuttke enjoyed more revenue as his piece of the pie grew, and the dust began to settle.

In the midst of these early battles in Germany, within six weeks of opening the office doors, Sparkman picked up the phone to hear Gifford's voice:

"Fred's had a heart attack."

"Oh my God, is he okay?"

"Yeah, f--k he's fine. He's going to get better, or I'm going to kill him. He's out for two months. In the interim, you work for me."

"Holy s--t. Okay, Jack."

So, says Sparkman, for his first quarter overseas, he worked with the Maxim CEO, as a 30-year-old kid in the Wild West of Europe. At first, he would talk with Gifford most days, as he worked to set up the office and catch up the backlog.

However, the rookie director would have to shoulder an even greater challenge that threatened to sink the Maxim ship.

"Günther owed us eight million dollars. My number one job was receivership. So, literally . . . I was approving every invoice that Spezial paid to get the debt levels down. 'Cause Günther would go spend [Maxim] money on all kinds of s--t . . . hotels, cars, boats . . . and he wouldn't pay us. So, I had to freaking take over the whole operation. And, you couldn't not ship in product, because that hurts the company."

Sparkman soon teamed up with Wuttke's right hand person to manage company finances. While Wuttke tried to cover his tracks, the young 'receiver' did his sleuth work and waded into innumerable conflicts with the older distributor. He says, many conversations would unfold like this:

"How much more can you pay us? Can you pay us 200,000?"

"I'll pay you 120,000."

"Gunter. That's not enough. You've got to pay us at least 180,000."

"I'll pay you 160."

"Okay, can you do 165?"

"Well, I'll do 163."

Then, says Sparkman, he'd call Gifford. "Jack, he can do 163."

And Jack would go, "163? That's bulls--t, 240! Middle Number. 240 or we are not shipping s—t."

"And then I would go back and negotiate between the two until . . . Jack said it was okay to ship the product."

Sparkman describes himself as "chief accountant" and receiver for years, one with "zero experience" in these types of grueling negotiations.

If the fledgling Maxim had sued to recover this great debt, says Sparkman, Wuttke would have gone into receivership, and the company "stock would have tanked." Maxim would likely not have recovered from such a large debt.

So the new team in Germany managed the business carefully, slowly retrieving "money and bleeding off whatever we could get back to the mother ship, so that we could get the debt down." By the time Sparkman left Europe many years later, he says, he had retrieved most of the outstanding eight million dollars, and Maxim was on a far more stable and profitable footing at home and overseas.

Months after he started working directly for Gifford, Sparkman received another shock phone call from the CEO that would further change his life. Jack informed him that the director of the rest of Europe had developed a serious health issue, concluding the conversation by announcing: "You run all of Europe now." So, within nine months, says Sparkman, he went from "just trying to fix the Germany problem, to running all of Europe … as a 30-year-old kid." He was soon travelling four days a week around the continent, overseeing three other country managers and hiring constantly. He describes one significant conversation during those days of trial by fire:

> "I remember hiring a guy called Karl Hans Zuche, who was in his 50s when I was in my 30s. I love Karl Hans to this day. Just a very sophisticated, well-spoken German professional. I said, 'Karl Hans, look. Something we've got to talk about. I'm a 33-year-old kid. You got a problem working for me?' And he says, 'Absolutely not. You are good at what you do. You know your s--t. I can tell you are a great sales guy. I'm in.'"

As with many Maxim endeavors in the early days, in the midst of frantic troubleshooting and his pursuit of company success, vital details fell through the cracks. Eighteen months into his stint in Germany, with the office at 20 strong, says Sparkman, a man came to visit the office. "This little German guy comes and knocks on the door…

"Are you Mr. Sparkman?"

"Yeah, yeah."

"How long have you been in Germany? If you are here longer than 90 days, you need a residence visa and a work permit."

"Oh? That's great."

"I'm at 70 days," which was really more like 450 days. "So, yeah, I'll take care of that the next 20 days."

"Mr. Sparkman, we might know how long you've been here."

"Oh s--t."

"Go get a work permit and get a residence visa."

Registered as the president of Maxim GmbH throughout his overseas stint, Sparkman had been hiring people, signing contracts, and doing business . . . without a residence visa. He soon discovered that the only way for him to get a work permit was to have the company president write him an introduction letter. "So, I literally wrote a letter that said, 'Tom Sparkman needs to be at Maxim GmbH, best regards. Tom Sparkman.'" Then, he says, the woman "looks into this little book that shows, sure enough, Tom Sparkman is president of the Maxim GmbH. She hands the form back to me, and I had a work permit."

Sparkman needed to learn German on the fly too. Early on he asked Gifford to sign an approval for him to take a German course. "I'll approve the courses," said Gifford, "but if you ever think you have time to take them, then I need to reconsider you as the guy running Europe." So, though he never did take German classes, within about three years he became fluent.

This pioneering season in Europe provides a prime illustration of Gifford's ability to gauge people. Somehow, says Sparkman, Jack looked at him and said, "This kid can do this," even though "I didn't know I could do this. And he threw me into the deep end of the pool, and I really didn't know how to do half this s--t. I mean, I was CEO, if you will, of Europe. I had that opportunity. It was unbelievable." By the time he returned to America, Maxim Europe employed over 200 staff, and Sparkman had helped open offices in Sweden, Italy and Spain.

Maxim Europe, like the US mother ship, grew exponentially as a result of big vision and unnatural confidence. Sparkman carried that DNA. During his term in Europe, he says, "I promised all of these guys I'd make them millionaires." He recalls a "scrappy guy" from National Semiconductor that he convinced to come work for Maxim. "My pitch was, 'Norbert, if you stay 10 years, I will make you a millionaire.' Norbert responded, 'Yeah, yeah. Look Tom, I believe in your mission. Let's just go forward. If I become a millionaire, life is good.'" However, 10 years later, Sparkman is walking in downtown Sunnyvale, California, when his phone rings and he hears a familiar voice.

"Hi, Tom, how are you?"

"I'm great, Norbert. How are you doing?"

"Today is the day."

"What do you mean?"

"Do you remember when you hired me, and you said you'd make me a millionaire?"

"Absolutely, of course I do."

"Today is the day, and I owed you a phone call."

The stock price had risen dramatically, Norbert's vesting had kicked in, and he was a millionaire. "We were able to do that for a bunch of people, which was kind of fun," concluded Sparkman.

Such financial rewards throughout the company were merely the fruit of wider business success. And, the foreign conquests in Europe and Japan, as described by Sparkman, Beck and Fullagar, set the stage for the eventual product surge into the US domestic market. The same product ingenuity that opened doors abroad would also do so at home.

16

PRODUCT REVOLUTION

"At one point we were introducing 500 new products a year.
As far as creativity and ingenuity, Maxim was head and
shoulders above all other semiconductor companies."

Dave Fullagar

The creative Maxim chip design team, in the early years, far outstripped its competitors, pumping out hundreds of new products with what we dubbed our "new product machine." I recall one of my illuminating moments as a young engineer, one of many that inspired the startup team during that season. This coincidental experience helped increase Maxim's launch into the newly budding power supply circuit market, where it ultimately became an industry leader.

One day, my brother, a digital engineer working for Chips and Technologies in Silicon Valley, said, "A lot of these laptop customers are having trouble designing all the power management for Intel's chips. And it's delaying their programs because they don't have good solutions for power management." A few weeks later, I ran into Jack Gifford at the coffee machine and told him my brother's story. As the decisive CEO he was, Gifford immediately declared, "That sounds like a really good opportunity. Why don't you go figure out what chips we should make and then put a team together. Let's go make these things." Jack believed in quick action rather than months of meetings, a mindset that continually propelled our rapid growth.

With a team of three designers, among others, we defined and created a chipset that would help charge the laptop battery, create an LCD display backlight, and perform all the functions required to power up laptop chips, including the processor. We soon learned that Linear Technology Corporation (LTC) was also working on chips for similar applications, so the race was on. As VP of Research and Development, I remember strategizing with Bill Levin, my boss at the time, about how to get the chip to market faster.

"Well," I said, "the only way you're going to get this done faster is if you relieve me of all my other duties."

"What if we segregated you from the other guys?" he asked.

"Yeah, put me in another building in an office that nobody else knows other than you and Jack Gifford," I suggested. "Let me work there nine hours a day, and I'll come back to the office for the last hour of the day."

"Let's do it," he exclaimed.

For three months, I worked in "The Cave." Even though LTC slightly preempted us with their product introduction, frankly, ours was better. The Maxim chip received huge traction and publicity, including a prominent *Electronic Engineering Times* article describing our achievement. As a result, by the late '90s, this lead product, the MAX781, and follow-on products like the MAX786, which was wildly more successful, were designed into about 80 percent of the notebook PC computers in the world. We probably offended Intel, however, by displaying their microprocessor chip in the block diagram as a tiny dot next to much larger Maxim power supply chips, as if they were the core of the notebook.

With this revolutionary product, our team was able to create a one-chip solution that helped power multiple computer subsystems from a higher voltage battery. For example, a microprocessor needing 3.3V, a memory that is powered by 5V, and other 12V components like PCMCIA slots. "At the time," Hood says, "you had a portable computer about the size of a sewing machine, and it was hard to pack around." This chip dramatically reduced computer size and "forced people to do business with us that would generally have liked to have multiple sources for circuits."

Only Apple, that had "cozied up with Linear Technology in the beginning," says Combs, wouldn't design the Maxim chip into its laptops. "I once went to meet with a development VP at Apple, and while I was trying to convince them that they needed to use our laptop chip, he ceremoniously comes in with his laptop and plops it down on the desk and flips it open. He looks over his shoulder and an aide comes in. She's got this 50-foot extension cord and plugs his computer into it. I go, 'Loser. If you use our chip, you won't need that extension cord.' At the time, our chip was boosting a three-hour battery life to nine hours. Eventually, the same thing happened in cellphones."

Despite the great later success of this power supply product, says Fullagar, it was the first of three proprietary chips (the MAX610, the MAX232, and the MAX690) in the mid-'80s, that put Maxim on the map and ensured its future success. The MAX610, designed by Dave Bingham, "took a voltage of the AC line and turned it into five volts DC," the voltage used in digital circuits at the time. He was able to substitute a big, bulky transformer with windings using a capacitor and a chip. It won the product of the year award. This revolutionary design had applications in smart power meters, microwave ovens (to power the digital controls and display), and a host of other digital devices.

"From a sales point of view," says Fullagar, "it wasn't that successful, but it was so innovative that people said, 'Wow, what's this company, Maxim, done? How did they do that?' The product got a lot of attention from the media . . . and became renowned." Next, the revolutionary MAX232 invention became a hit, according to Fullagar.

"A typical digital circuit board only has 5V power for the logic, memory and microprocessor. It was a pain in the arse to generate +/- 12V just for RS232. Most digital engineers designing these boards wouldn't have a clue how to do this. Charlie Allen recognized the need for a self-contained RS232 IC that would internally generate +/- 12V from the 5V. Dave Bingham did the CMOS design: quite an accomplishment. It was the equivalent in the old days of USB. Imagine having a chip that was the interface between all kinds of industrial and computer equipment before USB. Every desktop and laptop had an RS232 port, as did printers, industrial control equipment, etcetera."

Before this product, people used to buy two charge pumps, an RS232 receiver, and a transmitter, then put multiples of these on a board. The RS232 chip put it all on one IC. This circuit, notes Hood, compelled Compaq Computer, IBM and others to do business with Maxim, because "it took hundreds of dollars' worth of stuff out of their luggable computers."

"So," notes Gifford, "was born one of the company's most successful product lines."

"Chip sales took off like wildfire," states Combs. Tech companies everywhere wanted RS232 interfaces in their computers, he says, and "dumped what they were doing and bought our part . . . it went to millions of units a quarter."

One of Maxim's primary goals at the time was to be the lowest cost supplier. "A lot of these things had a market value, and we kept driving the cost down," says Combs.

> "So, the MAX232 replaced $10 worth of discrete components. We sold it for three bucks, but we started out making it for 90 cents and drove it down to 15 cents. So, we're selling something for three bucks that costs us 15 cents to make. Our actual [average product] gross margins were probably close to 75%, [though] our reported gross margins were typically 55%."

GE soon caught wind of this circuit and quickly demanded second source rights. We had no choice. However, since the legal agreement didn't stipulate that Maxim needed to tell them all the secrets, for years GE couldn't make the part work, despite us showing their team the chip schematics. In the analog industry, there's a lot of 'secret sauce' to semiconductor recipes that is not in a schematic diagram. These hidden ingredients gave us room to build customer loyalty and grow the business, making Maxim profitable enough to turn more of its attention to proprietary parts.

The third innovative proprietary chip to help launch the startup—the MAX690—monitored various aspects of a microprocessor's performance. Defined by Charlie Allen and designed by Dave Bingham, this product, says Fullagar, "could take corrective action, such as reset, if it detected erroneous performance."

This trio of chips spun out whole families of related products and emblazoned the name Maxim on the Silicon Valley map. The products also opened the doors to the corporate big guns of the Valley, like HP and Siemens, as well as the Hitachi powerhouse of Japan.

Though these proprietary products provided the greatest initial fuel for growth, they were built on the backs of the second source products produced in Maxim's first year or more. These second source circuits, which at first paid Maxim's rent, in almost every case improved some aspect of the original product. One of the first ads touted a radical improvement: "190 Circuits Without A Leg to Stand On." Previously, engineers would build products with "through hole" technology by joining circuit layers with legs soldered into holes. With the newly created surface-mount technology, designers removed the posts and placed leads on the PC board, dramatically reducing circuit size. Maxim's first ad announcing the simultaneous release of 190 such innovative parts added significantly to its revenue stream.

As a young engineer, my work on another early second source part, the MAX162, accelerated my career path at Maxim. I recall reading an analog product article claiming that an Analog Devices chip was "the world's fastest 12-bit Analog to Digital converter." It made 200,000 conversions per second, as slow as molasses by today's standards, but a big deal back then. After telling Fullagar that I could create this chip in CMOS, our technology, he gave me the budget and said, "Go design it." The part ended up doing 300,000 conversions per second, significantly better than the original part.

After completing the design, I was working in the lab evaluating the part, when Jack walked in with a bottle of champagne and two glasses. He excitedly congratulated me, shared a drink, patted me on the back, and left. That achievement and recognition was one of the best moments of my budding career, raising my credibility in the company and inspiring me toward new future achievements. The chip also boosted Maxim's reputation. Analog Devices (ADI) was shocked that this small company, Maxim, was not only about to second source their part, but also do so in only one year, with a simpler process technology that delivered 50 percent faster speed.

All these Maxim product entries into the market were strategic parts of the larger company story, one revolving around 'The New Product Machine.' This product creation system led to extraordinary early company achievements, says Fullagar. "At one point we were introducing 500 new products a year. As far as creativity and ingenuity, Maxim was head and shoulders above all other semiconductor companies."

Fullagar, as VP of Research and Development, bore great responsibility in this endeavor: "Every quarter it was my job to introduce more new products than the previous quarter, the cause of many sleepless nights. The results of this effort were published in each annual report, so there was no hiding!" One of the greatest stresses, he says, arose from the uncertainty of accurately predicting product success.

> "You don't actually know until it's out there whether it's really going to sell. It's just like building a car. Ford thought that the Edsel would be a big seller and it wasn't. Our methodology was . . . create whole s--tloads of new products all the time. Just keep the new products coming . . . and coming faster than the competition. We did that over a period of 20 years, probably. I think our competitors were amazed at how productive we were. That was a large part of the company's success. It was this idea that we were creating a whole range of products in all sorts of different markets throughout the '80s and '90s."

Though Maxim would often officially introduce products in batches at the end of each quarter, we commonly proclaimed to the industry, "We introduce a new product every day." Today, with the removal of outdated products and the introduction of new ones, Maxim sells close to 9,000 unique products and lists about 45,000 orderable part numbers.

Maxim's hard-driving DNA for chip production, spearheaded by Gifford, was built into the company from day one. However, some years into this IC-innovation sprint, Steve Combs created the official system, which he named the 'New Product Machine.' He broke the process into common steps for all products from inception to introduction. The team held weekly meetings with all key parties present. "[Designers were] held accountable to explain if they were not on schedule, then describe corrective action, and update the schedule only if no other options were available. The result was a more predictable outcome for product introductions."

At the regular meetings, says Combs, if engineers couldn't say, "Done," they better have a good reason and know that they're going to get some fury over missing their goal." This system helped streamline the beginning of the production process so that, unlike the earliest years, the company was keeping new product schedules 90 percent of the time . . . compared to zero percent before. At first, he says, he got some pushback from the designers, who said, "You can't regulate creativity." However, by breaking the problem into manageable pieces and having designers estimate and commit to completion timelines, scheduling became easier and far more predictable.

This structured production system proved highly successful. "There wasn't another company in the semiconductor world that introduced as many new products" during Maxim's early era, says Combs. "Companies talked about how they introduced a new product a week, while we were bringing out five new products a week."

Over the years, after the new product machine peak output, Maxim started producing fewer products per year, in large part due to increasing functional complexity. The more intricate circuits would take far more engineering time. Eventually, Gifford shifted our emphasis on product numbers to a measure of total engineering content instead. Today, we still introduce about one hundred fifty new products per year, but they are far more complex and integrate a multitude of functions on a single chip.

Our startup environment, which emphasized prolific ingenuity, attracted highly talented and sometimes eccentric designers. One of Maxim's best engineers, Lee Evans, was a big, burly Texan with previous start-up experience at Siliconix. He invented the industry's first dual slope A/D converters, which transformed the digital voltmeter industry. His technical leadership helped foster the environment for the prolific Maxim innovation. According to Fullagar: "[Evans] was a gifted circuit designer who tended to eschew computer-aided design in favor of an intuitive approach. He would describe circuit operation with a series of grunts, as if he could actually feel the flow of electrons through the chip."

Evans was also known for his mealtime eccentricities, says Fullagar. "His favorite lunchtime meal was pizza. He had a favorite pizza joint on El Camino Real in Sunnyvale where he would consume a whole pizza by himself. I remember once, as he finished off the last slice, he observed, "I think I've got this anorexia nervosa thing licked."

Then, there was Dave Bingham, creator of the MAX232, the MAX610 and the MAX690, among other ingenious circuits. Aside from his design skill, he was known to be a madcap prankster and often lightened the workplace mood, according to Fullagar. In retaliation for a trick played on him, he once placed a live tarantula spider in a colleague's brown bag lunch. Also, during the startup era he became annoyed that people kept borrowing items from his office. "So," says Fullagar, "he took a can of orange paint and sprayed everything with it: his phone, his computer, mouse and keyboard . . . even his chair." No one ever borrowed anything from him again.

Another engineer who made invaluable contributions to Maxim, Ziya Boyacigiller, was the first designer recruited after the hiring team launched the company. He was jokingly referred to as a member of the "Turkish Mafia" (along with myself). He made many significant contributions to Maxim, but is best known as the creator of the RODT, most often known as the RODENT scale. Fullagar explains:

"We always had more good product ideas than we had design engineers to work on them. Ziya developed an algorithm that took into account the cost of development compared with the anticipated revenue or profit stream . . . called the Return On Design (Engineering) Time, or RODENT score. The details of this are still considered proprietary, but this ranking system was, and probably still is, widely used to prioritize new product development."

During the founding season, the New Product Machine, combined with this scoring system and a team of brilliant inventors, helped turbocharge our company ahead of the competition in product creation. Building on this foundation, Maxim was able to create thousands of products that became the lifeblood of the tech world. These semiconductors were integrated into millions of laptops, cell phones, digital cameras, vehicles, health equipment, industrial machinery, military equipment, communications gear, and many other devices.

These products have helped launch a product revolution of very small and powerful semiconductors that today help run the world in significant ways.

17

TIGHT & TOUGH

"He'd look at the vendor and smile a genuine smile while
he's telling him, 'Your price isn't even close to right.
You need to drop your price in half.'"

Rob Georges about Fred Beck

While arranging a Maxim dinner event at the Barbarossa European Restaurant, Gifford told the manager that many key Silicon Valley influencers would attend and that he needed to do a "fantastic job," says Combs. After insisting on a pre-event demonstration, he states, Gifford and Rhodine arrived for dinner at the Redwood City restaurant. There, management began "knocking themselves out, showing what they could do." Soon, exclaims Combs, a figurative food fight ensued:

"About a third of the way through dinner, Jack goes, 'This food is s--t!'
He gets up and he and Rhodine walk out. The owner of Barbarossa was
just totally shook up, begging Jack for the next two weeks, 'Please, let me
do this. I promise I'll do a better job.' That was completely strategic in
Jack's view. He knew he was going to do that going in there. No matter

what they did, he was going to walk out."

As always, whether negotiating for an event, a product price, or a company purchase, Gifford always walked into the deal with a strategy in mind. "He's trying to get the best out of everybody," says Combs. "He's going to take whatever they said was their best and he's going to tell them it's crap . . . knowing that they were going to do better when the real deal came through." No matter the situation, "he had his game face and he used it. He knew how to push people."

This aggressive tone of 'tight and tough,' in both negotiation and fiscal restraint during the startup years, was forged and led by its hard-driving CEO. He and other team members, like VP of Sales Fred Beck, applied this cutthroat culture to most company endeavors, including procurement. At the beginning, when Beck was "wearing lots of hats," says Georges, "I just remember that guy was so smooth negotiating. He'd look at the vendor and smile a genuine smile while he's telling him, 'Your price isn't even close to right. You need to drop your price in half.'" Georges says he marveled at how audacious and smooth Beck was as he tightened the negotiating screws. And, as Hood previously stated, Beck would get three bids for everything, make use of the good cop/bad cop strategy, then have people begging for business and making outrageous commitments.

Rich Hood, who was mentored by Maxim's negotiator-in-chief, vividly remembers how vital this skill was in rescuing the German operation from going under, and in cutting costs. "Our culture at Maxim . . . was all about cost reduction," he emphasizes. "And we did that by really smart purchasing, tough negotiating, and streamlined manufacturing. We just had to drive the yields and reduce costs every which way we could." Eventually, when contracting with major packaging manufacturers, he says, "We would pit them against each other, and for a tenth of a cent difference, we'd move a million parts in a week . . . It was that tough."

Fortunately, adds Hood, they didn't have to make quality tradeoffs because Maxim "got good quality and good reliability from all our different package vendors." The company also made great use of its clout when it began making a hundred million chips or more. "It was a great time," he concluded with a mischievous smile.

Undergirding the frugal fiscal mindset at Maxim, says Bergman, was the belief, "If you want something to get better, measure it. So, Jack measured everything. He could tell you what cost a penny in the design, in terms of manufacturing . . . or a tenth of a penny." And, Gifford became deeply involved in the details of everyday operations, he notes, far more than most managers. Jack's extremely frugal bent, explains Bergman, stems partly from his childhood upbringing in a poor, working class family:

> *"He wanted to save every penny, everything to the bottom line. You never know what tomorrow is gonna bring. All of us grew up . . . in my era . . . all of our parents were depression kids. They'd all been through really hard times and understood how bad things could get. When the sun's shining, you gotta make hay, you know? And he was small in stature. If you're competitive . . . you say, 'Well, I may be little, but I'm tough.'"*

Philosophically, says Combs, the Maxim CEO "always believed that it's easier to save a penny than earn a penny as a company." That cost-cutting culture permeated Maxim at all levels. He recalls one of the direct labor staff walking into the copier room and asking him, "Do you really need to make all those copies? That's hurting our profitability." Clearly, he says, "they got the message" throughout all levels of the company. "There was an equality in the sense that everybody participated in the success of the company. It wasn't just

'You're here to do a job.' It was 'You own part of the company.'" At the time, this concept was unique within Silicon Valley.

Integral to the company's fiscally tight culture, says Georges, was a "pay freeze" during the first three years. "When I came over, it was a lateral transfer. I didn't get any raise ... I got stock options. But of course they weren't worth anything. It was beans, macaroni, and cheese ... and very difficult." He passed up other job opportunities, says Georges, not only because he knew and liked other team members and expected great success. He also understood "the potential of becoming wealthy because of these stock options if the company was successful."

During the startup days, with only the $5-million first round to work with, the company applied its radical penny-pinching approach in many instances, including that of office equipment. "We needed a copying machine," says Fullagar. "We had one on loan to evaluate from company A, and we sent that one back. Then, we had one on loan from company B to evaluate and then sent that one back. We never actually bought a copying machine for the first year." After the trial period, Maxim would send the machine back.

On another occasion, during the back-to-school season, management discovered that staff members were taking pencils home for their kids. So, says Fullagar, "Jack instituted a policy (that you had to turn in the stub of your old pencil if you got a new one) called, 'lose a pencil go to jail.'" Cost cutting policies also extended to furniture. "We started the company with second-hand furniture. For the whole time I was there as a Vice President my desk was something we bought at a second-hand shop. The Formica was all broken and lifted off the edge. We had to wear ties and it cost me a fortune ... because when you leaned forward, it ripped the tie. I had to buy new ones."

Jack's money-saving motivation even took him to extreme heights. With a chuckle, Fullagar recalls: "I have a photograph of Jack up in a tree in front of the building, pruning the tree because he didn't want to pay a landscaper to do it. In the second building there must have been hundreds of employees, and he's trimming the tree."

According to Levin, at various times VP of Engineering, U.S. Sales, and Product Line Management, Maxim's thrifty measures also meant that employees were "stuck with VAX computers" for years, seemingly relegating them to "the stone age of computing." In hindsight, he says, this slowness to update their computers may have temporarily disadvantaged the company. "A lot of people didn't understand" the frugal measures, says Levin. However, they helped make Maxim profitable. "We should treat it like it's our own f---ing money. I wholeheartedly endorsed the penny-pinching culture. The difference was huge in terms of how profitable it made us."

On the other hand, the company's financially conservative but pragmatic approach led to decisions that broke with industry-wide, corporate status quo while advancing effective decision-making. "We were one of the last companies on earth that embraced email," exclaimed Levin. "Jack felt that people having email and broadcasting [a problem] to 500 other people" often encouraged people to shirk their responsibility to take decisive action. In addition, email blasts can enable the avoidance of interpersonal communication, while staff procrastinated action with the electronic back and forth. Levin says, Gifford felt that, sometimes, to make the best and most inspired decisions, people needed to look each other in the eye and problem solve. Though Maxim eventually introduced email, the company continued to strongly encourage face-to-face decision-making interactions.

Gifford saw interpersonal interaction as so vital to the operation that he insisted that upper management attend all company functions. Georges and a group of colleagues found themselves colliding with this policy after planning a fishing trip to Raspberry Island, Alaska. Six months later, just before leaving on the trip, says Georges, they discovered that Maxim had scheduled an employee and family picnic at the same time.

Jack's policy mandated fines for executives who didn't show up at company events. A first-time offender would be fined $20,000, a second-time offender would pay $100,000, and a third-time offender would have to cough up $250,000. Georges describes their dilemma: "Rich and I had already paid for our trip, and Alaska Airlines only flew in once a day" to Kodiak, where they planned to board a boat to the island. After running the numbers, Georges and Hood calculated that it would be less expensive for them to charter a Lear jet. "We went to the picnic, took our pictures together, put it on the board so that Jack knew we were there, and then flew to Alaska and caught up with our friends."

You might ask whether this policy was merely an "official threat" to make a point or whether Jack would actually follow through with these fines. I can tell you from personal experience that he would, because I had to pay the first offender fine when my daughter's soccer team made it to the regional finals, and the match date conflicted with a company picnic at our Arizona Design Center. I had to make a choice, and I chose my daughter. I wrote a note of apology to Jack and included a check for $20,000 in the envelope. If I remember correctly, at least one other Vice President also paid the first offender penalty at some point.

Gifford tended to micromanage using this type of "big stick" approach and, at times, using the "big carrot" method through generous bonuses. Despite that pre-Maxim breakfast meeting with Fullagar and Beck where he declared his hands-off intentions, his colleagues knew he would not be able to resist getting involved in every detail. However, Gifford's close involvement proved highly effective during much of his tenure, notes Fullagar:

> *"He had an amazing ability to go into a meeting on a complex subject and peel back the layers of the onion. You could think you're completely prepared for any question and he'd find some fault somewhere. He'd*

*figure out what the weakness was when you thought there was no
weakness in your position whatsoever. Then for the next 45 minutes
you'd get reamed out."*

Though Gifford's routine brainstorming and interrogative grilling method
"was sometimes painful . . . it was also fun," says Fullagar. And, it was very
effective.

*"He ran the company by meetings. He would arrive at work at about
9:30 in the morning . . . He'd have meetings scheduled all day long. Any
time he sensed something wrong, he'd just, 'Call a meeting. I want so
and so and so and so.' They were scheduled for an hour and they always
lasted longer. That's the way he ran the company."*

Fullagar notes that this management approach meant that the executive
team always knew exactly how the company was doing in every area. "I've
been in other companies where the upper level management is very hands off.
Things can get a long way out of whack before anybody figures it out. Jack
would know instantly when something was going wrong because of his deep
level of involvement."

On the other hand, he says, trying to micromanage a billion-dollar company
is both dangerous and unsustainable. "We always used to debate: 'When is
Jack going to run out of gas as it grows?' He just kept doing it. He had a huge
amount of energy and dedication to making it work."

According to Georges, the micromanaging also extended to dress code and
executives' signing authority. As a vice president, his longstanding maximum
signing authority of $1,000 was severely limiting his ability to implement
decisions. Typically, Vice Presidents have far higher signing authority, as
high as six to eight figures. Humorously, after sending a memo to Gifford

requesting greater authority, Georges received the memo back with this hand scrawled note: "Rob, yes, I will expand to $5,000. Jack Gifford."

As an illustration of the company discipline, Combs describes an occasion when a manager arrived at a meeting in a suit jacket and a turtleneck. "What is that you're wearing?" questioned Gifford. "Get out of here and put on a tie." The manager had to leave the meeting to find the missing piece of attire. "When you went to a meeting with Jack . . . you put a tie on. He had an older fashioned kind of dress code expectation," says Combs, even though the Silicon Valley business environment was becoming less formal. Although the standards were relaxed somewhat for engineers and designers, Gifford still expected them to wear collared shirts and look professional.

"The Maxim CEO," says Combs, "had certain expectations like that of the dress code, which drove a rigor and discipline in the company that I think is needed, especially today." He describes many contemporary companies as "too loosey-goosey." These businesses, he says, "spend piles of money on all kinds of things and then they blow up."

Bottom-line rigor was practiced from the company's early startup days, especially in the manufacturing division. Hood notes that in Gifford's weekly meetings with him, the CEO wanted every detail measured. "The performance of the test equipment, the average test times, how many times a robot would jam, how many . . . everything! And, there was always something he didn't like," exclaims Hood. To top it off, Hood was required to present the many metrics to the board every quarter, and show them what he had improved and what wasn't working. "He was just absolutely . . . just so demanding."

This exacting culture was practiced with great detail in the setting of goals and objectives company-wide, says Fullagar. After some time, he says, Maxim created a system of goal setting. "Every engineer, every person in the company had a list of goals and objectives. Each one had a point score. Every quarter, everybody got graded." Staff members would first grade themselves, and managers would grade the people that worked for them. Then Gifford would take his red pen and slash it out and write in a new number. For example, he says:

> *"Let's say I had a goal to recruit 10 new engineers per quarter and I had 10 points for that goal. If I got eight engineers, I'd say, okay, I get eight points. He used to cross that out and say, 'Zero. You didn't meet the goal. The goal was 10 and you didn't meet it. You're zero.'"*

Years into this objective system, "Goals ran into the thousands." This detailed company-wide list of specific, measurable goals, claims Fullagar, "was a key part of our success." It helped streamline systems and product creation from start to finish.

> *"If you designed the product, but the test engineering people don't have that in their goal somewhere, there won't be a test program when you're ready for it. All these goals and objectives were totally transparent to everybody. We could look and make sure that we had the necessary support in the other areas because it was in their goals. If it wasn't we could say, 'Wait a moment, in test engineering I need a program by such and such a date. Let's get it in the goals.'"*

However, the system does come with a downside, he says. "If you need help from somebody in another group . . . he's going to say, 'I'm sorry, I don't have time. It's not in my goals.' It can create some inflexibility. But, overall, I think it was a very positive part of our success because everybody was quite clear on what they had to get done."

The big carrot or big stick associated with the goal setting came at the end of the year— the annual bonus time. And the amount of Gifford red ink on employees' goal sheets was often closely connected to bonus penalties. During company startup days, Gifford had circulated a memo mandating that he was the only one permitted to use a red pen. And, he tended to make prolific use of it. According to Fullagar, "If you got your goals back and it was covered in red ink, you knew you were in trouble. I can promise you, he never increased somebody's percentage. That wasn't in his nature."

In fact, says Georges, one year many of the executives received a memo reprimanding them for handing in their goals later than the quarterly deadline, which was two weeks prior to the end of the quarter. The memo listed the names of those penalized based on lateness of goals submission. Each executive received annual bonus deduction penalties of between 7 and 44 percent. Now, that's how to run a tight ship.

Though the many policies described in this chapter may seem extreme, most of us in the trenches at the time would agree that they helped propel Maxim's success during the lean make or break years. It was a time of competitive war. The company and its crew had to quickly learn to operate lean and mean, like their captain, whether through tight fiscal policy, detailed goal setting, or tough negotiating.

This lean toughness developed in Maxim's culture is no better illustrated than in a later company acquisition. With a tone of awe, Hood tells this story as an example of what he refers to as Gifford's unsurpassed, innate market sense and shrewd negotiating skills:

"When we bought Tektronix's semiconductor division, we bought it for pennies on the dollar, and when we bought the fabs, we always paid six to eight times less than they were worth. One of Jack's big secrets . . . he was always willing to walk away because he knew that there would be another opportunity. He was a very astute businessman and had no lack of ego."

18

POLAR BEAR IPO

*"I can't worry about which direction
the Merrill Lynch cows are running."*

JACK GIFFORD

Standing at the podium on October 19, 1987, in front of a full house, Jack Gifford was making a quarterly presentation to employees and the Board of Directors. He spoke in glowing terms about Maxim's next significant milestone—its imminent listing on the NASDAQ stock exchange. However, Gifford was unaware of the destructive economic implosion about to impact the company's November Initial Public Offering (IPO). The CEO was in midstream when, suddenly, someone interrupted the presentation, handing him a note. The room buzzed with anxious excitement as Gifford read the message. From the midst of the room, someone broke the silence, echoing the stunning words penned in the note: "The market's crashed 500 points!"

With characteristic optimism, says Fullagar, Gifford quickly responded: "It won't make any difference to us. People will continue to invest in strong companies. It doesn't make a difference." Standing at the back of the room, the Chairman of the Board leaned over and said to Fullagar, "Bull s--t. If Jack believes that, he must have his head up his arse." Sure enough, the shock waves of that infamous 'Black Monday' continued to devastate the US economy in the days to come, and the IPO lead underwriter, Goldman Sachs, pulled out and never did renew its commitment to Maxim.

That market event, during the 1987 crash, is still on record as the greatest single day percentage decline in history. On Black Monday, the Dow Jones Industrial Average fell 508 points to 1,738.74, a 22.61 percent decline. Few economic pundits foresaw this calamity when the market peaked just months earlier in August 1987, after recovering from the 1980s recession. However, astute observers could have seen the signs. OPEC had collapsed in 1986, and as a result the crude oil price decreased more than 50 percent by mid-1986, creating great economic uncertainty.

The Black Swan event arrived in the form of Iranian silkworm missile attacks on two US ships. America then retaliated by shelling an Iranian oil platform in the Persian Gulf. This unrest triggered the Black Monday meltdown and a subsequent domino crash effect in global markets. Economists worldwide predicted that "the next few years could be the most troubled since the 1930s"[1] depression.

Despite these predictions and the subsequent economic malaise, Maxim's team was determined to resurrect the IPO. According to Fullagar:

"We needed to go public to generate additional cash to finance our growth. We had burned through most of the initial venture funding by the third quarter of 1987 and were just starting to show a profit (11 cents a share for the last half of '87), so we could have grown the company from then on without going public, but it would have been a much slower growth than what we were able to achieve with a

significant infusion of cash from the IPO. Since we had met our goals and were profitable, it was the right time to go public. We had a good story to tell."

Maxim also needed the credibility of public company standing to win over large Original Equipment Manufacturers (OEMs), adds Combs. "Hewlett Packard is not going to risk their products on a small private company where they can't see what's going on. They can't see the books, and they can't see all the numbers. If you're public, it's open kimono and they feel a lot more comfortable."

Consequently, the company soon began to take its success story to potential pre-IPO investors and underwriters. The Maxim multi-city international road show, says Combs, was "beautifully orchestrated . . . we'd fly in, and the limos would be waiting" to shuttle the team from one IPO pitch meeting to another. He recalls the athletic Gifford going running in New York City's Central Park in the winter snow and sleet, dressed in just shorts and a t-shirt. Later, while both cars were driving down the road, one team member was handing the Nyquil from one limousine to a very sick Gifford in the other. "Jack's chugging the Nyquil, passing it back as we're driving down the street to the next appointment."

Despite their high confidence, the team received a chilly reception at IPO pitch meetings. During one presentation, says Combs, a man stood up to say, "I don't know why you guys would be going public in this market. Frankly, I'm not interested. I just came for a free lunch." Local papers referred to Maxim team members as "polar bears testing the water in the public market."

At another appointment with T. Rowe Price in Baltimore, the executive VP met the team in the lobby and took them up to the eighth floor. "I just wanted you to see this," he announced. When the elevator door opened, says Combs, the team quickly scanned a panoramic scene of 4,000-square-feet of desks with no people. Then the VP explained: "Last month, every one of those desks had somebody sitting at it. Do you want to know what kind of market you're trying to pitch this company in? That's what we're facing."

In his office, the VP explained that their company policy was to pick a good market sector, like analog IC, and buy 5 percent of every company in the sector. "If I buy your stock, I'll put it in a drawer, and three years from now, I'm going to pull that out . . . and see how you've done, and I'm going to either sell it or keep it." Just before the pitch, says Combs, Jack is "sicker than a dog" and says, "Combs, you're going to do this one. Don't screw it up." About 15 slides into the presentation, he says, Gifford "rises from the dead" and announces, "I got it."

While in San Francisco, the road show team rode an elevator down from the 45th floor with an investment banker, states Combs. The banker "told us we had to do a reverse split on our stock before we could go public because the price was going to be too cheap otherwise. Jack fought him all the way down in the elevator, but in the end, we agreed to do it." Although the Maxim team was concerned they wouldn't be able to finalize the IPO, states Combs, "a couple of surprise investors came through and we sold out our initial shares."

Though the core team had an impressive success story to tell, notes Fullagar, they were compelled to concede to a reverse stock split because the valuation, compared to today's "heady prices," was less than five dollars. However, he notes, though the company valuation didn't decrease, "some of my smartest engineers thought they were getting screwed . . . [despite having] . . . exactly the same percent position in the company." This second time out of the IPO gate, Maxim secured Montgomery Securities and Cowen Securities as underwriters. Ultimately, the fledgling company launched its IPO in March of 1988, five months after the crash.

Maxim's IPO represented a big risk, as it was the first tech company to take that initial polar bear leap into the icy waters of the post-meltdown stock market. According to Beck, "The market was still in shambles and people would show up to see what kind of idiots were trying to go public in this terrible market. And we went public. How fearless is that?" That fearlessness paid off. According to a *Funding Universe* article, the company's offering "was a big success and brought a hefty $16-million into Maxim's coffers. For the 1988 fiscal year, ended June 30, 1988, Maxim recorded sales of $28.3-million, about $3-million of which was netted as income. Within a year of the offering, Maxim's stock price had increased nearly 40 percent to about $7.50."[2]

One word of wisdom gleaned during the road show helped spur Maxim's future success, says Combs. "The same guy that made us do the split said, 'Look. Here's the formula for success: Grow your earnings a penny a share every quarter. Don't try to do any more than that, just a penny a share.' Jack took that to heart. That's what we did for 10 years or more." Pursuit of consistent growth became an in-house mantra, according to Combs:

> *"There are a lot of yoyos in the semiconductor industry. So, we would work our tail off to make a number and then, the next quarter we had to beat that . . . I remember in the beginning thinking this wasn't going to be so hard. But after a while, I tell you, we were really sweating bullets to make the penny. Jack was always extremely tough about setting goals. If it looked like we were going to make a goal, he'd raise it. So, we were always under water."*

Combs recalls many years, along with all his department staff, spending New Year's Eve in the factory shipping product. On December 31st, with the auditors in-house, the team would be sorting, labeling, and boxing in a final big push. "Overtime was normal time."

Meeting goals was serious business, notes Combs. The year following Maxim's IPO, the team worked feverishly through December 1989, despite freak disruptions from Mount Redoubt in Alaska. Repeated volcanic eruptions spewed ash to a height of 45,000 feet, catching planes in their plume and diverting others,[3] including flights carrying Maxim product. The ash blanketed an area of about 7,700 square miles and caused $160-million in damage.[4] On New Year's Eve, says Combs, delayed flights from Korea carrying company shipments into San Francisco were rescheduled for 9:00 p.m.

> *"We realized that there was no way we . . . were going to get the product cleared and out in time, so we sent a group of guys in Suburbans to the airport. They talked their way on to the airplane and got our parts off. As they were driving back to Maxim, they were sorting the boxes and getting them ready to stage for the test on the test floor. Those guys came in and, just like a swarm of bees, got the stuff on the test floor, cleared it out, packaged and shipped by midnight."*

This company culture of dedication and drivenness, he says, allowed them to achieve the seemingly impossible.

> *"You just figure out a way, and you do whatever it takes. That's what life was like. That didn't change, even when we were shipping $50-million . . . or $100-million a quarter. It was panic every quarter. I'd go walking with my managing director of operations and say, 'Buck, are we going to make it?' He'd say, 'I don't know.' He's always good at screwing with me. But we'd be working till midnight and then at midnight, he'd pull out a cigar and I'd go, 'Okay, we must have made it.'"*

This tough-nosed survival mindset helped ensure Maxim's success. That and its strategy of initial focus on second source products and foreign sales, followed by the kickstarting of the proprietary product machine and domestic marketing. "In addition," says Fullagar, "going fabless was the core of our early years strategy" that allowed the team to strut confidently into their IPO despite the opposition of skeptics. "If we had built a fab we would have had to raise a lot more money: the fab alone would have cost $10M. We felt it was wiser to put those dollars into product development."

After achieving its first fiscal year profit of 6 cents a share in 1987, Maxim posted consistent per share income growth in subsequent years of $0.30, $0.44, and $0.58, and continuing. In fact, as I'll outline in subsequent chapters, during its early years Maxim would become the most consistently profitable US company for at least a 10-year span. The company's growth success story, adds Combs, placed it in the top seven companies on the entire NASDAQ stock exchange during the decade of the '90s. Interestingly, Maxim was briefly featured on the stock market ticker tape in the 2013 movie *Wolf of Wall Street,* starring Leonardo DiCaprio. The relevant movie scene shows MXIM at a lofty $8¾ (the price it reached in October 1989, a year after the IPO). And, Maxim's price is shown alongside Texas Instruments (TXN) $6 ½, Oracle's (ORCL) $4 $^5/_8$, and Microsoft's (MSFT) $1/_2$ listings.

Maxim 'stars' in a scene of the 2013 Wolf of Wall Street movie.

During this birthing season, from the IPO launch and beyond, it was as if the founding team's self-assured foresight enabled it to succeed despite its many detractors. As Gifford once said in an interview, *"We would be the last company in the universe to be a leading indicator of any reduction in demand."*[5]

SNAPSHOTS OF MAXIM'S FOUNDING YEARS

Maxim founders at early headquarters ▲

Maxim founders in front of Sunnyvale headquarters on N. Pastoria Ave. From left to right: Jack Gifford, Dave Fullagar, Bev Fuller, Roger Fuller, Sam Ochi, Steve Combs, Lee Evans, Rich Hood, and Dave Bingham.

Launch party ▲

Left to Right: Rhodine and Jack Gifford with Roger and Debbie Fuller at Maxim's launch party.

▶

Maxim global headquarters

The four Maxim global headquarters buildings in Silicon Valley over the years: top image, 1983, original bank building at 920 W. Fremont Ave., Sunnyvale; second from top, 1984, 510 N. Pastoria Ave., Sunnyvale (building recently torn down and replaced); third from top, 1988, 120 San Gabriel Drive, Sunnyvale; bottom image, 2012 to present, 160 Rio Robles, San Jose.

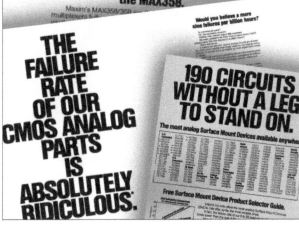

Maxim ads

Early hard-hitting Maxim ads

CEO of the year

Electronic Business Magazine selects Jack Gifford as "CEO of the Year" in 2001.

Maxim engineers

A group of early Maxim engineers in 1986. From left to right: Ziya Boyacigiller, Bob Underwood, Lee Evans, Ron Knapp, Roger Fuller, Yusuf Haque, Sam Ochi, Dave Fullagar, Dick Wilenken, and Dave Bingham. ▼

Business and baseball ▲

*Jack Gifford, Maxim CEO,
baseball enthusiast and
Maxim Yankees manager.*

▶

Calma layout work

*Tunç Doluca at a Calma layout
station in the early days.*

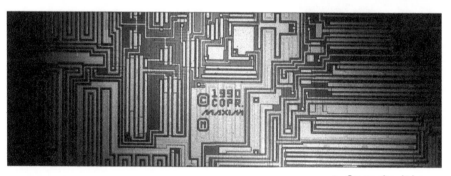

▲ **Cover circuit image**

*The Image featured on
the book cover—the
renowned RS232.*

◀

Executive managers

*Maxim executive management team
in late 1983. From left to right: Jack
Gifford, President and CEO; Steve
Combs, VP Operations; Alan Henricks,
VP Finance; Dave Fullagar, VP R&D;
Fred Beck, VP Sales & Marketing.*

Department Photos During Maxim's Early Years

Application Engineers ▲

▲ *Design Engineers*

Test Engineers ▲

▲ *Administrative Staff*

Test Operations Team ▲

▲ *Business Managers*

*Customer
Service Team*

*Test Floor
Operators*

Legacy & New Era

Recognition

*Jack at the University
of Hawaii graduation
ceremonies, May 2007.
He participated as the
commencement speaker
and received The Degree
of Doctor of Humane
Letters, honoris causa,
in recognition of his
humanitarian work.*

Passing the reins

*Jack Gifford hands
over the CEO reins
of Maxim to Tunç
Doluca in 2007.*

PART THREE

THREE

GROWTH

19

MEETINGS
FROM HELL

*"When people say something silly, you're going to get hammered,
so think about what you're going to say before you say it."*

JACK GIFFORD [1]

Walking into a meeting with Gifford to make a presentation, Matt Murphy, a Business Manager at the time, had no inclination that this would be one of the worst and, ultimately, the best encounters of his business life. At first glance, says Murphy, this routine quarterly Maxim meeting, a 2.0 version of one aptly nicknamed by insiders as the 'Meeting from Hell' (MFH), seemed to promise a warmly receptive audience. Murphy describes the occasion:

"I was doing my presentation and it was right before Christmas because I remember Gifford was wearing a Santa tie with lights on it. I thought, 'Okay, cool, he's going to be in a good mood.' Jack had said, 'Everyone has to give me your marketing advertising plan for your product line.' I didn't prepare well, and my thoughts weren't clear . . . it was kind of a new thing for me. I get some spreadsheet and . . . we're running ads in Russia. I'm trying to make sense of it. I sort of give him my plan and he's like, 'Why are you running this product five times here? Why are you running this product over here?' I just didn't know, and I started kind of flubbing it. At one point he said to me, 'I can't even understand a word coming out of your mouth.' Then I answered, 'You know something? I think we need to end this meeting. I'm not prepared. I'm not doing a good job and I need to come back to you.' He goes, 'Yeah, damn straight you have to get back to me.' So, I walk out. I was like, 'Oh s--t.' It was probably one of the worst meetings I ever had."

Walking out of the meeting, mortified, says Murphy, he sees one of his peers, Ron Clark, on the way in to do his presentation. Apparently, he immediately says to Gifford, "Hey, Jack, I saw Murphy on the way. He didn't look so good." To which Jack responded, "Yeah, he really f--ed up." To make matters worse, later, during the typical peer debrief, Clark returns telling the glory story of his great presentation meeting. It was then, says Murphy, as a young manager cowering in his cubicle, that he began to reconsider his future. *Oh man, I just suck*, he thought. *I'm not good enough for this place. Maybe I've hit my limit.*

Days later, still pondering his career, a second encounter would dramatically impact his decision. Murphy attended the annual Maxim Christmas party with a date. He briefed her first, saying, "Look, whatever we do, let's just not run into him because I'm not in a good place with him. He thinks I suck, and I think I probably need to leave anyway. Let's just avoid him at all cost." Fortunately, Murphy's wish would not come true:

> *"We had this great night and we're walking out . . . when I see Jack.*
> *There's a thousand people, and everyone's dressed up in tuxes. He's got*
> *some glass, some scotch or something. He's holding court with a bunch of*
> *people, and I'm thinking, 'Perfect.' I was getting out of here scot-free.*
> *I'm walking out the door . . . he looks up and sees me, points at me, . . .*
> *and signals us to stop."*

After sauntering over and charmingly introducing himself to Murphy's date, Gifford inquires about her work situation and discovers she works at IBM as an electrical engineer. Looking at Murphy, Jack asks, "Why isn't she working at Maxim? You haven't brought her over to join?"

Answering, "No, no," Murphy starts thinking, *Oh, my God, this is a nightmare!*

Then came the moment that would transform his life. With great emotion in his voice, and reflected on his face, Murphy continues retelling his story:

> *"Then I figured he's going to say something because I just had this*
> *horrible meeting [with him]. It was like the world just stopped.*
> *Suddenly, it was just he and I. He looked at me and said, 'I just want*
> *to let you know that I've been following you and your career here, and*
> *I think the sky's the limit for you. I have tremendous confidence in your*
> *abilities, and you're doing a great job."*

This experience, says Murphy, captures the kind of leader Gifford was. In this large company, he says, where . . .

> *"I was just another guy . . . when he was at his peak he knew every*

person. He knew where they were at, and he knew how to masterfully
coach them. He was incredibly intuitive as to where people were at.
Unbelievable EQ [Emotional Quotient]. His instincts, his ability
to pattern recognize, and read, like nothing I've ever seen. A truly
Six Sigma, off-the-charts, brilliant guy on business, technical, people,
leadership."

Somehow, Gifford knew that he had brought Murphy to the edge and recognized that night just what his young protégé needed. Though that was one of few compliments he ever received from the CEO, says Murphy, "He had me for five more years. I didn't need to hear that again because I knew he delivered that gift to me that night." This was one of three significant compliments Murphy would receive from Gifford, moments that ultimately helped propel his future career.

Murphy's traumatic encounter is not atypical of Maxim meetings in the early years that Gifford presided over. Most business unit managers (BMs) in these quarterly meetings came in with trepidation, and after a grueling interrogation would leave with great relief or with their tail between their legs. Few today would approve of Gifford's high-decibel management style; however, it was not an uncommon CEO strategy among early Silicon Valley pioneers. These Meetings from Hell (MFH) were so nicknamed for many reasons, besides their demanding test of the mettle, intellect, and research of every manager, as Jack sought to blow holes in their product presentations.

According to Fullagar, the infamous gathering of managers, originally designed to select the next products Maxim would design, was so named . . .

"because it lasted all day (sometimes two days), and the overseas staff in
Asia and Europe were on a conference call for the whole meeting—truly
hellish to be hanging on the phone for eight hours through the night."

In addition, Gifford gave too few bathroom breaks and often filled the air with spicy language during the continually challenging interactions, as he played devil's advocate and kept his managers on their toes. However, he did give everyone fair warning: "When people say something silly, you're going to get hammered, so think about what you're going to say before you say it."

Various Maxim meetings spearheaded by Gifford became an extreme gauntlet. However, this gathering started out, between 1983 to 1985, as a more sedate, weekly, Breakfast Product Planning Meeting at the Peppermill Restaurant. As Fullagar notes, "The breakfast meetings were quite congenial and didn't qualify as hellish," despite Jack becoming "a little wound-up." However, this weekly meeting, with the initial five or six participants, eventually became the MFH quarterly product presentation and discussion. About 20 or 30 participants would interact over dozens of new product ideas.

Like many of his strategies, for the sake of efficiency and mentoring, Gifford wanted all upper management and aspiring leaders to learn together the lessons of the MFH. He wanted each participant to learn from people's successes and to know what traps not to fall into . . . whether it was the product line or business managers (BMs), marketing managers, product designers or other top executives. He also wanted to hone each person's ability to problem solve and make better forecasting decisions about future products.

With more product ideas than engineers, this meeting became pivotal in the future and ongoing success of Maxim. Everyone recognized engineering resources as the limited company gold. Consequently, the primary goal was to select the best products that would generate the highest marketplace returns. Often, Field Applications Engineers (FAEs), with their fingers on the pulse of customers, would present their perspectives and interactive research of market needs. One of those FAEs, Charlie Allen, who coined the MFH handle, was one of the top engineers whose brilliant new product instincts and decisions helped Maxim successfully create and compete.

At first, the Maxim team made future new product decisions based on ballpark estimates of future yearly sales and revenue. No metric existed to compare products or refine the accuracy of estimates. That's when eventual business unit Vice President, Ziya Boyacigiller, got an epiphany that would revolutionize the decision-making process. In the mid-80s, he developed a metric that enabled managers to create a Return on Design Time score (RODT, but quickly nicknamed RODENT by the employees). He rationalized that if engineering creativity was the most limited resource, then they should develop metrics that determine which products had the highest and lowest return on design time. The formula for RODT was to divide estimated lifetime gross margin dollars generated by the product into the estimated design engineering time required to design the product (months of designer time). So, the units for RODT were millions of dollars per design engineering month of investment.

This metric was "absolute genius," says Sparkman. "You've got these 100 plus product lines going into 10,000 different applications across 20 or 30 different industries. And how do you decide between doing a product for an iPhone or doing a product for a Mercedes Benz?" RODT would help make this determination, whether the product had a life cycle of 18 months or 10 years.

Once a potential product's RODT number was determined, participants would indicate if they were for or against the product's creation. Gifford would make the final decision and sometimes exercise a veto vote after ranking the ideas. "These meetings were ordeals, and it was like going into the lion's den," says Levin. "You would present your idea, and Jack always favored people based on how much conviction they had for something and how aggressively they pushed. They had to be able to communicate it effectively. It had to be logical, but it had to be strong. He wanted to see their passion."

The key in determining passion and holes in product presentations came through challenging and sometimes humorous interrogation by Gifford. According to Levin, "Jack felt very strongly that the only way you could survive when you got to the high level in a company was by asking good questions. So, that's how he thrived." The barrage at MFH might include, "Why do customers need this? How many households are there? How can you sell 500 million of these ICs if there are only 100 million households out there? What specific application are we targeting? Why will this product be a winner?" The mandate was to be #1 or #2 in every market targeted.

Though other factors helped in product selection, the RODT concept helped shape a structured, rational process. It allowed managers to rank products and compare product lines to one another to determine best investment potential. Though the forecasting of future revenue and engineering was still subjective, at least it created some order, with educated estimates within the product selection process. Managers researched their RODT numbers, like most businesses do, through market studies and discussion with customers. Then, they'd bring their findings to the MFH. For instance, they'd say, "This product is going to sell into PCs. Here's the PC forecast for the next five years—20 million units per year. Each one is going to need a MAX232 interface chip at $1.50 per unit. Here's the whole market. We can maybe get 30 percent of it."

The greatest challenge in implementing this selection metric was the tendency for managers to want their products to go to the top of the list. Though they did their best with forecasts, managers would sometimes encourage engineers to underestimate design time. And, estimates also seemed to be influenced by Jack's initial determination that a product wasn't worth producing if it didn't have a RODT greater than $1-million per month. Consequently, many manager forecasts came in around $1-million to at least get on the list, and because the BMs didn't want to risk their credibility by estimating too high.

However, by meeting's end, based on the RODT metric, conviction, and individual votes, Gifford would rank ideas. BMs would leave knowing the products Maxim would create that next quarter. Eventually, we refined the RODT metric to include Internal Rate of Return (IRR), which accounts for the time value of money. In making our product decisions today, we consider whether the product will yield its revenue within one or more years, depending on its potential lifecycle. Some chips eventually far exceeded RODT estimates, like the MAX786, which knocked out a profit 10 times what was expected.

Whether it was the official Meeting from Hell, or other unofficial business meetings with Gifford officiating, this CEO held all participants to high standards. In manufacturing division meetings, says Fullagar:

"Jack was insistent that every aspect of the company be measured and reported . . . wafer starts, shipment to schedule performance, and a host of other metrics. When we first purchased the semiconductor operation from Tektronix, their design engineers couldn't believe I was demanding that they each say precisely what they were going to get done in the next working week, and then be held accountable for whether they had gotten it done seven days later."

Gifford would call meetings any time "he sensed something was amiss," says Fullagar. "A typical day might include half a dozen or more meetings. That was his management style."

Jack often espoused the philosophy that people could only be motivated by fear and greed. As a product of the hard-driving Fairchild ethos, he implemented a 'take-no-prisoners' approach to management. Gifford believed this style got the most out of people, and to some extent it worked. But you had to be thick-skinned to work for him. He would regularly heckle other managers to keep them on their toes.

In her *"Book of Jack,"* Pratima Rao, Director of Business Management, compiles humorous and quotable Gifford statements. Here are a few of his typical zingers:

> *"Be advised: your boss may think you know what you are talking about, but you don't."*
>
> *"Hell, my grandmother could make a pager. There is no proprietary advantage to a pager."*
>
> *"No amount of electronics can fix incompetency."*
>
> *"I don't need to read anything. That way I can listen and see if you know what you're talking about."*
>
> *"Sounds pretty flimsy to me. What's the next excuse?"*
>
> *"I know that I am right, and you are f---ing wrong."*
>
> *"You all get a vote, but the only vote that's important is mine."*[2]

Senior management were not spared. In one of these meetings, says Levin, he was still new to the company and asking lots of questions about the chip business. That's when, in front of the group, Gifford dismissed one of Levin's comments, saying, "It will be five years before anything you say matters."

Levin recalls another MFH-like encounter, this time over the phone, when he called Gifford from Oregon to discuss some business matter. As a long-time friend of Gifford and knowing the CEO's tendency to test people's certitude about an issue by their passion, Levin usually felt free to engage in heated discussion. At the time, the company legal counsel, Tony Gilbert, a polite, cultured gentleman, was sitting in the CEOs office. As was his habit, Gifford put Levin on speakerphone.

Soon, a typical war of words broke out. "He just pissed me off about something. I'm sure I pissed him off back, and so we're both really screaming at each other," explains Levin. Later he discovered that "the door was closed into Jack's office and all of the admin people were sitting just [within] earshot." Eventually, a shell-shocked Tony exited the office. As he walked away, the staff, assuming he was the target of Gifford's outrage, were heard to say, "Oh, poor Tony."

Despite Gifford's seeming relish of verbal pugilism, says Hood, "He had just fantastic leadership qualities. And when you got your butt kicked, he was probably right. There weren't many times when I felt like I got scolded that I couldn't have done a better job. I think he got more out of us than we would have gotten out of ourselves in other situations in other companies. He improved all of our performances. He forced us to look at things in different ways."

One legendary Meeting from Hell illustrates Gifford's tough-minded, combat-zone mentality when business managers were being interrogated for missing their quarterly revenue forecasts. I was sitting next to him and watching him yell at people. Suddenly, his face turned white, and he stood up without saying a word and rushed out the room. We sat there for at least 10 minutes, wondering what had happened. "He was really upset. Should we go get him or are we dismissed? Is the meeting over?" Eventually I said, "Let me go look for the guy." After leaving, I discovered a big commotion in the bathroom. Jack had collapsed on the floor while passing a kidney stone. At least 20 people crammed into the room to find out what happened. Some even wondered out loud, "Did we do this to him?"

Eventually an ambulance arrived, and Gifford was taken to the hospital. I imagine he was probably in excruciating pain throughout much of the meeting. Yet, he continued to run the conflict-zone meeting until he couldn't stand it any longer. However, Jack quickly recovered from that crisis incident and was in fine form again at the next Meeting from Hell. As usual, in his mind,

Maxim's MFH boot camp was vital preparation for aggressive engagement with the competition and in achieving the wild success necessary to win our war.

20

EPIC MAXIMS

"These principles . . . represent the guidelines I use to approach my job and my daily life and have played an important role in my successes—and I believe Maxim's."

JACK GIFFORD

H e would have likely been disciplined or fired at most other companies, says Murphy, for his implementation of Maxim's unique cultural principles the way he did as a young Strategic Account Manager. In that role, Murphy noticed the company was extremely late in shipping one of the products he was responsible for. The delay was creating serious issues for Maxim's customer, HP Singapore, in the production of their Palmtops, a device that preceded the smartphone. "Maxim had two power supply chips in them . . . and we were eight, 10 weeks late. The Singapore factory was going to furlough HP employees. It was a total disaster," exclaims Murphy.

While managing this product, he discovered that during the final test phase before shipment, the parts were being placed in a queue at the Sunnyvale, California test facility. "I'm like, "No, no, no . . . there's an expedite list, we need this prioritized." Then, once the team started testing the chips, the machinery jammed. "I come in at five in the morning on the Friday to personally check. Put on my lab coat, go on the test floor . . . the thing's jammed, but some units have tested." Quickly, Murphy instructed the test floor operator to "split the lot" so that the units already tested could ship.

"Now in manufacturing operations, splitting a lot is super inefficient . . . The guy that was running the test floor at the time was just a brutal guy . . . a menace." Both the test floor manager and his superior refused to split the lot. So, Murphy decided to go to the top by writing a memo to Gifford explaining the dilemma and the necessity for taking extraordinary action. "I laid myself on the tracks. I took this thing over to the office and gave it to Gifford's admin . . . 'Can you please have Jack look at this?'"

Then, says Murphy, "I'm just pacing around going, 'Either he's going to approve this, or I'm going to get called into his office . . . [and] he's going to maybe fire me. Because honestly, I totally went rogue because I knew I wasn't going to get s--t out of this other guy.'"

Remembering some of the Maxim Principles—*Stand up for what you believe is right; Don't accept the status quo; Challenge everything and everybody*—he decided to just do it and let the chips fall where they may. "I was probably 24 years old. I felt like that was what I was supposed to do," explains Murphy.

"All of a sudden . . . they say, 'There's a note from Jack's office. It says he signed your memo.' I see his admin and she hands it to me and there it is, signed with the red pen. I wheel around and there's the manufacturing guy walking toward me, looking all ticked off. I walk toward him and I say, 'Hey, I'm not sure if you've seen this.' I

confronted him . . . he [was a] managing director, which is like a VP—
brutal guy. He reads it and he starts cursing:

'You effing piece of s--t, how [did] you do this? We're not this late,
your date is wrong.'

'No, you're wrong. The date is right, Jack signed it, split the lot.'

'F--k you,' as he walked away.

All of a sudden, three of his guys come into my office: 'We're going
to go split the lot.' That was that. That's how Maxim did it and that's
how we saved the customer. But without that cultural framework, how
would you ever do that? My boss was gone that day . . . so I did it on
my own. Any other company without that DNA . . . I would have just
given up. Later on, I remember thinking, if someone did that to me, I'd
be wondering, 'How do we promote that guy?' Some company CEOs
would say, 'How do I fire that guy?'"

This illustration of several Maxim principles in action demonstrates the
culture that inspired the best in its employees. Like many highly successful
entrepreneurs, Gifford conducted his life and his business by a strict set of
principles. These guidelines for conduct, eventually codified in the company
culture and named "Maxim's Principles," provided a rigorous standard for
management and employees. Sometimes referred to as 'Maxim's Maxims,'
these 13 principles became rules for the road at every level of the company
that inspired the challenging culture and its stratospheric corporate success.
Here's what Gifford said about them:

"These Principles, although they may appear ethically or morally based,
are really not. They have been developed over time, based upon my
experiences, my successes, and, mostly, my failures due to violation of
one or more of them. They may appear straightforward and obvious.

*However, they represent the guidelines I use to approach my job and my
daily life, and have played an important role in my successes—and I
believe Maxim's."[1]*

Like most others at Maxim, says Murphy, these principles have shaped how
he lives his personal and professional life:

*"I saw him [Gifford] lead by example on these things—and they became
more real. By my own wiring I am not a conflict-oriented person . . .
but I became very tough working there. Not only because . . . you had
to make it through the wringer but because of the values that Maxim
stood for. It was okay to do those things. They were encouraged."*

In many companies, corporate slogans and values mean very little, says
Murphy. However, at Maxim, the culture supported employees making the
effort to align with company values, just as Jack supported Murphy's challenge
of his superior's product test system. Here are Gifford's 13 Principles that
became a way of life to employees at Maxim:

1. Don't accept the status quo:

"Do not accept a situation just because it has always been that way; find a
way to improve it and go beyond the results of the past."

"That's what happened," says Georges, "when Tunç [Doluca] innovated
his power solution; that's what happened when Dave Bingham and Charlie
Allen came up with the MAX232." Then, he adds:

*"I think if we just accept the way things are, then you don't innovate.
One of the cultural things at Maxim is we're always looking for a
different way to do things, a better way to do things. It really doesn't*

matter what your job is, doesn't matter whether you're a secretary, an admin, or an engineer or a product engineer or designer, whatever your job is, there's always something that you can do to make it better."

When it came to chip innovation, says Ochi, Gifford made sure he always employed people "who had the skillset to implement pretty much whatever design he wanted. In fact, Jack did not place any limits. He just looked at a market and said, 'Let's figure out what they need, and let's design a product to get at that need.'" For example, he says, Maxim became a leader in DC-DC converters because the engineers broke with industry norms by combining a small controller and two separate power switches on a single chip. Simple but revolutionary.

Lee Evans, he says, would also buck the system with extremely simple designs. "Where I may use 20 devices to do a circuit, he would use five. And his five devices seemed to work better."

The test team applied the same principle #1 in yield improvement and in reducing packaging and manufacturing costs, according to Hood. "We would go over the cost of every product continuously. We had really high gross margins . . . but they still weren't good enough. We were constantly driven to reduce costs, improve yields, make stuff better, faster, cheaper."

2. Question everything and everybody.

"Don't accept a solution or procedure just because you were told that is the way it is or the way it has to be done. Question your supervisor, because he and I can be wrong, because we do not always know the facts as you do. We need you to keep us straight."

Maxim leadership emphasized the importance of asking good questions to expose flaws or weaknesses and to brainstorm the best solutions. At the Meetings from Hell, as previously described, Gifford demonstrated a honed question-crafting skill during his regular, tough, question sessions. Company employees were encouraged to follow suit, says Ochi, not just in refining solutions or processes, but even in questioning their supervisors and everyone around them. For instance, he says, Fullagar's engineers rarely designed in the manner expected of them. "We all had our ways of designing. Everybody was looking for better solutions, so they were questioning things, and they were trying things differently. There was no set way of doing anything."

3. Stand up for what you believe to be right.

"Make your opinions known; do not be silent regarding things that you believe are wrong or you don't understand."

Georges provides an example for this maxim in action. During a meeting about a new wireless product with Saeed Navid, the new Vice President of the wireless business unit, Jack declared, "The test time on this thing is two and a half seconds. This test time ought to be one second." But Georges disagreed: "It can't be one second, Jack. We're testing noise figures on this. There's no way." The two men continued strongly debating the test time, while Saeed sat in the middle, says Georges, likely thinking, *What did I get myself into?* Eventually, says Georges, he made his final argument: "It's not right. I couldn't go to my test development engineer and say, 'Hey you've got to do this in a second.' You physically can't do that. Jack, what do you not want to test then? You can't do this whole test list in one second, so just tell me what you want to test and we'll do that." At that point, Gifford changed the subject.

Jack deliberately challenged others, often to determine what could really be done. He especially questioned employees in areas in which he wasn't very knowledgeable. "That's how he really got to the answer." And, at times, says Georges, "People stood their ground and said, 'No, that's unrealistic.' If you kept pushing back, [he realized] you were probably right."

At Maxim, especially in the early years, people would air their disagreements publicly and, often, loudly. "You had to be brutally honest," says Hood. "There were always situations where the design guy would think what he did was right, the process guy would think what he had was the best, and then my results would be different." However, often the data would be unearthed, and the best position would stand. "We were a data driven company; we measured everything. And, sometimes you'd have to just stand up and say, 'Hey look. It's not what you think.'"

4. Do not suffer fools.

"There are always individuals, although few at Maxim, who are not focused on the goals that need to be achieved. Do not let them waste your time; be polite and move on."

As Levin explains: "If you let somebody say something to you in front of a bunch of other people that is patently non-responsive, or they're trying to cover up for something . . . that doesn't help the company. So that may have been a major ingredient of why Jack was so vocal. I know it's why I have been." Gifford believed that to get the best results and solve problems, you couldn't cover up issues and mistakes, or accept BS excuses. Everything needed to be laid on the table.

"There weren't very many people who tried to pull the wool over your eyes," says Hood. And, employees who did "typically didn't last very long . . . because people were watching what they did. Developing a new product involves a lot of people. So, if you weren't doing a good job it stood out." He says that even in sales, staff typically wouldn't waste time with some salesperson misrepresenting products. And, they wouldn't tolerate those in the company considered "bellyachers." To people like this, Gifford would quickly respond, "Okay, I'm tired of listening to you complain. It's yours. Go fix it." Company culture mandated that rather than belaboring the problem employees go find the solution.

5. Try as hard as you can.

"Always give 100% effort to everything you do. Nobody at Maxim has ever been let go, no matter how serious the mistake, if they have given their best effort."

This principle, which is similar to #6 and #7, will be elaborated on below.

6. Don't give up until you've won.

"Never sell yourself short of achieving the results you want. The most important accomplishments occur through perseverance, not brilliance."

Like many of these principles, this idea of persevering until "you've won" is rooted in Gifford's passion for competitive sports and often applied in engineering new innovations, says Georges. Whether it was difficulties making a measurement or challenges getting a circuit to work, designers would try everything they could think of until they "finally found a way to make this thing work. You just had to use your best engineering judgment and figure out how to solve it."

As Hood says, "You had to work until you got a result. There weren't very many failures." And, because his test equipment was so costly, he says, his team would . . .

"save every second they could . . . because every second is money. We worked very closely with the circuit designers to make a circuit test faster. We knew what the packaging cost was gonna be, we knew what the die size was, we knew the steps in the process technology. So, we figured out the cost of each product down to the nit."

7. When you work, get a result. Don't waste your time.

"Focus on what you want to accomplish and work toward that goal. Don't hesitate to modify the project so that your work will have a useful and not wasted result." Goal setting was key.

At Maxim, says Ochi, the teams would focus ruthlessly on completing their many written goals. And, not only would everyone be held accountable for achieving goal-related results, they would receive bonuses based on those accomplishments. When team members' efforts seemed to meet with a dead end, they would brainstorm together other viable or creative routes that could produce the success they were pursuing.

8. Work as a team.

"Get help as soon as, and whenever, you can. The sum of the parts is greater than the whole when there is teamwork."

Gifford understood the power of teamwork based on his decades playing semi-pro baseball and participating in competitive tennis. He believed that the characteristics of good ball players—discipline, hard work, persistence, and working together for a common goal—were transferable to the workplace. "Development of a new product involved a lot of people," explained Hood, "and you just had to be a team. It's like a sports team; you can't play without a shortstop."

Certain aspects of an analog chip design process, says Ochi, called for teamwork. For instance, when it came time for simulations, other engineers "would help you finish up the project or design. Tunç, for example, would help me with full chip level simulations . . . and sometimes it would take nights or weekends."

Even though Jack encouraged designers or teams to compete against each other to get the best results, cooperation for the larger good was mandatory. In test development, says Hood, employees often collaborated. His managers and directors became intimately involved with engineers who were writing test programs. "I'd go down and sit with them on test equipment with an oscilloscope, making sure that what was coming off the machine was accurate."

9. Be proud of your results.

"Be proud of what you achieve. Communicate your results so that they can be followed, valued, and used by others."

Gifford certainly encouraged employees to celebrate their results, like the time he brought over a bottle of champagne and two glasses after one of my circuit design successes. He also wanted everyone to share their results, so that others could learn from each other's significant achievements.

10. Give credit; don't plagiarize.

"Always give credit to the individuals who help you. This is the key to Principle #8. Your teammates will make you successful if you give them credit."

Because of this maxim, team members usually knew the various achievements of others within the company, which complemented and supported the next Maxim, #11.

11. Teach—pass on knowledge.

"This principle must be met in order to be promoted within Maxim. The ability to pass on knowledge to others is the key to a civilization's and our company's survival."

As a result, within Maxim, says Ochi, "people pretty much knew what was going on in terms of chip development. I could literally go from one group to the next and just sit down and query people about what they were doing. Based on that, I would either come up with my own ideas or come up with an improvement on what they were doing."

Typically, says Murphy, companies don't do a good job of mentoring employees and expect that new hires will take responsibility for their own development. However, because Jack didn't believe in Human Resources (HR) departments in the early days, each manager performed their own HR functions. "You're responsible for these people, and so you trained them, you made sure that they were good," says Murphy. "You're so happy to get a resource, you just invested the crap out of these people. Today people just want to get headcounts, bodies." Such investment in personnel, he says, also played out in other parts of the company, like business management and sales. "It's a really powerful thing."

Murphy says, he always viewed it as his job to help his team members succeed, and that it was his fault if he couldn't get them to perform. "That means I need to invest my time. I need to be the one that sets the tone ... and is making sure that everybody that works for me is developing. I'd send people to Stanford to study or make sure that I gave them really challenging career opportunities." Development of staff was so valued, he says, that managers would provide rotational opportunities. For instance, he'd say to someone: "Hey, you know what? You're really good. You're a top performer. But if you go transfer to this product line you'll actually learn more and you'll be better later for it. So, I approved the transfer even though you're my key person."

Those at Maxim that fully applied the principles, he says, practiced this "freedom of movement" idea, and made great effort to mentor others. This teach-and-pass-on-knowledge concept, says Murphy, is extremely valuable because it "lifts the whole organization."

12. Don't intentionally miscommunicate, not communicate, or lie.

"Changing facts, not communicating the whole story, or lying will lead Maxim in an incorrect, fatal direction. It is the only principle whose violation will result in immediate termination."

Gifford recognized that when brainstorming or problem solving, says Georges, that miscommunicating can sabotage a project or the ability to make effective decisions. "His way of reaching quick decisions and early decisions is trust ... if he can't trust you, if you're going to lie to him, it's bad. You can get fired for that easily. Intentionally miscommunicating or not communicating or being quiet is the same as lying."

13. Take direction enthusiastically once a decision is reached.

"Don't take decisions that go against you personally. After a decision has been reached, each member of the team must work toward this goal in order to ensure a successful result."

For example, says Georges, "Frequently you'd get in these meetings and people would be arguing on one side or another. Finally, he'd just say, 'Okay we're going to do this.' He didn't want to hear you come back and say, 'But I thought we were . . . 'No, the decision is made. You're going to take that decision enthusiastically and you're not going to take it personally that your side, your argument, didn't win. You're going to march forward because we burn too many calories just trying to argue for our case. After the decision is made, the decision is made . . . move forward."

Though these 13 principles encouraged healthy conflict, both within and outside the company, they also created an environment of competition that boosted the success of everyone. During the Wild West days of Silicon Valley and the dramatic burgeoning of entrepreneurial companies, it was a war zone. These Maxim maxims provided the front line playbook for the company's analog team to both survive and thrive.

21

CONQUESTS

"Jack pulled us aside and said, 'Okay, what's your decision, do you want to do it or not? We made the [acquisition] deal on Super Bowl Sunday . . . exciting times."

RICH HOOD

An executive team from Maxim, led by Gifford, gathered in the boardroom of Dallas Semiconductor on Sunday, January 21, 2001, interviewing the local management team and board members to evaluate an acquisition opportunity. The CEO of this Texas company had recently passed away, and the board had approached Maxim about merging. This was the first large semiconductor acquisition that Maxim had seriously considered, as Gifford preferred to grow his company organically from within. This day there was a strong sense of excitement and enormity in the air.

213

Six Maxim executive managers, sworn to secrecy, had flown into Dallas to complete their due diligence. During that top-secret weekend meeting, participants were even prohibited from calling home. As both companies were public, it was imperative that word did not get out about a potential deal. The Maxim team began grilling the other management team members sitting across the table from them, completing dozens of interviews during marathon sessions.

Though some previous discussions had led them to believe this acquisition could be a home run, many of the logistical details needed to be worked out and the final decision made. The away team dug in for hours to determine the compatibility of the two companies, and the valuable product lines and human resources that Dallas Semiconductor brought to the deal. However, the Maxim executives were also trying to find any weaknesses they could highlight and exploit in hammering out the best final deal possible.

After gathering all the strategic information necessary, says Hood, it was decision time: "We were in a big board of directors meeting . . . with the top guys at Dallas Semiconductor. Jack pulled us aside and said, 'Okay, what's your decision, do you want to do it or not?' We made the deal on Super Bowl Sunday. It was an exciting time." After negotiating a sterling deal, the company instantly added hundreds of complementary new products to its analog and mixed signal stable. Also, by default, the company gained many highly qualified new engineers, the greatest treasures of the analog semiconductor industry.

After a period of pruning and aligning, this new tech conquest added significantly to Maxim's bottom line. "For a long time," says Georges, "we grew as fast as we could grow, and Jack wanted to be very careful about the destruction often inherent in an acquisition. He looked for bargains that did not pose a lot of risk." This semiconductor acquisition fit the bill. Gifford understood full well, from observation and history, that unwise acquisitions can destroy a company.

In its analysis of 2,500 acquisitions, global consulting firm L.E.K. determined that "more than 60 percent of them destroy shareholder value." After this extensive analysis, L.E.K. suggested, in the *Harvard Business Review*, that "such deals should come with an official warning: 'Acquisitions can result in serious damage to your corporate health, up to and including death.'"[1]

However, in this case, not only did Maxim get a new injection of life, but also "Dallas was a major milestone in Maxim's history," says Hagopian. "Enormous time went into the evaluation of this acquisition. The entire board was involved." At the time, he says, "Maxim was doing very well and was under no pressure to make deals, especially one this big." In fact, adds Hagopian, Gifford put it this way: "The easiest thing to do with the deal is to just walk away. No one will ever know what we might have missed. But if we do the deal and f--k it up, we are going to look real bad." On the other hand, declared Gifford, "Doing the right thing for the shareholders is what we get paid for."

And that's what the team did, starting that Super Bowl weekend with the purchase of the Texas company for $2.5-billion of Maxim stock. They took a calculated risk and executed it well. At the time Maxim was valued at about $20- to $25-billion. For 10 percent of Maxim market value, within a couple of years we added 20 percent to company earnings with the combined manufacturing synergies. According to their forecasts, says Hagopian, the Maxim team raised the "Dallas gross margins from 50 percent to the Maxim Margins of 70 percent." The dot com bubble burst right after this deal was struck, slashing the combined companies' revenues by one third. However, he says, "We weathered that storm without ever losing money. In fact, in fiscal year 2002 ... Maxim reported a profit of about $230-million after tax." Maxim/Dallas recovered quickly.

Although this Maxim Super Bowl 2001 victory was the first that involved more than just fab capacity, the company had already stuck its toe in the acquisition waters, starting in 1990. At the time, Gifford made an eleventh-hour deal to purchase the bankrupt wafer fabrication plant, Saratoga Semiconductor, in Sunnyvale, California. After securing this asset for a huge bargain, a team of 20 set to work getting the idle fab running. "We managed to do it though," says former Maxim VP, Robert Scheer. "We worked 24/7 for a week on the first wafer run and got record yields! It was just fantastic."[2]

Before this purchase of manufacturing capability, as previously mentioned, in its first seven years Maxim stayed financially liquid by contracting foundries to make its chips. "We're certainly the first analog company to use foundries for wafer fabrication," says Combs. "It was way too expensive to have a wafer fab when you're a small volume operation."

Linear Technology, according to Fullagar, took the other approach, building a fabrication facility. "That could be one of the reasons why we overtook them, because we could do more product innovations . . . They spent half of their founding money building a factory." During Maxim's startup years, the company contracted five foundries, Tektronix being the most significant. This semi-conductor company in Beaverton, Oregon, gave Maxim expanded fabrication ability, in addition to high-speed bipolar processes for wireless RF and fiber-optic products.

As stable, established foundries didn't exist in 1983, says Fullagar, "We ended up doing business with some tin pot companies that scared the s--t out of me." One foundry, he says, located in Scott's Valley, "started the business out of a trailer with diffusion tubes." Though the company had upgraded to a building by the time Maxim started doing business with it, the foundry was still a "shaky" operation.

"Quite early on, he didn't pay his air-conditioning contractor, so the . . .
contractor came in over the weekend, took the crane and yanked all the air-

conditioning off the top of the building and drove away. He was our number one foundry. Then the guy got into trouble by not paying withholding taxes."

Despite Gifford's determination to stay foundry based, says Fullagar, "eventually, he changed his mind, thank goodness . . . In my mind, that was our biggest vulnerability. It could have shut us down."

Fortunately, though Maxim subcontracted the assembly and wafer production in those days, it always operated a captive test floor for final testing. The test team, says Combs, set up a cutting edge "full lot traceability system," that ensured they placed a wafer lot code on every package. "If there was ever a quality problem, we knew exactly where all the parts were . . . we had 100 percent traceability, which I don't think any other company had at the time."

Eventually, the time was ripe for growing Maxim through non-fab-related acquisitions of semiconductor companies. That's when the Dallas Semiconductor deal was sealed, ultimately triggering many more acquisitions over the years. (See the list of 17 acquisitions in the Appendix.)

Just after the 2002 market recovery, Maxim took a leap into consumer electronics, including chips for laptops, smart phones, and digital cameras. Unlike the industrial market, the margins were 50 percent or less, rather than the 70 percent the company was accustomed to. In addition, Maxim could no longer rely on a 7- to 10-year product life cycle. Most consumer products lasted two to three years before the newer and better product arose. And, the greatest challenge—missing the consumer manufacturing schedule— would be far more punitive to the company's reputation and bottom line. As Hagopian says, "A three-month slip meant we could miss the market window entirely or lose half or more of the lifetime profit."

The management team, he says, decided that this larger market was where the money was, and that "reduced margin points with higher volume," would boost profits. Consequently, after great effort to overcome challenges, successfully hit their market windows, and create game-changing products, the Maxim team's gamble paid off. Soon, Maxim had created and sold hundreds of millions of market-dominant laptop, smartphone, camera, tablet, palmtop, flat-panel TV, and LCD monitor analog semiconductors.

Besides its consumer market wins, Maxim made great competitive conquests in the areas of quality and reliability (see Chapter 16). Initial quality far superseded that of competitors, with 100 percent burn-in and semiconductor failure rates up to 30 times lower than competitors, at an unheard of 9 failures per billion hours. Such astounding numbers gained widespread attention from media and the industry, and brought customers knocking.

Maxim also consistently beat competitors by driving down costs. "You'd introduce a part... for, say, five bucks," explains Fullagar. "Within five years that had to be a dollar, or 75 cents. It was all about yield improvement. You get a wafer and you think you're gonna get a thousand good chips out of that wafer, and you might only get six hundred. Because the design needed to be tweaked, or the process needed to be tweaked, or the test program needed to be changed." However, the driven team would work tirelessly to create the solutions that allowed them to set more competitive pricing.

Aside from the achievements described above, including the landmark Maxim acquisition of Dallas Semiconductor, one other stands out in the company timeline—the Tektronix Semiconductor purchase. As previously noted in Chapter 17, Maxim landed this corporate catch and many others for "pennies on the dollar . . . six to eight times less than they were worth," according to Georges. This purchase, he says, "was critical for acquiring and enabling high-speed SiGe technology for our fiber optics and wireless product lines." Tektronix had decided to exit the semiconductor business, and so the deal added to Maxim both semiconductor operations and a wafer fab in Oregon, along with a wide range of new products.

Gifford and the Tektronix CEO struck the entire deal—"buying the fab, all the team, and the people—over lunch on a napkin," according to Murphy. "He and Jack. Old school. That's just how you did business then, and these guys were both CEOs of really successful companies." Both CEOs were "larger-than-life personalities," says Murphy, and they had been friends for years, since their days working for GE.

After this deal, Hood commuted to Oregon two or three days of the week, working to integrate the operations. Eventually, with great effort, the Tektronix products were woven into the merged manufacturing operations, and product costs were dramatically reduced.

Following the Tektronix and Dallas Semiconductor acquisitions came many others over the years, as Maxim continued to make its mark in the analog world. And, whether conquests in the form of acquisitions, superior quality, or product innovations, the current incarnation of the company will assuredly continue to make strides into the future.

22

MAXIM MAGIC

> *"No one got fired. A lot of them retired because they made*
> *so much money they didn't need to work anymore."*
>
> Jim Bergman

As a young engineer during the founding years, Ochi had no idea how exceptional Maxim's achievements were and would continue to be. After the company's IPO reverse stock split, he says, "I recall going into Jack's office and complaining that I got half as many shares as I was supposed to. 'So,' I said, 'I'd like to try my dream of trying to get into another startup . . . sort of like Maxim.' Looking back, it's amazing how everything came together for Maxim. So, I thought: *Well, gee, this startup is so easy. I have to do another one. Why do I need Jack? I know all the secrets.*" So, Ochi left and subsequently joined forces with two other startups, which, one after the other, went belly up. In hindsight, he says, if he had simply stayed at Maxim with his eventual increase of stock wealth, today, "I'd have an island all to myself."

Clearly, with only 1 out of 10 tech startups succeeding, companies that managed to thrive like Maxim were usually the benefactors of many positive converging forces. "It's not easy to duplicate. It's almost like magic. Everything has to be just right," declares Ochi. One of the fortuitous growth factors, as previously mentioned, included the founders' ability to ride the industry transition from bipolar analog to mixed signal CMOS analog technology, and from multiple-micron to sub-micron technology. "Today... if you were doing a semiconductor startup, you'd have to go into deep sub-micron, which is prohibitively expensive. It's a lot more difficult to get off the ground." Today, as a result, most successful startups are Internet and software based, like Facebook and Google. Very few startups focus solely on hardware.

Without a doubt, Maxim's monumental numbers, as summarized earlier by Gifford and other founders, provide definitive proof of some secret sauce. Those numbers include the forty-nine percent growth rate per year for fourteen years straight, plus many more years of dramatic growth, and the hundreds of analog products produced annually for many years, peaking at 500 one year. As Gifford declared about the company: "So ... we're a legend." And, as Fullagar notes matter-of-factly: "As far as creativity and ingenuity, Maxim was head and shoulders above all other semiconductor companies."

Many students of Silicon Valley may not have heard of Maxim and its achievements, feats that seem to have largely flown under the radar. "People tend to be glamorized by microprocessors and all the digital things that are going on. The analog stuff is sort of buried in the background somehow. When Intel announces a new microprocessor, everybody perks up and listens. When we announce 50 new products in the analog field, which probably took the equivalent amount of effort, nobody notices."

In this chapter, I'll continue to examine other ingredients in Maxim's recipe for success. Though I've already referred to many of them so far, I want to first summarize some of those factors that stemmed from wise actions and the recognition of strategic market waves. Then, I will investigate, specifically, some of the mindsets, attitudes, and leadership factors that propelled the company's meteoric rise. One of the early successful and observable strategies and actions included the Maxim efforts to becoming the lowest cost, highest quality analog company. So, products like the MAX232 not only fulfilled a great market need but also replaced $10 worth of separate components in a combination circuit. Following its introduction, the team drove the initial product unit costs down from 90 cents to 15 cents, while charging $3 per unit. You can do the margin math.

The company pioneering focus on second source products, as well as it's opening foray into the foreign market, helped provide early profits and a lifeline for future expansion. The markets in Europe and Japan helped raise Maxim's quality control and reliability far above its domestic competitors, while helping to raise its capacity at a more manageable pace than if it had launched domestically first. The company also avoided the likelihood of being overwhelmed by domestic demand. This twofold strategy gave the US team time to create the big breakthrough products like the MAX232 and the MAX690 chips described in Chapter 16.

Also, greatly spurring Maxim's success was Gifford's ability to gather an ace team of veteran managers and designers from the start. This experience capital dramatically accelerated the analog company's ability to scale financially and grow swiftly. These veterans, says Georges, brought with them "business sense and market sense in terms of managing money very tightly and understanding the market that Jack was going after . . . They also knew how to get stuff manufactured. Jack had great designers, but he also had a team that could manufacture and distribute and get those products to the customer." Experience in the trenches of Fairchild, Intersil, and AMD had trained them well.

This expertise, along with intense market research and instinct born from years in the industry allowed the Maxim crew to anticipate market needs and produce the right products at the right time. As Beck noted, "Revenue, profit, and leadership products were exceptional. The whole environment at Maxim was to exceed. There were no limits. It doesn't matter what it was. Whether it was a sales budget or an expense reduction, whatever it was, it was always to outperform whatever the goal was. It was just a state of mind . . . 'the sky's the limit.'"

Foreseeing the dramatic growth of the analog market in the draft of the digital market explosion formed the foundation of Maxim success. Plus, the benefit of analog product life cycles of 15 to 20 years, as opposed to the typical two- to three-year life cycles of digital products, fed the company's exponential growth.

"It's quite a profitable business, once you get into it," says Bergman, "though it takes a while to build up a portfolio of products that can get you a sufficient amount of revenues to break even." That's where Maxim's top-notch team and new product machine kicked into overdrive.

With so many moving pieces in the company's success puzzle, Gifford's ability to manage the details ruthlessly and juggle many balls at once were vital to the company's early survival and success. In this culture of micromanagement, of constant challenge and teamwork, as defined by the 13 Principles, every team member was continually held to a higher standard and to extensive lists of quarterly goals. And despite Maxim staff's constant pursuit of goals in known areas of the market, company culture constantly provoked ventures into the unknown.

The automotive market was one of those ventures. "Jack was a real car nerd," says Sparkman. "He always loved cars. And, so he said, 'Look, someone needs to figure out what we have that would be applicable to automotive.'" For the next two years, Sparkman says, he would be investigating the potential for entry into that market. During the research period, "I visited probably every automotive subcontractor around the world . . . to map our product lines into their potential products." Sparkman's investigation also determined the costs of market entry and the higher automotive standards Maxim would have to meet. Gifford realized how integral to company success that auto market entry was, says Sparkman. "Jack was one of the first to realize how important high-performance analog would be and that the automotive guys would pay for it."

Maxim's dramatic growth, whether in automotive or other markets, was greatly accelerated by marketing and sales savvy in the organization. Gifford's marketing skills and the sales expertise of Beck were essential success ingredients. In the next chapter, I'll examine in more depth the Maxim sales organization's essential contributions to company productivity.

Besides the more obvious success ingredients already described, the Maxim culture was infused with many more intangible, cultural motivations, often inspired by Gifford. "He had a huge ego and unbounded self-confidence. Even when it wasn't justified, sometimes," says Fullagar laughingly. He was fond of saying . . . about some failing company, that 'they need Jack Gifford, but there aren't any more Jack Giffords around anymore.' He would talk about himself in the third person."

Though Gifford emitted this sometimes-excessive self-confidence, says Fullagar:

> "Every now and then he would back off and be realistic [and say], 'The important thing is you make a decision.' He'd rather be right 51 percent of the time. It's better than making no decisions. So, he would make decisions on the fly. Some of them were right and some of them were wrong. But that's true of every CEO."

Clearly, Gifford never succumbed to analysis paralysis. "When push came to shove, he wanted results more than perfection," explains Fullagar.

One of the greatest skills of effective CEOs, notes Georges, is the ability to make decisions on insufficient information. "Jack was a master of that. He would say, 'Hey, if we have an assumption and it's wrong, we'll adjust our course, but let's not wait for too much information." Georges notes that leadership guru, Patrick Lencioni, says that many CEOs become paralyzed waiting for "enough information" to make perfect decisions. Consequently, many of their decisions come too late. Gifford, on the other hand, made decisions quickly and fearlessly, states Georges. And, if necessary, he would be quick to say, "Okay, we were wrong. Let's change our minds." He brainstormed collaboratively, with the best information available, then would quickly decide: "'Okay, let's do this,' or 'No, this doesn't make sense, we can't do that.' I really appreciated that."

This power trait of decisiveness contributed greatly to Maxim's success and the team's selection of leadership product ideas that became runaway revenue producers. It was that quality that kicked in at the coffee machine when, after I told my brother's story to Jack, he spotted a prime opportunity (the eventual MAX786 chip) and immediately appointed me to put a team together and "go make these things for laptops." Today, when I speak with interns during our "walk the block with the CEO" events, I tell them that one essential key to Maxim's early success was a team that saw opportunities and decisively jumped on them, without meeting for months and belaboring decisions.

Another one of the Maxim success intangibles was a fierce competitiveness that permeated the company from the CEO down. Hagopian elaborates: "Jack was an intense competitor . . . confident, cocky, driven. He knew every aspect of the business. He understood manufacturing. He understood fab. He understood selling. He understood marketing. He understood finance. I mean, he was his own CFO for the first five years." The executive team would keep tabs on the competition; however, the competitive hunger for new levels of achievement caused the team to continually race after new goals and raise the bar at every turn.

Discipline, says Sparkman, was one of the primary mindsets contributing to Maxim success. "You didn't waste a lot of time. You got your job done. If someone had to tell you to do it, you probably wouldn't make it. You had to be self-driven ... get this done. Jack had incredible discipline for how he ran his life. He imposed that discipline on the company." However, he says, this expectation "wasn't a yoke to us" because "we knew we did it to be successful."

On the front lines of this competitive tech war, states Sparkman, radical commitment was a closely related cultural expectation. "You really did feel like a band of brothers ... you looked left and you looked right, and you knew that these guys were on your team. They were kind of an ace team. In [Maxim] Europe we called it the Storm Troopers. I mean, you just knew that if we were going in, they were going down." The team's confidence in the company "was unbelievable," he says. "It was an amazing collection of talent. They were the best at what they did and were in the right position at the right time. Almost an unstoppable force. You just had this feeling that no matter what happened, it was destiny that this company was going to survive."

Originally, he notes, this confident pursuit of survival was rooted in fear: "It's going to be so painful for you to fail" that you had to be successful. However, Maxim was so stacked with experienced "winners," that success became contagious. "Winners like to be with winners, right? It's good to win, and you get addicted to winning." Sparkman compares the early Maxim team to the repeat Super Bowl-winning team, the Patriots. "You just got so used to winning ... that's all you did. And, wherever you were, you just figured out a way to win." Customers, in turn, became persuaded by the winning "sky's-the-limit" mindset.

He says applications engineer, Charlie Allen, was able to work with customers to tailor winning products for them. Allen's creative ingenuity allowed him to take "three seemingly unconnected pieces of information and synthesize them into a new product." After listening to customers describing several problems, he'd put the solutions into one IC, as he did with the record-breaking, revenue-producing MAX232.

Within this winning, disciplined culture, Maxim implemented stringent individual and departmental goal-setting policies as an accountability tool. Though this tool acted as a motivational stick, even more powerful was the incentive carrot, including generous stock bonuses and the success inspiration that came with seeing rising stock prices. Bergman says Gifford generously "compensated his people heavily with stock. He felt these guys were gonna be part of the success here . . . 'We'll give them enough equity that they're not gonna be attracted away.' So, a lot of early people made an awful lot of money because they stuck with the company. No one got fired. A lot of them retired because they made so much money, they didn't need to work anymore." Even secretaries retired as millionaires.

"Jack was driven by performance compensation," states Bergman. "His strategy was to pay very low salaries but give out tons of stock. And that served us well. Jack was the same way. He'd never take a high salary. And neither did any of the other founders. But they all got chunks of stock. We made a lot of millionaires and multimillionaires over the first 25, 30 years of the company. Eventually, we had to go back to more conventional compensation plans." However, in the early years, "even contractors reaped the benefits of shares," notes Fullagar. He recalls saying to contract engineers: "I can either pay you $20,000 to get the circuit done for me or I can pay you 20,000 shares. They would definitely have been way ahead if they had taken the shares. Some of them did."

At first, every staff member, including receptionists, owned company stock. "Jack really cared about the financial security of his employees," says Ochi.

"That's not always true about other companies. Top executives tend to take away all the money and all the stock. That wasn't true with Maxim, and I liked that." Maxim founders through most levels of the company started with about 25,000 or more shares and gained tens of thousands more bonus shares throughout the years if they stuck with the company and held onto their stock.

The stock appreciation proved astonishing. For IPO shareholders in February 1988, with splits the stock grew from $0.35 to a peak of about $87 per share in 2000, an almost 249 times or 24,900 percent return. Selling stock in 2018 at a share price of about $55 would give a return of 157 times. Despite the extraordinary returns, says Fullagar, "no one I know purchased stock at the IPO and sold at the peak, just like I don't know anyone who won the lottery. Equally significant for stockholders is the fact that for the next 18 years the stock went nowhere. I'm not sure what caused the anomaly in 2000. If you look at Analog Devices (ADI) and Intel (INTC), you will see similar very short duration spikes."

Many employees, he says, because of market instability and the uncertainty of startup success, "sold stock for multiples of four or five to put aside money for their kids' college, buying a house, or setting up a retirement account. If the company had subsequently failed, that would have been a brilliant move. In light of what actually happened, it wasn't so smart." One employee, claims Sparkman, bought the most expensive BMW in history "because he sold at eight dollars per share, so he could buy a BMW." Tragically, if he had waited five years, he could have bought that same car for very few shares.

Sparkman recalls a conversation with Fullagar one day about share price. "Dave, this stock's at 18 bucks. I can't believe it. I've got to admit, I never freaking believed this stuff would be 18 bucks." To which Fullagar responded: "Tom, you know what? Neither did we."

However, for early Maxim employees who stayed patient and sold at the right time, life was especially good. According to Ochi, at a 2009 Maxim staff reunion, another founder told him the story of an accounting clerk that joined Maxim straight out of college, grew with the company, and retired after selling his shares before the 2001 market crash. "He took the Maxim money and bought himself an island off the coast of the Carolinas."

Whether they benefited as greatly as this employee or not, everyone who joined the analog team out of the gate or along the way enjoyed a charmed ride. The Maxim Magic lifted and propelled all boats in its rapid rush to success. Though not at the same breakneck speed, this analog vessel continues to quietly make its waves in the tech world.

23

GROWTH SPURTS

"That's why we're broken into groups here—
so each little fiefdom could have their own neurotic ideas."

JACK GIFFORD, 2005 [1]

Addressing newly hired college grads at Maxim, the company's CEO humbly proclaimed: "I am not the smartest person in the company. I might be in the 50th percentile. Maybe I'm higher than that, but I'm not the top. I'm probably in the middle." That, according to Murphy, who was present at the meeting where Gifford's young audience was taken aback by the admission. "Of course, when you're right out of school, you assume the CEO is the smartest guy because he's the top guy," explains Murphy.

Continuing, Gifford alluded to one of his hiring philosophies for success and growth. "We've got a lot of smart people at Maxim, really high IQs in this company, but the one thing I have, that I possess, that nobody else has . . . I have tremendous experience. I've been doing this for 32 years . . . I co-founded Advanced Micro Devices. I ran a fab. I was running sales for Fairchild. I was the CEO of Intersil. I've been there. Everything that you guys are going to bring to me, I've seen it before. I've probably seen it five times, and so that's why I have the job I have." That's Jack's take, in Murphy's words.

Though not every one of his colleagues may agree with Gifford's modest estimation of his IQ, his thoughts provide a window into some of the initial team selection rationale that greatly contributed to Maxim's seasons of growth. Clearly, he believed that experience and street smarts were of greater value than raw intelligence. However, in the early years, once he and his fellow founding executives had fielded a great team of highly experienced veterans, they transitioned into hiring some of the brightest young minds. He also sought out those with potential for quick advancement within the company.

Even then, says Murphy, Jack placed a premium on experience. He would often say to those considering returning to college to get an MBA: "Don't waste your time. Maxim is your MBA. The only thing you should focus on if you want to learn business is accounting. Other than that, you'll get your MBA here." Jack was "very financially sophisticated, and savvy," notes Murphy. "He believed that fundamentally, in an engineering company, you could always wrap a financial or data-driven framework around every decision you make."

When he joined the company in 1994, at age 21, says Murphy, Maxim had recently reached $150-million in revenue, was still in its primary growth phase, and was in the process of hiring many young people. "Jack wasn't opposed to hiring experienced people, but . . . he preferred to just hire people right out of school." That year, he says, Gifford hired around 30 young people he referred to as his "farm team." He believed in the "rotational concept where you join and get rotated through different parts of the company."

Many members of this farm team, including Murphy, were recruited into product management or marketing. Unable to get sales reps to devote the time to scout out the specific needs of clients, Maxim shifted direction. According to Levin, "We went to young people out of college that maybe didn't even have an engineering degree, and we told them what we wanted to do. This stuff is not at the technical level. This is at the book report level. It was more effective to do it that way. These young people would go out and do the sleuth work for you that the sales reps didn't want to do. Then we'd bring in the field apps engineers on the appropriate customer opportunities."

After working in one of these roles for about two years, Murphy states, he began to take the fast track from associate business manager, to business manager (BM), to business management director. "I got to run my first product line at age 27. They put me in charge of a $20-something-million product line ... I was the BM of." And during those six years, he says, as part of the Standard Products Business Unit, he saw the company explode from $150-million to $1-billion in revenue. Within 10 years at Maxim, Murphy moved up to BM, then co-General Manager (GM) of a business unit (BU), then VP of Worldwide Sales in 2006, at age 33. This is just one example of the Maxim fast-track approach for young up-and-comers.

Besides the Maxim team draft strategy changing from veterans to young, talented players, various company organizational decisions also contributed greatly to certain seasons of growth. One of the essential training grounds for aspiring young executives like Murphy, as mentioned, came in the form of the somewhat novel, vertical-market-oriented Business Units, which were launched in late 1993. Years later, Gifford humorously referred to this organizational structure and the rationale for it, saying: "That's why we're broken into groups here—so each little fiefdom could have their own neurotic ideas." Despite the former CEOs tongue-in-cheek description of them, BUs were strategically significant in the second Maxim growth surge starting the same year. The company's development from a minor to major league team can be divided into four stages:

Stage 1: 1983–1993: $0 to $110-million growth. (From $10-million revenue by 1986, to $50-million by 1990, to $110-million in 1993). Company milestone products during that time included the MAX232 and MAX690. Maxim turned its first profit by 1987, before going public. At the end of fiscal 1993, the company employed 638 staff, according to company records.

Stage 2: 1993–2000: $110-million to $865-million revenue. (Yearly revenue breakdown: $110/154/251/421/434/560/607/865M in 1993-2000, all in fiscal years that ended in June). Maxim growth was driven by company milestone products, including notebook/laptop power supplies, the MAX786 and follow-ons, and many other power products, interface products, and analog switches for battery-powered equipment. The first Business Unit was formed in 1993, preparing Maxim for explosive growth. Employee numbers grew dramatically from 638 to 4181.

Stage 3: 2000—2010: $865-million to $2-billion. (Yearly revenue breakdown: $0.87/1.6/1.0/1.2/1.4/1.7/ 1.8/2.0/2.1/1.7/2.0B in 2000-2010, again in fiscal years ending in June). During this stage, Maxim made the major Dallas Semiconductor acquisition in 2001, launched many milestone products, and increased its presence in consumer markets. Staff numbers during this stage more than doubled, from 4181 to 9200.

Stage 4: 2010-2018: $2-billion to $2.5-billion. By now the company was very diversified with presence in all major analog markets except for Military/ Aerospace. The mid-2000s decision to go after the automotive market was paying dividends with explosive growth as well as growth in smartphones as the company shifted R&D from laptops and LCD TVs to smartphones. Employee productivity improved dramatically, while some downsizing occurred. As a result, company headcount declined from 9,200 to 7,100 despite growth in revenue. Maxim recovered from its option backdating issue and loss of Gifford, and relisted on the NASDAQ by late 2008, preparing it for the next growth spurt. In 2010, Maxim was one of the first analog companies to transition to 300mm technology for analog wafer production. Consumer groups took on their final form by 2011. All the preceding factors inspired a new season of further growth.

As evident in the stages above, each period involved significant revenue and employee force advances. (For a more detailed overview of all the significant Maxim milestones over the decades, please refer to the Appendix.)

A significant portion of this company growth came through the BU's vertical structure that assigned Business Managers (BMs) to oversee a product line, and BU VPs to oversee several BMs and their respective product lines. BUs replaced typical tech company horizontal structure of the day.

The brainstorm for the launch of business units arose at an October 1992 offsite meeting in Hawaii. That's when I explained to the team the merits of segregating employees who did product marketing, product development and other functions into a group (later called a business unit) to create specialization and a crystal-clear objective for success in a specific market. No longer would product lines rely on Maxim's wider horizontal marketing and product development strategies, or even test development, which didn't take intimate ownership over specific markets. Over time, these teams would become experts in the markets they owned. Thus, they became more competitive and able to deliver better results. Each BU group had VPs who separately reported to Gifford.

Jack asked me to put some "meat around the bone" of this BU idea, which I began developing throughout 1993. At the time, I was the VP of R&D and thus was directly responsible for the product development or design of all new products at Maxim. At Gifford's request, starting in September, I relinquished my previous role and pioneered the first such group as VP for the group, eventually called a BU. Thinking back, I was giving up a more prominent and bigger role (R&D VP) for the excitement of a startup within Maxim—maybe subconsciously I was missing the startup environment. It was very exciting because we were now a lean-and-mean team of 25 employees of whom only eight were design engineers—tiny in comparison to the Maxim mothership. Most of us moved to a new building, which ironically was the "Cave" building, the place where I designed the first laptop power products. The group was initially called the Battery Management Group, then Portable Power business unit, and eventually the Portable Equipment BU.

At the time, this BU oversaw two product lines—the Notebook PC product lines managed by Dave Timm, and the Information and Communications product lines with BM, Chris Neil. The next Maxim BU, Fiber, was formed in 1995-6, reporting to Bill Levin. Other subsequent BUs included Signal Processing & Conversion, Wireless, and Standard Products.

The genius of this structural concept allowed each BU to operate like a small business startup. During the '90s, BUs became a powerful Maxim growth force, as they placed accountability for a product line's success squarely on the shoulders of a person and not a community. To support this structure and fuel the growth, the company placed entrepreneurial, aggressive, and competitive managers in charge as BU VPs as well as product line business managers. When somebody is running a very large organization, a few products could fail, while the whole enterprise succeeds. On the other hand, a BM makes one person responsible for growing a product line, and that individual can only succeed if the line flourishes.

Let me first explain the role of a business manager. The germinating idea for BMs likely came from Ziya Boyacigiller. Similar to his creation of the RODT metric to sort out which products to develop, he was also thinking about how to ensure market success. I was not a witness to discussions between Jack and Ziya, and since both met untimely deaths, we will likely never know how the "business manager" idea developed. But the concept was rather straightforward, as many great ideas are. We should simply treat each product line as an independent business; and to run a business one needs a business manager. This BM will decide which markets to go after, which products to design, which customers to target, what merchandising material to prepare, where to run advertisements, which products to manufacture, how to set the prices, and more. It's almost like running a small company or a business, hence the title.

Early BMs filled a tough and lonely role, even more than today. He or she had no direct reports, had to survive tough MFH interrogations, and had to fight for resources like design engineering, while competing with other BMs. They needed the ability to cajole, convince, or court others over dinner to get the resources they needed. I would tell new potential BM hires that they had to be comfortable with a lot of accountability and responsibility but no authority to direct resources. Over the years, the BU structure has grown dramatically, and today Maxim operates six BUs, which oversee approximately 80 product lines.

Chris Neil tells some classic BM stories about his encounter with Gifford while working as an associate BM for Power products. After receiving an assignment to create a design guide for customers about Maxim product solutions, he was summoned, along with about 60 managers, into an emergency meeting with Jack. Neil describes the brief, but forceful, Gifford speech:

"He got up in front of everybody, and he says . . . 'I've got this really great idea. We're going to do these design guides. They're going to feature the best products we have. They're going to really speak to the engineers. I know they're going to be a success. The reason I know they're going to be a success is I'm not going to let any one of you guys f--k them up for me, okay? That's all I got to say.' He bounded off the stage and he was gone."

Neil, who had experienced little interaction with Gifford till then, says he left stunned that day, wondering, *What did I get myself into?*

Another time, after rising to the associate business manager position, an engineer told him they only had the equipment to test 100,000 chips, yet they needed to test 200,000. He had made this calculation based on their average test time per unit. After hearing the engineer's appeal for him to ask Gifford for approval to buy more capital equipment, Neil knocked on Gifford's office door. As a relative rookie with such CEO interactions, he had no inkling what was about to come:

> *"What do you need?"*
>
> *"Jack, we need to buy new test equipment."*
>
> *"Why do we need to buy new test equipment?"*
>
> *"Because I got an increase in my forecast."*
>
> *"Let me ask you a question. How many seconds does it take to test this thing? Why can't the test engineer cut the test time in half?"*
>
> *"I don't know. The test engineer just gave me that information and told me to come and tell you."*
>
> *After pausing, Gifford raised his voice and delivered an explosive counter: "Never come into my office again telling me that you don't know the answer to questions like that. When you come in this office, you're supposed to have all the answers of the person you're representing. Don't come in here half assed!"*

Through these initial interactions in the furnace of the BM structure and Gifford expectations, Neil began to rise to the occasion. He soon learned to do his homework meticulously, sell problem-solving product benefits, and excel in every assignment or role.

In later years, starting in 2006, Maxim pioneered a structural reorganization that created new dynamic growth. In a transformation unique to Silicon Valley, the company shifted from end technology to end-market organization. This change was triggered when managers found customers reporting that reps from different Maxim groups were making back-to-back presentations to the same person, says Neil. For instance, the power management group would present their product to a cell phone customer, followed by the audio group, and later the radio frequency group, he says. Then the customer would complain: "I just had Maxim people in here twice in the past two months. Why are you bringing people in again? I'm still waiting for answers on the first two things."

Consequently, Maxim began to organize based on end markets, such as cell phone or laptop sectors. In such a consumer end market, "You'll have a power guy, an audio guy, and an RF guy. So, when you talk to the customer, you can say, 'Tell me about all three of those things at one time, and I'll see if I can come up with an answer for you that addresses all three." Neil recalls creating a huge spreadsheet to trace out the intersections of product lines and the many end markets, such as automotive, communications, medical, computing, and industrial. Previously, the audio rep would be competing with the power products rep. "Neither of them wanted to give up their control of the customer, and you had this conflict. But if you put power and audio under the same leader . . . [he or she] would just decide they're both important and provide the solution for them."

In addition to the BU and consumer group organization growth factors, certain milestone products were also responsible for adding a significant portion of Maxim's bottom line growth. During the Stage 1 opening season, the big growth was spearheaded by MAX232 and MAX690. However, in the first decade, all product lines grew strongly, with robust analog switches and multiplex online chips catching fire as well. That first stage was followed by a growth season led by supervisory chips. A third wave arose when Maxim introduced its notebook and smartphone chips, which became huge growth drivers. In the fourth stage, Maxim was led by its automotive chips.

Maxim's launch into the auto market was inevitable. However, in the early years, Jack forbade Maxim's presence in automotive because he was concerned about unlimited liability resulting from loss of life. However, we all know that it is not easy to forbid a customer from designing in your product; they don't follow the supplier's CEO's instructions. So, in the mid-2000s Jack somehow got wind of Maxim selling products to some car companies and was apparently pretty upset over it. In classic Jack style he called a meeting and instructed sales and BMs to get to the bottom of "What's going on here?" I was not at the meeting, but he apparently stormed into the meeting in the infamous MAX232 conference room and demanded answers regarding how much automotive revenue we had, and more importantly "why" despite his orders not to. Apparently, by the end of the meeting he said something like: "I forbade you guys not to win any business in automotive and we now have $20-million in revenue? I wonder what would happen if I told you to go win more automotive business?" It was classic Jack. He turned completely from the beginning to the end of the meeting and decided, then and there, to start an automotive business unit!

Once Gifford decided to pursue the automotive market, he turned to Sparkman to help conduct preliminary research. "Jack was a real car nerd. Always loved cars," says Sparkman. "So, he says, 'Someone needs to figure out what we have that would be applicable to automotive.'" With that observation, Gifford quickly assigned Sparkman the task of considering existing Maxim product potential with the auto market and with researching market needs. "Over the [two] years, I visited probably every automotive subcontractor around the world," he exclaims. In addition, he considered extensively what it would take for Maxim to enter the automotive market, what the revenue would be, and how company products could be adapted to the higher grade required for automobiles. Today, we have a fast-growing automotive business that is around $500-million in revenue.

During the many stages of significant growth at Maxim, it seemed like Gifford and the executive team had the magic Midas touch. Almost all strategic decisions turned to gold … sometimes even in non-Maxim-related matters. Neil illustrates: after producing rough drafts of some BU ads for Gifford's review, he was called into the CEO's office with his boss, Dave Timm. This time, after the somewhat uneventful completion of the business aspect of the meeting, Gifford said, "Okay, guys. Anything else you want to talk about?" As Neil notes, "Jack would get in these moods where he just wanted to talk." That day he was in a storytelling mood. Neil went along with the changing tone of the meeting: "I heard that you previously worked at AMD?" Gifford then began regaling his captive audience with tech-world stories. One of them involved the troublesome op amp, a notoriously temperamental technology. The device was low power and extremely sensitive.

Neil quotes Jack's description of his encounter with the design engineer: "The guy kept complaining to me that he couldn't get the damn thing to work because it would saturate [the output would change dramatically] even if someone walked into the room." Immediately Gifford responded in his out-of-the-box manner, saying, "It sounds like you just invented a really nice, low-cost motion detector. Why don't you just go market it as a motion detector?" Then, Neil says, Jack slapped the table and laughingly exclaimed: "I made that guy a few million dollars with that suggestion."

That same business savvy was implemented through structural changes, competitive business strategy, and product acumen throughout the four historical stages of Maxim growth. Throughout the years, this uncanny and instinctual know-how dramatically propelled company progress. It also inspired Gifford to make big claims like this one in a 1989 *Wall Street Transcript* interview:

"We are the preeminent company in the CMOS era. We pioneered the technology that allows analog mixed signal designs. It is called mixed signal CMOS. It means we put both analog and digital on the same silicon chip. Our people pioneered these circuit techniques in the mid-70s while at other companies. Our people have developed the most important techniques that have made possible mixed signal CMOS analog. By combining digital circuitry on the same chip with the analog circuitry, this is what has really allowed this growth to occur. We were an early pioneer and today, a very important player. Ninety percent of our business is in this area alone, contrasted to 35 percent of Analog Devices and maybe 5 percent of Linear Technology's and 5 percent of everybody else's. So, we are really the unusual ones."[2]

24

WAR & HOSTAGES

"We were comrades in arms and it was kind of a war. We were competing against the outside world and we were working inside in a very competitive way..."

STEVE COMBS

I t was August 1993 when communist rebels invaded Maxim's assembly facility in the Philippines, capturing the plant and holding operators and engineers hostage. "We were going to hire a SWAT team . . . to go in there and blow these guys up and get our people out," states Combs matter-of-factly.

"I had to go to Jack to get a PO (purchase order) signed for flak jackets and a commando squad. He started arguing with me:

'How do you know this is a reasonable rate to pay in the Philippines for a commando squad?'

"Jack . . . our guys are being held captive!"

243

This violent incident was triggered when the company started planning to move the facility from a communist controlled location to a free trade zone. When insurgents caught wind of the imminent move, they took the facility hostage to prevent Maxim from moving their equipment out. By contracting commandos, says Combs, the company was only able to get "a few of the people sprung." So, he says, he took the case through the Philippine court system by claiming the company had been aggrieved by an illegal seizure. "It got to a very high level of the Philippine court that was controlled by the communists, and we lost. They took our facility."

Then salvation came in the most unlikely form. After local community members learned of the hostage crisis, says Combs, "The women in the community got pissed off and they got their brooms and pitchforks, stormed the facility, and said, 'You guys, get out of here!' And the communists said, 'We're not going to mess with the Philippine women.' So, he concludes, a team of angry local women rescued the facility and employees, when even commandos and the courts couldn't.

"I've got dozens of stories like that!" says Combs about his many years of tenure in the conflict zone called Maxim. When life at the analog company didn't involve communist combatants, it certainly involved competitive marketplace conflicts. "We were comrades in arms, and it was kind of a war. We were competing against the outside world, and we were working inside in a very competitive way, mostly with each other, sometimes against each other." However, says Fullagar, "The camaraderie was good, even though we were under pressure. We were still joking and laughing and having a good time."

The following 2003 Maxim application note aptly captures the battle-ready tone of the analog company culture:

"It's a jungle out there. A small tribe, in the dense wilderness, is much sought

after by headhunters from the surrounding plains. Known throughout the land for their esoteric expertise, this is the tribe of the Analog Engineers, who live in the farthest regions of the left half Plains, past the jungles of Laplace. The guru of analog engineers is the Analog Filter Designer, who sits on the throne of his kingdom and imparts wisdom. You never get to see him, even with an appointment, and you call him "Sir."[1]

This culture of tribal warfare permeated the company at all levels. "We were always having fights, Jack and I," says Combs. "Yeah, it was a war zone. That's how we did our business." As an executive with regular contact with Gifford, says Combs, he quickly learned that timing was everything.

"Jack usually started at about 10:00 in the morning, and he usually went home around 7:00 or 8:00 at night. If you had to deal with him during the day, he'd tear you to shreds. So, I always timed it so I knew just when he was finishing up and was getting ready to go home. Then I'd go in there and say, 'Hey, we got to get this done today.' I knew it was the only chance I had, and we would go through it and sign POs or do reviews. It was always . . . brutal."

During the in-house battles, each executive implemented a different strategy. Fullagar, for instance, recognized that he was "one of the few that could get away with certain things with Jack. He would just be yelling in the conference room, and I felt he was being unreasonable. I'd just say, 'F--k you' and walk out." In the early days, Fullagar says that he and Beck would compare tactical notes on Jack:

"'Okay, how can we quiet him down? We're going to start losing people.' Because until we went public and people could see the gains in the stock, they

could move if you didn't treat them right." After conferring, one would say to the other, "Okay, today it's your turn to tell Jack to calm down. You don't need to be so tough on people. You're going to start losing people. Fred would give it a try and I would give it a try. I don't think it ever worked. It was just part of his nature."

Ochi recalls regularly overhearing loud disagreements in the large office space, where only cubicle partitions separated regular staff and managers. These verbal battles, he says, "you could pretty much hear throughout the building. A lot of times, when there was a heated argument, the other engineers would put down whatever they were doing, and they would listen. And Jack was fine with that." It was all part of the interactive culture of discussion and brainstorming that most staff engaged in.

During his tenure, says Fullagar, as the tech industry was aggressively expanding, "Jack was kind of a take-no-prisoners kind of guy." Everyone understood that any Maxim in-house conflict was always for the good of the team. Though colleagues may not have relished being on the other side of a conflict, they recognized that having Gifford and the other company warriors on their side would inevitably lead to their winning most competitive corporate battles.

Often, in this hard driving company culture, says Georges, no sacrifice was too great. On one occasion, Roger Fuller's chip design was expected back for evaluation. Georges notes that when Gifford discovered that Fuller was about to leave on a planned vacation, he put his foot down:

"You're not going on vacation . . . you've got to evaluate the chip."
"Well, I've already paid for my trip," objected Fuller.
"Fine, I'll buy your tickets from you."

So, Gifford bought the Hawaii tickets from Fuller, and the designer stayed back to work on his chip. "Jack was kind of serious about getting things done," notes Georges.

Maxim's "challenge culture" created an environment that helped expose decision-making flaws that nothing else could. Once, says Georges, "We had a really successful product and one of the business managers . . . came in and said, 'Hey, Jack, I need to buy $10-million worth of capital equipment to test this product, so we can sell it.'" Based on the product's approximately $200-million revenue forecast, the manager's request seemed reasonable.

That's when Gifford thought he'd run the decision through the gauntlet:

> "How accurate is this forecast? Do you believe your forecast?"
> "Oh, it's accurate, I believe it," replied the manager.
> "I'll bet you $1,000 you don't achieve your forecast," came the challenge.
> After a pause, the manager lowered his head and refused to accept the wager.
> "I'm not buying that capital equipment. You don't believe in it." Jack announced his decision like a gavel striking a sound block.

On other occasions, the challenger would win the matchup. At one meeting, says Georges, Gifford was complaining about the price of laser trimmers. Then, says Georges, "Jack, I don't think we're going to get the price any lower. I think these guys aren't making really big margins." However, Jack insisted that the margins must be over 50 percent: "I know we can negotiate the price down." The debate continued between various meeting participants while Georges quietly pulled up the trimmer company's balance sheet on his laptop. The margins were 35 percent. Then came the typical showdown.

> "I'll bet you that their margins are over 50 percent," stated Gifford adamantly.

"I'll take that bet," countered Georges.

"Jack, he just looked it up on the Internet. I wouldn't take that bet," warned another.

"Why are you telling him?" objected Georges. "I had him."

Gifford's hard-nosed style contributed greatly to company success in the tech wars. However, says Georges, the Maxim CEO's manner was sometimes counterproductive. "The way Jack confronted people was sometimes demeaning. He'd say, 'You're an idiot. My grandmother could design this better than you could.' I don't think that's necessary. You can communicate that you're disappointed, and you can raise your voice without berating them or using foul language to convince them that you're serious. Sometimes I think he carried it a little too far."

Yet, many who knew Gifford would agree that his confrontational style and words were calculated to achieve a certain result, adds Georges. "I wouldn't say Jack had a temper. I've seen him really rip somebody in a meeting and then walk out and say, 'Man, I hated to do that.' That was his way of getting the guy's attention, right or wrong."

Bergman says, in the boardroom Gifford could be "a bit of a bully." If someone wasn't pulling their weight, "he would yell, and scream at them," but he wouldn't fire them.

"He was kind of like a stern father. That was just Jack's approach to trying to get people to pull their oar correctly. He didn't have any showmanship to him. Whatever came into his mind . . . he would deliver it. Oftentimes, aggressively. Maybe it was a bit of a Napoleonic complex. He definitely wanted people to know he was in charge. I think he felt that—not as an ego thing—he felt that the company needed strong leadership."

Most employees on the receiving end of Jack's fury would admit that when he shouted them down, he was usually right. However, he didn't come down hard on everyone. For some reason, he was a lot easier on me than some others. I don't know why. I never asked him. He probably sensed that I responded better to encouragement than searing criticism.

I also recall that he listened to me more. In the '90s, one method Jack used to print quarter-after-quarter of a penny a quarter earnings-per-share increase was to hold back shipments to customers to "manage revenue and earnings." (Such an aggressive practice would be taboo today.) While the withholding of shipments was great for financial consistency, it was a nightmare for customer service employees. Customers would be begging for shipments and manufacturing would hold shipments until the new quarter started. Gary Berman, who managed customer service, wanted Jack to "release shipments" to relieve customers, apparently with no success. This must have been one of many loud arguments mentioned earlier in the chapter. After a team meeting, one of the managers suggested I be sent into Jack's office as the messenger. I remember saying, "Fine, just give me the shipments delinquency data plotted over time to show how dire the situation is, and I will try my best with Jack. The worst-case scenario is I get thrown out of Jack's office."

So, I requested the meeting, put the single page chart in front of Jack on his desk and said, "I think we need to release more shipments to customers." He looked at it for 30 seconds and said, "Fine, go ahead and tell Berman." A minute after I entered Jack's office I walked out with the "yes" answer. Berman, waiting outside, was in disbelief. The entire customer service staff was elated and celebrating.

However, such low-key problem solving wasn't typical. In this company culture where speaking your mind was encouraged, company executives would often loudly collide over strategy. According to Beck:

"Jack and I were close. But we fought a lot. [We] . . . had no trouble making sure each other knew where we stood and there was never any doubt that we would come to an agreement and would execute exactly. We also realized that making a wrong decision was not a serious consequence because we were quick to correct that. We were interactive and very responsive. It gave us tremendous freedom to just keep moving."

Although Gifford was very gifted at vision, marketing, and product planning, said Beck, "He was a dangerous guy to have in front of the customer. He would say yes to whatever the customer wanted, whatever they asked, and not mean it." Then Beck would find himself exclaiming, "Do you realize what you just committed to?" Thus, in the early days, Beck created a shield between customers and Gifford. However, he said, at the height of Maxim's growth, when the sales team developed great relationships with large companies like IBM and Samsung, Gifford became "much more of a customer man."

Jack's "promise-them-anything-but-commit-to-nothing" mantra created numerous problems, say Combs. "He'd allow them to book orders based on what the customer wanted, not what we could deliver. Then he would beat me up to try to meet the deliveries." I'd say, "How could I commit to shipping in six weeks when the material for that order is 14 weeks away?" His response? "Figure out a way to make it. You've got to do it." Some thought Gifford just held unrealistic confidence in his team's abilities.

Throughout its greatest growth eras, Maxim tackled many challenges head on. During one of our in-house skirmishes, I remember a real "Come-to-Jesus" meeting, when Jack gathered the designers and business managers to discuss our new product development execution. He'd noticed that the whole company was slipping its schedules. We were setting general goals such as, "Let's get this product out by August 1989," but without any tactical details of how to fulfill the goal. Gifford read the riot act to the teams, and I left pondering a solution.

After the meeting, I remember deciding that a more granular scheduling system would make the difference. I then hammered out a project management template on an Excel spreadsheet that would eventually be adopted company-wide. It was a crude version of the project management system that everybody uses today, and it helped streamline the process and defeat our new product development execution challenge.

Maxim faced many other challenges during its exponential growth. "Our technology was light years ahead of our manufacturing," said Beck.

"Our customer engineers loved our products. [But] our customer purchasing and management were hostile to Maxim for the first 15 years. We invested in new products and were slow to deliver [during production]. We had the door slammed shut with many customers, doors that were difficult to reopen. Technology won every time and the door would reopen."

As the company developed its proprietary products, the team developed many more significant relationships with key customers. According to Beck: "We could then start dealing with them on futuristic needs and develop products that really met and exceeded their needs and exceeded competition." However, although Maxim was considered excellent from a technical and quality standpoint, it was "deficient" from a manufacturing perspective. "We did not have dependable delivery," he declares. "We were loved in the engineering departments and hated in the purchasing departments, and the two would fight. We would complicate their [purchasing managers'] lives by not delivering or meeting our commitments. That was really who we were."

Maxim's engineering departments, said Beck, were able to understand and develop products that met customers' future needs. "From an analog mixed-signal point of view, there were none better. In terms of leadership products, we were out in front of our competition. In my opinion, we were absolutely number one." However, he says, if Maxim had put more emphasis on being reliable suppliers, "We would have been twice the size. There would have been no limit at all."

Combs would grapple with Gifford over 'optimum management' solutions to this company challenge:

> *"If I just had more inventory, if you let me keep wafers that I know are good, then I'm only three to four weeks away from shipping."*
>
> *"Okay . . . the other thing is we've got to increase our capacity . . . take our in-the-line cycle time from three weeks to one week," replied Gifford.*
>
> *"The only way you can do that is with twice as much equipment," observed Combs.*
>
> *"Well, but then they're not always going to be operating," objected Gifford. "If the handlers that run the parts on the test floor [aren't] clicking, we're losing money."*
>
> *"No. Actually, if they're all clicking, we're losing money because that means we don't have enough capacity and you got all this inventory built up in the line that you partially paid for instead of flushing it through and shipping it."*

Eventually, says Combs, another part of the solution came through implementing a statistical process control system, originally created by Nobel Laureate, W. Edwards Deming. It took some time to convince Gifford, he says: "This was really foreign to him. He certainly didn't want to leave decision-making to a bunch of numbers. So, we fought for a while on that, but ultimately, when he saw some of the results that we were getting, he was able to buy into it and sell it to the company. That made a big difference."

Besides efficiency, results also came in the form of greatly increased quality, says Combs, so, "We didn't have to sort wafers anymore. After the final test, the yields were so good that we didn't have to throw away a lot of product. We saved a tremendous amount of money by not having to do that upfront operation."

Through those high growth years—49 percent per year for more than a decade—Maxim was often caught short of supply and missed deliveries. Part of the blame lay in conservative business forecasting. It didn't help the company in the future because once you build that brand it's kind of hard to get rid of it. It was always a fire drill, with serious crisis management and overtime at deadline. However, another aspect of the supply challenge came because customers didn't always give an accurate heads up on how many parts they would need. In this booming tech culture, at one time they may want half a million, at other times millions—with little forewarning. Riding the boom and bust cycle of the semiconductor industry, companies just didn't know how successful they were going to be.

In the end, Maxim solved this painful problem by developing a more flexible manufacturing strategy rather than just owning its own fabrication facilities. Owning our own fabs meant a high cost of being idle, while using somebody else's might create a slightly higher cost, but it also gave us more flexibility in ramping up production. We eventually shifted to producing far more of our circuits in outside facilities, greatly remedying our supply challenge.

One of our last big battles during the Gifford growth era came during our enormous success with the newer generation, pocket-size digital cameras in 2004. As the first and only semiconductor company to dramatically shrink power supply chips to fit such a product, we were suddenly scrambling to meet great demand. Soon, we had a great crisis on our hands fulfilling the orders. Again, we found ourselves explaining to customers why we couldn't fill their orders, while at the same time working to tie up fabs that could help relieve our production bottleneck. We eventually secured a Japanese manufacturing partner to take partly built wafers from us and complete the second half of the process. Ultimately, we were able to make an agreement for them to build the entire analog chip. Maxim maintained its competitive advantage for two generations of cameras before competitors copied our chips and began selling at lower prices. We exited when that happened.

With our power chip for the notebook market, another of our skirmishes, we held on for about 10 years before it was time to exit. Nothing's forever in this business. Anybody who tells you otherwise is lying. It's a never-ending war.

Another of Maxim's typical front line battles arose when we were being fleeced by a corrupt fab in Arizona, says Combs. This time, to exit the contract, he says, the team hatched a plot to rescue our equipment and wafer plates, held hostage at the facility. The stakes were high—many millions of dollars of equipment and mask sets. While Combs courted the executive management team over lunch and warmed them up to the fact that Maxim was hitting the road, he says, other team members were smuggling company property out of the facility. When we returned to the fab, things got ugly, "but that's the way it was. We just had to do things," declares Combs. The Maxim swat team loaded their equipment onto a truck and locked it in a rented storage facility. Then, "We booked airline reservations for a guy under a different name. It was a regular mission impossible scenario."

In this instance and many others, amid ferocious competition and ongoing battles, the Maxim team executed their plans, overcame, and survived to fight another day.

25

THE BIG LEAGUES

"We thought that if you had somebody that was a really good athlete and a team player, they're going to be successful in business because they're competitive..."

STEVE COMBS

Maxim was founded on the lessons taught by competitive sports—hard work, discipline, persistence, competition, and teamwork—as reflected in the 13 Maxim principles. Though Gifford exchanged his early Major League Baseball career aspirations for a life in big league technology, he continued playing competitive sports all his life. And, he often went to extremes to weave the culture of his athletic passion for competitive sports into the cultural fiber of his analog business.

"Jack was [a] crazy competitor," says Hagopian. As described in Chapter 22, his competitive drive compelled him to become knowledgeable in most every area of the company. Gifford also took calculated risks—at times "he was . . . reckless," states Hagopian. "He was one of those guys who didn't like to spend a lot of time asking for permission. He liked to just forge ahead and . . . ask for forgiveness" later if he had to.

Hagopian recalls his surprise the day Gifford called him to say he wanted to "put a professional baseball player on our board." This first baseman for the LA Dodgers, Eric Karros, was a smart guy who was "admittedly a terrific long ball hitter," he says.

> *"I didn't know how to explain what his qualifications were for our board. But Jack really wanted to do this. We were performing great. And, to use a military metaphor, with Jack it was always best to choose carefully which hills you were prepared to die on. This wasn't one of them. And, so we got Eric and he did a fine job until his baseball schedule intervened too much. He also hit 30 homeruns that season."*

In Gifford's mind, as a pro ball player, Karros would help lead their company in raising its competitive and team spirit.

Gifford not only recruited baseball players for the Maxim board, he also hired them . . . not just to play on the company team. "We used to hire guys out of the UCLA baseball team," Combs notes.

> *"They'd graduate from UCLA and they were star players on the team and they'd come up and interview and Jack would say, 'Hey, I just hired somebody for you.' I'd go, 'Oh, yeah? What base did he play?' A lot of these guys worked out great. We thought that if you had somebody that was a really good athlete and a team player, they're going to be*

successful in business because they're competitive and they know how to
work with other people to achieve a goal."

Clearly, Gifford's love of sports, especially baseball, continued throughout his life, during workdays or outside of them, according to Levin.

"Jack played baseball for many, many years. We used to go down to the
baseball games at UCLA, where we went to school and he was on the
team. He continued to fund a lot of stuff on the athletic side, baseball
in particular. We had this Maxim Yankees team. He played on it till he
was in his 60s . . . He worked out and could handle high-speed pitching.
It was unbelievable to me that he was still competing at that level."

In 1994, Gifford founded and began managing the semi-pro team, the Maxim Yankees, recruiting mostly college players on summer break. Initially, he played first base for the team, and later—up till 2008, at age 68—pinch hitter. "You'd think . . . what's he doing out there, playing hardball, with a bunch of young guys. Many of them played baseball in college and were in their 20s and 30s," says Bergman. "But he loved it. He was in good physical shape."

Gifford also financially supported many college baseball and tennis programs and pioneered a free, three-day, baseball camp in Hawaii for kids. He recruited college coaches and former pros to participate. Amazingly, in addition to his many business, charitable, and baseball interests, Gifford was enthusiastic about many other activities. "He loved fly fishing. He liked to play tennis," says Rhodine. "For a while, we skied as a family. We played a lot of golf together." Obviously, he believed in both working and playing hard, and that the character and skills learned through sports prepared people for success in business and every area of life.

Consequently, Gifford decided during the early Maxim years to purchase a corporate membership for employees in the Decathlon Club, striking a deal with the financially ailing facility on Central Expressway in Santa Clara. "So, we had the Decathlon Club at our beck and call," says Combs. "We were small then and it wasn't a big deal. Then as we grew we said, we're going to limit you guys to 100 memberships." Staff members would regularly play racquetball or tennis, work out or go swimming. And, Jack would encourage staff to make use of the membership.

"He believed in eating properly and the running joke was . . . we have board meetings and Jack would serve turkey on wheat with no mayonnaise or anything. It was just dry turkey on wheat and the board guys kept going, 'Jack, I mean, come on. Why are you feeding us this crap?' He goes, 'I don't want you to get fat, and I want you to eat properly.'"

Gifford applied his philosophy of athletic, lifestyle, and business discipline to the competitive technology market. Early on, he realized that consistently good corporate performance over the long haul is always superior to unexpected high revenue followed by a miss of a market expectation. For instance, says Combs, at times, one of their main competitors, Linear Technology, would report higher gross margins:

"People would say, 'Wow! Look at them. They're even better than Maxim.' However, we were hiding our true gross margin. We would report 55 percent; they'd report 60. Jack would always report earnings as late as possible after a quarter closed . . . because he wanted to see what everybody else would do. If everybody else was having a really banger quarter, then he'd siphon a little bit from inventory and put the

numbers up ahead of them. If their quarter was not so good, then we would reserve more against inventory and report numbers only slightly better than theirs."

Call it 'within-the-rules' based stealing, or an effective, competitive strategy. Either way, similar aggressive plays permeated every corner of Maxim, even within the company's four walls. As Levin notes, different groups within the company often found themselves "competing against one another for resources, attention, and mind share [engineering talent]." In fact, he says, Gifford "didn't mind two different groups that had different solutions to the same problem competing with each other . . . and you just see who won."

Such 'self-competition' even applied to Gifford's other sporting love—fishing. He didn't just relegate the conquest of big challenges to the business world. "We fly-fished every blue-ribbon river in the western United States," declared Beck. And every occasion was memorable. The two Maxim executives even took on the Williamson River, in Southern Oregon, a river that boasts "the largest trout in the United States," he says. "They're huge . . . some of them would be three or four feet, 30 pounds." On three occasions they recruited an Indian guide who "knew every fish in the river by name. He would scuba dive and go down there and just study them." To fish for the big ones, said Beck, "you couldn't get closer than 40 to 50 yards, and he would allow you one false cast and then you had to hit the mark."

Catching the "big ones" was an endeavor also pursued at Maxim, especially among the sales and marketing staff. Landing deals with the biggest tech players in Europe, Asia, and America was led by sales VP and veteran, Fred Beck. However, because of his sales/marketing background and affinity, Gifford took particular interest in launching the department's strategies. After some early years of sales success, says Levin, Beck became sick and took a sabbatical. Gifford decided to split Beck's international responsibilities.

"So, Jack took the international stuff, and I took the domestic stuff," explains Levin.

However, Gifford continued, as he had done before, creating catchy ad campaigns, which he felt were essential to reaching the engineers who helped make decisions for potential customers. Back in the '90s, says Levin, Maxim sales were $100-million and "we spent $10-million on advertising." In these pre or early Internet days, print ads "were where engineers would look . . . Jack used to personally get very involved and look at every ad that ever got created . . . and with coaching people how to do these things right with the right headlines."

According to Levin, "The whole name of the game was to get your product designed into other people's products, and that's how you got the bigger volumes." Today, these attention-grabbing—and sometimes sensational—ads are legendary at Maxim for their wording and effectiveness as the company forged new paths in analog advertising.

They included ads entitled "190 Circuits Without A Leg To Stand On," (as previously mentioned)—which promoted its surface-mount technology that saved space and eliminated typical post design; and the ad taking a tongue-in-cheek jab at the competition with this: "How To Get Hard-To-Get Intersil Parts. Just Ask. They're Not Just Available. They're Better." Then there were the ads touting Maxim's industry-leading breakthrough technologies: "Complete Flash Memory Programmer in ½ Sq. Inch," or "12-Bit DAC+Amp+Ref In One Package." According to Levin, "Jack felt you could mass merchandise these kinds of products, which was a very different concept in the way chips were sold." Previously, engineers would always need to wade through huge data books from different companies to find products.

The Maxim sales team also sharpened its competitive edge by giving reps a unique new mandate. Managers started telling the reps that they were to go into other tech companies as corporate scouts and learn about each client or potential client, their specific needs, and what types of products would be most beneficial to them. Sales reps were commissioned to look for prime opportunities in different industry sectors. However, says Levin, discovering the inner workings of other companies "gets a little touchy because companies are not wanting to hand you on a silver platter exactly what they're doing." That is the case especially if they're interacting with sales reps.

Consequently, Maxim eventually created an applications organization that would send out specialized engineers to interact with customers' engineers. These interactions were successful in inspiring ideas for many breakthrough products. That happened in one meeting between Maxim's Len Sherman and Motorola about its next generation phone, says Levin. They were able to create a compromise over "some feature that would drive us crazy analog-wise that wasn't at the center of what they really needed, while there was something else that we could do very easily that they were starving for." The final negotiated design solution, he says, "was fantastic." Such successes also led Maxim to eventually start offering custom circuit solutions.

Pioneering another industry-first competitive strategy, Gifford and Fullagar took to the road to launch their 'Dog and Pony Show.' During this entertaining analog tour, the two put on tech slide presentations of Maxim product lines, leveraging Fullagar's technical expertise alongside Gifford's gift of the gab and flare for the dramatic. "We got a reputation for these presentations being interesting. They weren't sales pitches; they were engineer-to-engineer. We presented the product lines to customers, either in-house at their locations (big customers like HP or Siemens), or in hotels with invites to all the surrounding companies."

Such presentations were unique to Maxim in those days, says Fullagar, and could be rather entertaining. "Jack was wonderful. He wasn't a circuit designer, but he'd insist on presenting part of the dog and pony show. Sometimes I would cringe at some of the things he said because they weren't strictly technically accurate." But Gifford's enthusiasm was a great advantage during these presentations. Eventually, Maxim became the number one supplier for big tech companies like IBM and Samsung.

Another prime example of the company's extreme in-house competitiveness came in the form of the quarterly sales team meeting over a three- or five-day period. "Jack ... you know, he's an intense guy," says Sparkman. "And you would be presenting to him in great detail ... your sales plan: orders, bookings, sales process, prospects ... reps, the whole deal. And he required 100 percent knowledge. I mean, it was not enough for you to come in and think that you can swagger or answer two thirds of the questions." Each team member would prepare to answer every possible question. "It was very, very stressful," notes Sparkman. The process, he says, was like "Captain Kirk scanning your anus and looking for Klingons."

Everyone soon realized that Gifford could "see the matrix ... he'd find every possible flaw or weakness." Sparkman says that the CEO was renowned for his seemingly 'supernatural' abilities. "You go in with a slide deck of 150 pages. And, Jack would go, 'Tell me about that.' And he'd point to this one cell in your 50-page Excel spreadsheet, and it would be the weakest part of your argument. Uncanny, uncanny."

In addition, he says, Gifford could overlay, in his head, the 4D interaction of every part of the company with 100 plus product lines, markets and segments of markets. "This is where it gets religious. He was a visionary. He understood fundamentally what the electronics market was going to do before the electronics market knew ... he could spot these trends, large and small, before anybody else recognized them. It was a true gift."

And, though management wanted sales staff to make a certain sales number, says Sparkman, Gifford didn't care about the number. "Jack wanted to build the future. He's just like, 'Look, today's revenue will take care of itself. We need to keep building the base.'" So, for many years, sales reps weren't paid on revenue. "We were paid flat salaries with stock. We believed in the company. We worked like dogs, not because you get a bigger paycheck. Because the stock would go up. We were all on one team."

Despite in-house competition at times, teamwork in sales and other divisions was still vital to company success. And, like every good ball team manager, Gifford believed in shuffling the team at times, or allowing them to grow into other positions. For instance, Fullagar notes, that after returning from a sailing sabbatical, he was switched from VP of Engineering to VP of Applications Engineering for the greatly expanding global company. Then there was Murphy, who rose through the ranks to VP of sales, Sparkman who started as a sales rep and went on to run Maxim Europe, and many others.

For Beck, as VP of sales, mentoring the all-star team and watching them rise in the tech big leagues was incredibly gratifying, he said. He described watching "guys that just came in as sales or customer service guys who ended up running countries, running big sales organizations in Europe or Asia or the U.K. or the United States." Those dramatic promotions, and many others, took place as the company grew from 12 founders to 10,000 staff (at its peak) around the world.

And, throughout the years, as with all teams that enjoy cohesive camaraderie, they certainly enjoyed some good play times together on or off the field. Whether it was the lunch breaks smashing balls on the racquetball court or laughing over the 'goof chart' set up in test development to keep track of individual goofs; whether it was taking helicopter rides during the Hawaii company planning meeting or enjoying a Maxim staff outing to the San Mateo racetrack . . . the company continued to finely tune its team's skills and spirit.

On this latter all-company field trip to the races, says Ochi, "we'd sit in some of the best seats at the track . . . and when one of the horses came in that was a favorite of Jack's, they would go down to the track and get pictures taken with the jockey." As usual, Gifford was very excited and high energy, even about his equine wagers, notes Ochi. And, undoubtedly, employees later seemed to carry this contagious enthusiasm back to their in-company adventures.

In Jack's case, especially, off-campus play or recreation times were often tied to company goals or leveraged for future team success. Levin describes his Tahoe vacation with Gifford in 1990 as a springboard to his recruitment to Maxim. He and his wife joined the Giffords on this mountain adventure to Tahoe. In the car on the way, Gifford began sharing the great feats of Maxim thus far and the incredible potential he saw in the future. After describing the financial rewards of his previous corporate experiences, he described the possible rewards for Levin should he join the team.

"Jack had been successful throughout his career and been rewarded for it financially. I had done okay, but nothing like what he had done, and to have this happen in my personal case when I was 50 was great timing for some really huge win." Soon after the Tahoe getaway, Levin joined the intense Maxim big leagues for several seasons, initially as VP running engineering, while Fullagar embarked on an extended sailing trip. Nine years later, he was able to retire, after adding his significant efforts to the World Series tech team's many successful wins.

PART

FOUR

LEGACY

26

FAMILY &
BENEVOLENCE

"He was kind of a father figure to a lot of us ...
family was really important to him ..."

RICH HOOD

O ver the years, Maxim hosted many fun gatherings for employees—great
family affairs. One event, a summer employee family day at Marine
World in Redwood City, says Combs, was particularly poignant for him and
Gifford. During this family adventure, he says, when Maxim took over the
place from 5 p.m. to midnight, he vividly remembers looking across the crowd
at the whale show, taken by the thousands of faces of moms, children and staff
members.

"I got really emotional about it. I was walking out with Jack in the parking lot, and we were looking at all these cars, and a lot of them were new. I said, 'Jack, look at that. Look at all these new cars out here because of what we've built. I mean, this is fantastic. Look at all these families that we have affected.' Jack was totally emotional about it. It's easy to be tough on the employees when you're inside the war zone, but then when you see what the success has brought, it's really gratifying."

As illustrated in Comb's anecdote, though Gifford was hard charging, he cared deeply about his Maxim family. And, according to Bergman, "Though he was a tough taskmaster . . . he was also a benevolent father." This benevolence was dramatically illustrated after one Maxim board member's troubled son ran away from school, later to be diagnosed with schizophrenia. Though he found his 19-year-old son and brought him back home, the young man needed full-time supervision. When Jack learned the board member needed to leave for a few days, unsolicited he sent a security officer down to keep watch over the young man for several days. The grateful father provides further insight:

"I wasn't one of his employees. I was a friend . . . and a board member. But Jack was concerned enough that he would take one of his employees and have him come down and watch my son. Because he cared. To watch him in a meeting, sometimes, you'd never guess that he had that side to him. He just had a big heart . . . when somebody had a family issue, Jack would step up and find a way to help them."

As Hagopian notes, when staff were loyal to Maxim and within his immediate corporate inner circle, Gifford would do everything he could to meet needs he discovered. Jack thought of his employees as "part of his family," says Rhodine, and felt responsible for those experiencing hardships:

medical, financial, family or otherwise. He always prioritized his family life and children at home, and the priority bled into his company. Hood elaborates:

> *"You had to respect the guy. We all did. In many ways, he was kind of a father figure to a lot of us ... Family was really important to him, and my family was to him too. He could be very personal and very helpful ... He was a nice guy. He was just hard to work for ... there were no excuses—he was driven to make the company better and get the most out of us."*

Bergman adds: "He was somebody that could be tough on you at one point in time and then be your buddy soon thereafter." As Hood illustrates, "I'd get through a tough meeting with him and he'd say, 'Hey, Rich, let's go fishing ... or, I went fishing last week.'" And he'd be left wondering: *You just kicked my butt. Now you want to talk about fishing or the baseball game?*

Gifford's rough style, says Combs, was not only his method for challenging people to higher performance at Maxim, but it was also his way of getting staff to reach their potential. "I think he struggled a lot of times. He would threaten to fire you, but he would almost never do it ... you had to really mess up to get fired. He really did care about people, and I think it was probably hard for him to balance the two at times." However, regular acts of kindness to the Maxim family, as described in later chapter anecdotes, constantly helped express that care and strengthen company loyalty.

As in a typical loving family environment, Gifford was also quick to forgive, says Hood.

> *"There were times in my career where mistakes were made. I learned early on that if you made a mistake, admit it. You didn't lie with Jack. You admitted your sins right away, and you come in there with how*

you're gonna fix it, or you'd ask him for his advice on how to fix it . . .
you'd just go to him and say, 'I screwed this up. What do I do now?' In
those situations, he'd roll up his sleeves and help you. But don't ever try
to pull the wool over his eyes. That was the end of you if that happened."

However, says Bergman, Gifford didn't hold grudges. "If he got mad and thought you did something stupid, he would tell you, pretty aggressively. But then, he'd put his arm around you later, and say, 'You've gotta do better next time, let's work on it.'"

The family culture of Maxim was also practiced in its hiring practices, says Murphy: "Right or wrong, Jack . . . was okay with nepotism . . . family members working at the company." Many family members of Maxim executives and other employees worked at the company, including the Gifford daughters and sons-in-law, Bergman's and Georges' family members, and many others. Maxim didn't enforce the typical corporate prohibitions against such nepotism. As Rhodine explains:

"Jack believed in hiring relatives and friends . . . He believed that if
you recommend a friend or you recommend a relative to work for a
company, you're going to be personally responsible for them, to a degree,
and you're not going to recommend somebody who's not going to work to
the Maxim standards and have the Maxim culture."

In addition, says Levin, Gifford thought that families taking care of one another "built commitment and involvement." Maxim hired many high school students as interns, and typically those students were relatives of employees. "They learned what working really was about. They learned what their mom or dad, or aunt or uncle did, and many of them . . . came back to Maxim after completing their education." After interning at Maxim, says Georges, his son decided that Maxim was the only place he wanted to work; it was his ideal company.

Another source of Maxim's success stemmed from the ethnic diversity of its corporate family, according to Hagopian. "Almost half of our top people are foreign born," he said at a company sales conference presentation in 2010. "Think of it. A Turkish CEO, and an Armenian Chairman. Only in America." That's in addition to a high percentage of foreign-born engineers and staff in other roles. Hagopian adds:

> "We used to joke . . . that if you put up a list of our top 50 executives, most people couldn't pronounce [many of] their names. It's the great thing about the classic melting pot of America. Jack didn't care what country they were from. He didn't care if they were female or male. It was all about merit. So, by being colorblind, or country-of-origin blind—just focusing on who's the best—we ended up with some incredibly talented people."

Despite the many varying backgrounds, Gifford nurtured the family environment through caring gestures. For instance, says Georges, at one time Jack would send flowers to every female Maxim spouse on her birthday. "One guy came in mad one day. He says, 'Some guy named Jack is sending my wife flowers. I don't even know who this guy is!'" Georges says he calmed the staff member down by explaining the Gifford custom to him. Eventually, this gesture became politically incorrect, and the flower gifts stopped. "It was just one of those things he tried to do to care about employees," explains Georges.

In this family environment, says Murphy, people would often meet, get married and have children. "I know so many couples that met while they were there," he says. Unlike many workplaces today, Maxim did not discourage or stigmatize company romances. "At some companies it's like you've got to report to HR even if you're in different groups" if a relationship develops. At Maxim, he says, "It was like, 'Cool, they're getting married. OK, awesome!'" Many of those couples and their children grew up together around the company and at Maxim events.

"Company parties were always a huge deal" for the entire family, he adds, whether it was the summer picnics, Valentine's Day parties, or Christmas bashes. Not only did Maxim make it mandatory for executives to attend these gatherings, with large fines handed out for missing them, he wanted them to be grand community affairs that bonded employees and their families. According to Combs, the first company social event, the Christmas party, started with 12 staff members and their wives at a restaurant in Palo Alto. In the early years, these events were very child-friendly, and included Santa and gifts.

The party grew dramatically, along with Maxim, until the company was renting the Civic Center in San Jose. However, eventually it became challenging to find a place that would accommodate thousands of Maxim employees and spouses in a relay of multiple Christmas events at a reasonable cost. So, company management agreed to switch the time. After celebrating Christmas in January for a while, the event eventually became an annual Valentine's Day company party in multiple locations. Other corporate family affairs included summer picnics.

Georges recalls one fun company gathering, the IPO party, at the Decathlon Club, when he and his wife Judy were sitting at the same table as Jack and Rhodine. "My wife grew up in a very conservative household that didn't dance," he notes. "The music started, Jack jumps up, grabs my wife's hand, and says, 'Come on, let's go dance.' Out they go and they're dancing. It was traumatic for her, and funny . . . good memories."

Another great annual employee and family bonding occasion came in the form of the *Clean Up Day*, based on a Japanese company tradition. It took place on a Saturday every December in the spirit of cleaning out the old to prepare for the new year. The company brought in recycling and trash bins, and provided cleaning supplies and shredders, says Murphy: "You could bring your family, and they'd have a little brunch thing . . . so, my kids would be running around, squirting each other, running through the cubicles, meeting the other kids." Children would also draw on chalkboards and be able to see their mom's or dad's workspace. Many Maxim employees describe this unique company event as highly memorable.

Though the company was an intense workplace, the fun and games still took place in various contexts. Georges describes the company's Friday afternoon pizza and beer parties in the early days. "People would just sit around the table and talk . . . they'd bring in pizza and soda and beer. Nowadays most companies limit alcohol to after working hours." He also remembers employees examining spiders on the electron microscope or joking around with the paging system:

> "People used to have fun with guards that would run the paging system in the company. The guys would call up and page somebody, 'Ima,' and they'd say, 'Last name please?' 'Dumbgard.' So, they'd page, 'I'm a dumb guard' to a number. The guy would get halfway through paging and then he'd realize the joke. Fun times."

Fullagar recalls other Maxim fun at celebrations for Fred Beck's birthday party, and his own wedding, attended by many staff members. He retells stories of helicopter tours and Jack's deep-sea fishing expeditions during Hawaii business meetings. Other founders also describe backpacking and fishing trips with colleagues.

The Maxim culture's value for its corporate family was also reflected in its generous stock options and bonuses. Company generosity extended much further. For instance, says Georges, when auto companies started offering safety options like antilock brakes and airbags, Jack sent out a memo, stating: "If you buy a new car, Maxim will pay for these options . . . we care about your safety." In addition, in the aftermath of hurricane Katrina on the Gulf Coast of the U.S., Gifford offered to pay the salary of any employee who wanted to volunteer to help in the cleanup efforts.

Besides such instances of company-wide generosity, Maxim employees readily tell stories of Gifford's personal benevolence to individual employees. During my early days at Maxim, I became a fortunate beneficiary of Jack's thoughtfulness. Though living in the US, in order to maintain my Turkish citizenship, which I didn't want to lose, I was required to serve a three-month stint in the military back in my homeland. That meant that as an engineer at a startup, I would need to go hat in hand to Jack and ask for a three-month leave. My wife and I expected that he would just let me go from the company. Instead, he surprised me by his response: "So do you need any money? Because we can't pay your salary when you're gone, but I'm sure this has some expense." So, he loaned me money till I returned. Instead of suggesting I resign from the company, he helped me financially, which made me loyal for life to him and the company.

In another notable situation, Gifford helped care for the baby of a department manager. He contributed very generously toward the medical treatment of the child's heart condition. Sparkman tells the stories of two other employees who benefitted from Maxim benevolence. One woman needed to flee an abusive husband, so "Jack handed her his credit card and said, 'Use this. He can't trace it. Leave the country.' He paid all the bills." Gifford looked after her until things calmed down and she was able to return. Sparkman also describes the situation of a woman who once worked for him: "She had MS. It was tragic. Ten-year Maxim employee and still young . . . in her 30s." So, he approached Gifford:

"I want to keep her on Maxim's healthcare. She's going to have to drop off. And Jack's like, 'Absolutely.' I think we paid her for probably a year. She never came to work, I mean, she couldn't. And then . . . she gets through the MS—it goes into remission—and she came back. She still works for Maxim."

In these types of situations, Jack took off his CEO hat and put on his Dad hat. "None of this stuff made economic sense. You couldn't go to a board of directors and say, 'Here's the return on this employee,'" exclaims Sparkman. "But that was Jack. It was not a question of money. If it was the right thing to do for a committed employee, he did it."

Georges says he was also deeply impacted by the Maxim family culture of benevolence. After returning to Maxim following a few years in Colorado, he says, he realized he couldn't afford a house in pricey Silicon Valley.

"So, Jack offered to loan me money to buy a house, knowing that stock options would [eventually] be worth something. I looked around for houses and I found one in Saratoga that I thought was pretty nice. So, I came to Jack and said, 'Here's what I'm looking at.' He says, 'Nope you don't need that house. You're looking too high. You need to lower your sights a little bit.' So . . . I found another house and we were very happy with it. He loaned me money; we paid it back. I appreciated that he gave me advice about what to do and where to go."

Many years later, in 2006, Gifford again surprised him, says Georges. After doctors diagnosed him with prostate cancer:

"Jack called the head of the UCLA medical center. The guy called me back within five minutes of me telling Jack . . . and he says, 'Hey, we

have a guy on our staff, Jean deKernion, who's on the national cancer research board. He's an expert urologist. When can you come down for him to see you? He'd like to consult with you."

Within three weeks, Georges arrived for his appointment: "They had valet parking for me. I walked right into an exam room. He [the doctor] went through all my paperwork. He spent 45 minutes to an hour with me . . . because Jack had contributed a huge amount of money to the UCLA medical center, so he had their ear."

The "simple-minded" danger, says Levin, of helping employees like this is that if you provide aid to one staff member for a personal need, some may think you need to do it for everyone. Jack disagreed. "He would do what he thought was right . . . and in those cases, he would do things that other people—just out of an abundance of caution—wouldn't."

Gifford's care for many employees also extended to concern for their careers. In Georges' case, he recalls saying to Jack, "Hey, I want more visibility. I think I can do a lot more than I'm doing, and I want an opportunity to do something else." Jack quickly advised him: "Well, just keep doing what you're doing well, and those opportunities will come." Within eight months, in 2000, notes Georges, he was promoted to vice president.

The Maxim culture of benevolence and charity extended beyond the corporate four walls. Gifford provided extensive financial support for many college baseball programs, tennis programs, children's sports clinics, and various educational and health-related causes. He believed in giving back to the support systems that helped him on his educational journey and that would help the less fortunate thrive as he had.

Jack's charitable and family culture, expressed at Maxim and beyond, were ultimately an extension of his home life values. "At home he was not the type A personality [seeking to] do everything you've got to do to win. He was a husband and a dad," says Rhodine. And though he sometimes traveled for business and worked long hours during the week, at home he was a devoted family man. "On Monday nights he'd put the trash out. He was just Dad." In addition, he enjoyed family dinners and coached his daughter's softball teams, played family tennis, helped with homework, participated in father-daughter dances, helped plant a pumpkin garden for the grandchildren, and got rid of the woodpeckers on the house roof. "He was always there for us," says Rhodine. In addition, he regularly let his wife and children know, that they "could do anything . . . and be anything they wanted to be."

At Maxim, it was that same sense of belief in each person's ability and value that fueled the company, even during competitive battles. That culture was spearheaded by Gifford and all the founders, and perpetuated by staff members. The Maxim value of treating people well and creating long-term employment opportunities for them created great loyalty within the company, says Murphy.

To illustrate, he describes a recent conversation with someone who has worked for Maxim for 17 years:

> "He met his wife while he was a business manager guy . . . she was an applications engineer. They got married; they have two kids now. Even when Maxim went through its really hard times after Jack left and we had the stock option backdating issues and we couldn't file our financials and it was a total mess, he and his wife were saying, 'We didn't even think about leaving.' That's just what you do when you're part of a family. You have the good times and you have the bad times . . . and it worked itself out."

27

SHOCK WAVES

"Jack was devastated by it . . . and he felt responsible to the employees, who were like part of his family. He just thought he was so careful . . . just didn't see it coming."

RHODINE GIFFORD

Starting in 2006, a series of shock waves hit Maxim with reverberating and traumatic impact. Multiple major sequential crises seriously tested the mettle of Maxim's management and its employee loyalty.

To begin with, the Securities Exchange Commission (SEC) initiated an investigation of illegal stock option backdating, as announced by Maxim on June 7, 2006. Then a shareholder derivative action was filed in Delaware on June 12, 2006, asserting that Maxim issued backdated stock options, based on a report by Merrill Lynch, which indicated that Maxim stock options returned annualized returns of almost ten times annualized market returns in the same time period. Maxim's board appointed a special committee and independent counsel to investigate the allegations of stock option backdating. In September 2006, Maxim notified the SEC that it would delay its financial filings and thus began the great "Blackout Period" when Maxim was delisted from the NASDAQ exchange and employees could not exercise any company stock options, truly testing employee loyalty. Numerous additional shareholder derivative lawsuits were filed in California against Maxim's directors and officers. A shareholder class action suit was also filed in California against Maxim, and its former CEO and CFO.

For months Maxim employees watched their company endure a barrage of lawsuit allegations, press articles, and ultimately the resignation of their founder CEO, their CFO, Treasurer, and Stock Administrator, while having their income threatened by a delisting of the stock by NASDAQ. This meant that their income from stock options was not available to them, at least temporarily and maybe permanently. Everyone, but especially Gifford, was shaken to the core.

For many, the first warning of a problem came in a lead article in the *Wall Street Journal*, according to Fullagar: "Out of all the CEOs in the country, they picked on Jack to analyze his stock options . . . he [the author] looked at the price of the options and said the probability of Jack picking the low point each month for any options that he was granting was like one in a billion."

After the SEC launched a major investigation, "Jack was devastated by it," says Rhodine. "He was so proud of the company . . . and he felt responsible to the employees, who were like part of his family. He couldn't believe that something like this would ever come up. He just thought he was so careful . . . just didn't see it coming." Jack was so hands-on with Maxim, she says, "but you can only be hands-on so much when the company is growing."

At the time, Gifford was grappling with some health issues, though he shared very little with work colleagues. However, I could see that he was not the same Jack. I think other co-workers saw that too. After the backdating scandal struck, his health continued to worsen. Near the end of 2006, his doctor told him, "You can't work anymore, or you'll kill yourself." That's when Jack approached me, and we had this brief, urgent, and life-changing conversation at the Dallas Intercontinental hotel lounge after Maxim's Christmas event:

> *"I'd really like you to be the CEO. Of course, I have to sell this to the board. But first I need to see if you want to do it."*
>
> *"Yes, I'd like to give it a try."*
>
> *"But you're gonna be CEO in like two weeks."*
>
> *"Okay."*

Within three weeks, just after Christmas vacation week, I took on the role of CEO, along with the immense additional challenge of cleaning up the accounting mess. Unfortunately, the backdating issue escalated, and Jack needed to also officially resign his strategic advisor role on the board, before eventually ceasing all interaction with the company. Jack's sudden exit from Maxim came as the second shock for me. It was a trial by fire.

Gifford's resignation also came as a great surprise to company employees. To most of them he was the invincible leader who would be carried out on a stretcher before retiring. However, employees were aware that he had some health issues because he was losing his voice. It was also evident that he was trying with great effort to control his emotions and not get upset at meetings. These challenges were contrary to his personality and did not go unnoticed.

On December 19, 2006, *Business Wire* announced the retirement news:

> *". . . John (Jack) Gifford, Maxim's founder and CEO from 1983 to the present, has, on the advice of his doctor, elected to retire as CEO. He will remain with the company on a part-time basis as a strategic advisor focused on product planning and business direction. Mr.*

Gifford's continuing role will facilitate a seamless transition to a new CEO. Tunç Doluca has been named President and Chief Executive Officer of the company, effective January 1, 2007. Mr. Doluca will also become a director of the company at that time. To limit management representation on the Board of Directors, thereby maintaining the independence of Maxim's Board, Mr. Gifford will relinquish his seat on the Board. B. Kipling (Kip) Hagopian, who has been an independent member of Maxim's board since 1997, has been elected interim Chairman of the Board."[1]

During the transition, Jack set up a consulting office for himself. Many employees would visit him, drink some coffee, and converse with him about Maxim opportunities, challenges, and other business matters. I went out to lunch with him occasionally, and he dropped by Maxim a couple of times for the same purpose. He advised all of us on many matters because he enjoyed mentoring leaders and wanted to contribute to Maxim's future success.

Maxim was delisted from the NASDAQ exchange in the Fall of 2007. The investigations and court proceedings continued at a snail's pace while Maxim and its two auditors worked on a multi-year restatement of earnings due to massive backdating of rank and file employee stock options. It was a miserable period in the company's history, for employees, management and shareholders. Since Maxim was delisted from the NASDAQ exchange, in-the-money options of employees that were granted in 1997 and 1998 expired without employees having any ability to exercise in late 2007 and 2008. Management was emotionally devastated. In response to this challenge to Maxim's employee centric culture, Maxim instituted a goodwill program offering rank and file employees the equivalent of the money each lost due to the expirations of options during the Blackout. This goodwill program cost Maxim hundreds of millions of dollars, but it was worth every dollar for employee morale. Moreover, Maxim management and board never questioned that it was the right and fair thing to do for our employees.

Had I known how long and painful the financial restatement would be when I accepted the CEO role, who knows, I might have declined. I thought it would take a few months, not twenty! However, since I had accepted and was not the type to run from responsibility, I decided to stick it out and dig in till the storm passed.

I soon switched into crisis management mode. Besides the backdating and retirement shockwaves, the global financial crises struck the world, and Maxim, during 2008 to 2009.

The financial crises, considered by many economists to have been the worst since the 1930s Great Depression, began with the subprime mortgage meltdown in the US. Next followed an international banking crisis, crashing stock markets, the bursting of the real estate bubble, and the global Great Recession. Ironically, just when we announced our restated financials in September-October of 2008, and said "it's now back to work," Lehman brothers collapsed, marking a deepening of the financial crisis which followed the Great Recession.

The executives of Maxim and I managed the converging crises as best we could—one day at a time. Even though it was painful, we shared the challenges with employees as transparently as possible, describing the problems and our strategies for dealing with them. For the first time, we were regrettably compelled to do something Jack had never done before— lay off employees. The news came as a culture shock to the company. When the inevitable blowback came, I responded the only way I knew how . . . by telling employees the brutal truth about the situation and not withholding information or spinning a story.

Just over a year into navigating Maxim's storms, we were struck by a fourth one that left most employees and founders reeling emotionally. On the fateful morning of January 12, 2009, while commuting to work, I received the text: "Jack died." I was shocked. In my lunches with him during the transition, he was very engaged and frankly looked much healthier than he had during 2006, his last year at Maxim. Quickly, I pulled my car over to absorb the news, gather myself, and begin to give thought to my next steps. Although shaken at the passing of my friend and mentor, I could not afford too much reflection at the time. I would soon have to communicate the distressing news to Maxim employees and amplify our crisis control measures.

I think many employees were just as surprised as I was because I had heard some rumors suggesting that he made his illness up to escape the backdating issue. However, this sad news of him dying at an early age (by today's standards) proved them wrong. Tragically, according to Rhodine, the ongoing trauma of the backdating investigation of Maxim had taken its toll: "That actually killed him. That's what killed him," she exclaims.

In response to the sudden passing, there was a strong outpouring of sadness and gratitude from many employees, which eventually filled a *Book of Remembrance* (extensively quoted in the final chapter).

Here's an excerpt from the LA times obituary:

> *"It is with great sadness that John F. Gifford passed away unexpectedly on his birthday, January 11, 2009, at his family home in Hawaii. After spending a beautiful sunset with his wife, Rhodine, he suffered a fatal heart attack. Jack is survived by his wife, Rhodine, of 49 years. Rhodine was his best friend, confidante and love of his life. He had three wonderful daughters and their husbands . . . and leaves behind eleven adoring grandchildren . . . A beautiful traditional Hawaiian memorial service, held for his many local island friends, took place outdoors on the Mauna Kea grounds in Hawaii, on Wednesday, January 14, 2009. A local memorial service for friends and family is*

*planned for today, Thursday, January 22, 2009, at 1:45 p.m. at the
Stanford Memorial Church in Palo Alto, California. A reception will
follow at the Sharon Heights Country Club, in Menlo Park.”²*

News of Jack's passing spread quickly throughout Maxim and Silicon Valley.
Thousands mourned the loss of a man, friend, family member and CEO
who had made a remarkably wide and deep impact on their lives. Fullagar,
one of Jack's longest standing business associates and friends, provides these
recollections:

*"I had just got off a plane at JFK when a series of e-mails
announcing his death showed up on my iPhone. Like most people, my
first reaction was 'This can't be true,' but a call to Chuck Rigg [Senior
Vice President] confirmed that, alas, it was true. Jack was always so
physically fit, often talking about his Marine Corps exercise regimen,
so much so that I always assumed I would be the first to go. In fact,
a number of years before his passing I had a dream that I was on my
deathbed and Jack came by to say farewell. He was on his way to a
ballgame and had his baseball bat slung over his shoulder, bouncing
up and down on the balls of his feet, looking like he was still in his
twenties. Even today, this dream is quite vivid in my mind!*

*My wife and I visited Jack and Rhodine at their Hawaii home a
few months before his passing. He and I spent a few hours resolving an
electrical problem on his fishing boat. Jack seemed, finally, to be enjoying
retirement, so when I heard the news of his death my first thoughts
were for Rhodine and their family. Measured in years, 68 was way,
way too young. On the other hand, Jack achieved more in his 68 years
than most who may enjoy another 15 or 20 years. He founded two very
successful semiconductor companies, was an entrepreneur in several*

other enterprises, from the first digital wheel balancing system to custom athletic shoes to his various farming endeavors, to name just a few. In addition, he was instrumental in setting up a number of philanthropic organizations, including the very successful EPATT (East Palo Alto Tennis & Tutoring) and a baseball team for underprivileged kids in Hawaii. By these measures, Jack outlived (in the literal sense of the words) most of his peers."

As a father of the analog industry, an aggressive and brilliant tech pioneer, Gifford left us a memorable heritage to build upon. As far as the restoration of Jack's business legacy, it wouldn't be until May 2010 that the ravages of all the legal proceedings would be repaired and cleaned up. However, before his death, at the end of 2007, Jack was able to settle with the SEC for $800,000 to clear up his personal side of the case, neither admitting nor denying the Commission's accusations.

In the SEC case specific to Maxim as a company, we were able to clear the charges in late 2007 and restate our financials by October of 2008. Maxim also entered into a memorandum of understanding in 2010, according to a Maxim press release, "reflecting an agreement in principle to settle all claims asserted against all defendants in the putative class action concerning the Company's stock option accounting practices . . . The agreement in principle provides for the payment of $173-million by the company. The after-tax cash impact is estimated to be $110-million."[5] No criminal charges were brought against Maxim, and it was determined that not one backdated stock option was ever granted to an officer.

As a result of the litigation and the financial crises, Maxim stock had taken a beating. However, on October 8th, 2008, amid great celebration, we relisted Maxim on the NASDAQ and remotely rang the market's closing bell. We were one of a few companies that went public *twice*.

With great relief at navigating another storm, I was again able to focus solely on the business and righting the ship through the remainder of the financial crisis. It would take some time to restore our significantly reduced revenues and our stock price. By 2010, the economy and market bounced back like the release of a catapult, and we soon had shortages of many products. This same downturn and sudden recovery applied to the entire tech industry.

Quickly, our stock price rebounded, and we embarked on several significant growth years. From Maxim's stock price bottom around $11 in December 2008, the company dramatically recovered to the $60 plus range in mid-2018. The hardships of that Maxim multiple-crisis season became a distant memory. Within a few years, we were riding the Samsung smart phone wave at the height of some of the greatest analog chip demand in company history. What is most remarkable, from a Maxim financial perspective, is that we were always profitable and prolific new product producers, even in lean times.

In retrospect, as with most serious life challenges, the 2006 – 2010 period of our company timeline, though greatly trying, strengthened both Maxim and its people. A newly determined and toughened team, forged under the pressure of prolonged ordeals, rose from the ashes to enter a new era of analog success.

28

NEW ERA

BY JIM BERGMAN

[Note: This book has largely focused on the early Maxim founding and dramatic growth periods, spearheaded by Gifford and other founders. However, it seemed important in this one chapter to enlarge the book's lens and provide a brief overview of the company's most recent years. In the interest of providing a more detached perspective of Maxim's New Era under my leadership, Jim Bergman, longtime Maxim board director, graciously agreed to provide his perspective in this chapter. Tunç]

For years prior to Gifford handing over Maxim's helm, the board knew that Tunç Doluca had been designated as heir. As board members, we had been observing Doluca's steady leadership and quiet but impressive performance. Also, our veteran CEO had repeatedly told us that Tunç would assume his leadership role some day. However, to confirm this direction, the board interviewed company senior managers. Unanimously they agreed that Maxim should recruit the next CEO from within, and that Tunç be that person. Even when managers were asked to include themselves in the consideration process, they agreed that Tunç was most prepared to steer our corporate ship.

Once the decision was made, we summoned Doluca to a board meeting where we engaged him in a short but pivotal conversation:

"Do you want to be Maxim's new CEO?" we asked.
"Yes, I do. But I'm going to need a lot of help and support from you."
"OK, we'll do whatever we can to support you."

With that simple and humble dialogue, a new era at Maxim was launched. Tunç officially assumed the CEO role on January 1, 2007. Though he had no experience running a public company, we all believed that Jack had prepared Tunç to take the lead of his corporate legacy. Doluca started with the company at the age of 26 and developed his leadership acumen in many areas of the company. Jack had quickly recognized him as a budding talent and groomed him for this moment for over 20 years.

It was as if Tunç, like many other young promising staff at Maxim, was one of the corporate kids Gifford had helped raise and mentor over the years. And, as the eventual choice as heir, Doluca rose to the occasion. As the new CEO, he deftly steered the company through a very turbulent season and kept the ship aright through the series of storms already described. He also continued to develop the monumental legacy that Jack and the founders had created with such aggressive genius.

In meetings throughout the years, Tunç was fairly subdued and didn't talk a lot. However, when he did, he was impressive. His thoughts were always well reasoned and on point. He wasn't a showboat, but when it was important, he offered his opinion. Tunç didn't go out of his way to avoid offending Jack, and I think that over the years Jack developed a deep respect for him.

Ed Medlin, our company General Counsel, who closely watched this milestone transition, shared these insights with me: "Jack had complete trust handing off Maxim to Tunç. After Jack had stepped aside, he once told me: 'Tunç is smart; he *is* Maxim. Trust him, support him, and help him succeed. He'll get things done. But you've got to help him with one thing. Tunç is too damn nice . . . However, Tunç is looking at things we should have fixed long ago."

Everyone who knew both men recognized their vastly different management styles. Tunç is not somebody who's an in-your-face kind of person. He's very analytical. Jack was very quick to react to things . . . a ready, aim, shoot type of leader. Usually he was right, but once in a while he was wrong. But Tunç tends to be super deliberative. He really thinks it through from every possible angle. Still, he makes his decisions in a timely enough manner. He's very analytical. He's smart.

As Matt Murphy put it, in decision-making style, Jack was like Captain Kirk, while Tunç was like Spock—fair, meticulous, and exceedingly data driven. At the same time, those who get to know Tunç appreciate his great sense of humor, endearing personality, and sincere care for people. Also, Jack was willing to cut deals with people by giving a little more stock here or a better deal there. He would often customize his approach to the situations, especially during Maxim's early days. Although such individualization works when a company is smaller, it becomes more challenging to apply once the company becomes large. Everyone ends up getting different deals. Consequently, Tunç's more fair-minded approach helped create an even-handed system that worked better for our now sizeable operation.

At the beginning of this new season, and in preparation for greater streamlining and scaling, Tunç was well suited to take over as Maxim's CEO.

He challenged staff to think a little differently in order to get more organized, apply more even-keeled decision-making, and develop more precise systems. Thus, Maxim executives began to implement a more measured leadership approach, resisting the temptation to make exceptions and honing systems that emphasized fairness more.

Gifford's style was ideal for Maxim's early years as a Wild West Silicon Valley startup. In addition, because of Jack's incredibly high leadership aptitude and intelligence, he was able to apply his approach effectively even throughout the company's dramatic growth. Doluca's style seemed to be well suited to a more established company. This transition, the change of corporate style, was inevitable. Though Tunç operated differently from Jack, he was the right choice for CEO. He revered the past accomplishments of Jack and the other founders, yet still had a fresh, clear vision for the next stages of company development.

Doluca's gradual elevation to CEO was quiet and surprising to some. Born and raised in Turkey, he moved to America for his post-secondary studies to take advantage of the safer US university environment and benefit from the reputed engineering programs. Tunç came to Maxim as a kid recently graduated from UC Santa Barbara's Master's program. He had long hair and was just a down-to-earth guy. A while after joining Maxim, the young chip designer returned to Turkey to complete his military training. Many of us at the company remember the pictures of him in his army fatigues. He returned from overseas to work again at the little Maxim startup lab. That's where he determinedly focused on helping develop some of the cutting-edge designs that would carve out a name for our company in the semiconductor world.

As previously mentioned, Doluca's first major contributions to Maxim came during his designing days. That's when his retreat to "The Cave" inspired the creation of the MAX781 lead product and the greatly successful MAX786, eventually housed in most of the world's PC notebook computers. Tunç holds eleven mixed signal design patents. He went on to serve as Vice President of Research and Development. Later, as previously mentioned, after proposing a new way of organizing the company into Business Units, Tunç established the first vertical BU for portable power management products. In May 2005, he took on the role of Group President of Portable, Computing, and Instrumentation Electronics group, overseeing ten business units.

Throughout Doluca's management of BUs, he learned more about marketing and defining products, as well as working closely with customers. In these roles, Gifford saw the younger executive's ability to take a chip design idea from seed form to a full-fledged business within the larger Maxim organization. Then, when Fred Beck retired as VP of sales in 2006, Gifford suggested that Doluca would gain valuable experience by taking over sales. After some negotiation, Tunç agreed to take on that function, while still overseeing eight of his ten business units. Gifford consented to handling two of the BUs for a while.

As Tunç explained to me, "Jack was trying to get me to learn more— prepping me. After about six months, I realized that running sales was not my thing. But it gave me good experience and helped me form a bond with the sales country managers." Months before Gifford's departure from Maxim, he agreed to find another VP of sales, while Doluca continued running his BUs. However, that season overseeing sales would be the final experience necessary to prepare Tunç to shoulder the role of CEO.

Yes, the new Maxim era started in serial crisis control mode. However, Doluca's ability to remain calm and methodically implement a clear strategy brought the company out of the storm relatively unscathed. When faced with the decision between an easy choice and the right choice, Tunç consistently does the right thing. During the turbulent times, and beyond, he was able to make great advances within the company, including large reductions in new product development and manufacturing cycle times, supply chain enhancements, and the recruitment of outstanding new managers. He was also able to make dramatic improvements in customer relationships, which eventually placed Maxim on preferred customer lists for 11 of our top 12 customers.

In addition, Tunç and his management team also supported Murphy's impressive strategic initiative to dramatically expand Maxim's distribution business. This resulted in improved margins and increased revenue. New investment in information technology and design software as well as infrastructure helped improve development productivity significantly. Also, by conducting a tactical review of product lines and business units, Tunç was able to discard the least profitable lines and boost investment into lines that promised the highest margins and greatest growth. Finally, the staffing of an acquisition and merger group resulted in 17 acquisitions of various sizes during this new era.

The most ambitious new undertaking under Doluca, *The Maxim Manifesto*, mandated an aspirational path for Maxim's recognition by investors, customers, and employees as the indisputable leader in the analog and mixed signal business. Within this plan, Tunç identified about 20 different areas at Maxim that needed attention. Areas like marketing, manufacturing, and human resources were compared to those of competitors and scored from one to five. Then, a plan was drafted for taking each area of the company to the next level.

Under its new CEO, the Maxim culture began to shift too. Management increasingly listened to company staff and, if their suggestions made sense, trusted them to introduce changes. The company sharpened its focus on improving employee well-being, environment, and growth, and on increasing corporate involvement in local communities by supporting impactful donations and volunteer work.

A capstone of the new Maxim era, one that frames the successful legacy of its past and the continuing achievements of the present and future, was the acquisition of its newest facility. When he became CEO, Doluca made it his objective to foster a more collaborative approach within the company. It was difficult to foster such a cooperative environment with staff spread around 10 buildings in Sunnyvale, California. Tunç also saw growing unhealthy internal competition and an occasional dynamic of blame shifting in the company as other signs that Maxim needed a cultural shift.

Shortly after assuming the role of CEO, Tunç gathered the approximately 40 senior leaders at the Doubletree Hotel in San Jose. Each participant was encouraged to introduce one opportunity or challenge and then a solution or action plan. Tunç wanted everyone to see his leadership style was different than Jack's; he expected more collaboration across the various groups and divisions of the company.

Maxim had grown up with business units competing against each other, a dynamic that had effectively advanced the company through the dramatic technology industry growth periods. However, as the semiconductor industry matured, more companies began competing for limited market share. That's when Maxim needed to transition into a more cooperative corporate structure and mobilize its team to increasingly work together toward the same goals. Sometimes that meant we would sacrifice an opportunity for the greater good of the company.

Doluca realized that the best solution for improving and fostering a collaborative and problem-solving culture was to bring all staff together in one facility. People work a lot better, achieve alignment, and resolve differences of opinion best with face-to-face discussions. As he would say, "I wanted an environment at HQ where it was easy for people to walk over and talk."

Though the hunt for a new home began in 2008, the financial crisis convinced company management to shelve the campus project. It didn't make sense to spend millions of dollars on a facility during a season of tightening budgets and industry crisis control. However, the team resumed its search efforts two years later.

By happenstance, or perhaps providence, Tunç arrived at the site of a CEOs group meeting one day in 2010. This is how he described the occasion to me:

"I not only arrived at the same time as the CEO that owned the building, but I also ended up parking right next to him. He offered to walk me into the building and to the conference room. I noticed that most of the building was dark with no employees working. When I inquired about this, he said it was going to be sold. After finding out the square footage and other details about the campus, I realized it was a perfect home for us."

The building structure looked old and needed a complete renovation. But by gutting the interior and modernizing, Maxim was able to create a new, terrific home—with its courtyard, rest areas, and cafeteria—for greater community and cooperation. Also, before the move, company sales people didn't want to invite customers to visit our old Sunnyvale buildings. The new facility, however, became a place that highlighted Maxim's achievements and where everyone could proudly invite customers and other industry professionals.

This 430,000 square foot campus in Silicon Valley became the launch pad for the new iteration of this leading analog chip innovator. In June of 2012, the new campus, at 160 Rio Robles in San Jose, became the new Maxim home, headquarters for many thousands of employees at home and around the world today.

Thus, a coincidental meeting in a parking lot led to the purchase of corporate ground zero for Maxim's new technological impact on the world. As Tunç rhetorically asks: "Isn't life full of coincidences?"

Maxim Global Headquarters today—the Rio Robles campus in San Jose, CA.

29

LEGACY OF
IMPACT

*"In thinking and acting beyond ourselves,
we enrich our own spirits immeasurably."*

JACK GIFFORD, IN A LETTER TO EMPLOYEES,
THANKSGIVING 2006

"*We show up at Chantilly [restaurant]. We sit down, meet the owner, and tell him we're waiting for Jack. He starts telling us stories about Jack coming in 20 years ago and always having a really nice holiday dinner there, tipping fabulously every year . . . a super generous guy. Then the door blows open, and he comes in:*

"Hey, how you guys doing? Do you guys have any money?"

"What do you mean?"

"I forgot my wallet at home. Do I need to run back?"

"Jack, we're taking you out to dinner—we're paying for you."

"Oh cool, all right, thanks."

299

At the "epic" dinner, continues Murphy, "We just had this really amazing night with him. He was so open, so candid, so personable, and so kind to us." This milestone meeting was hatched by Murphy and his fellow Maxim VP, Chris Neil. After Gifford's swift departure from the company, says Murphy, in the shadow of serious health concerns and the backdating issue, no one had given the CEO a proper farewell. Unbeknownst to many, Jack had rejected multiple requests from Tunç to set up an event to recognize him and say farewell.

"After Jack left, Chris and I were sitting around on some business trip a few months later saying, 'This is just terrible. Nobody said goodbye to him, nobody threw him a party, nobody did anything nice for him.' We were talking about how he did so much for us. He gave me a career, financial security . . . this tremendous individual. If you think about the thousands of people that came through the company, their families, the college educations that were paid for . . . tens of thousands of people were impacted by this guy. I was one of them. We decided to take him out to dinner . . . to say thank you."

Gifford quickly accepted the two younger VPs' invitation. However, on the day of the dinner, Murphy and Neil found themselves nervously wondering out loud about their imminent encounter with the high-powered former CEO. Murphy was following Neil north on the 101 freeway, when his cell phone rang. "Why did we do this to ourselves?" asked the familiar voice on the other end. "We're going to go have dinner with *Jack*. What are we going to say?" Nervously, they discussed the anticipated grilling by Jack about the past nine months of decisions and actions at Maxim since the CEO's retirement. "We were ready for an earful."

As Murphy explains, Jack was a larger-than-life personality, a much older veteran, who was a "very sharp-elbowed, sharp-tongued force. He was not a guy that you hung out with. He was somebody in this very high position who I couldn't relate to . . . not the soft and cuddly type." However, they were both pleasantly surprised by the congenial dinner conversation with their mentor.

Eventually, says Murphy, he mustered the courage to ask Jack the question that had plagued them both for years: "Hey, we've got to ask . . . you were really hard on us, especially Chris and me. Was this your strategy to push people this way or is it just how you are?"

Then, according to Murphy, came this surprising response:

"No, my approach was very thoughtful. I would just push everybody in the company when I had a chance. I'd find the right time and the right place, and I'd push really hard, and then I'd watch and see if they could come back from that or not. How would they respond? Would they come back with a better proposal, or would they crack in the meeting? Then, ultimately, I'd find over time that they would get to a point where I couldn't push them anymore. They would rise to the highest level that they could rise to, and then I was okay with that."

Next, Gifford dropped the bomb that would reverberate in the two men's psyches for the rest of their lives:

"With you two guys . . . you just kept coming back. Every time I'd push you guys, I'd give you more stuff, you just kept coming back and you'd do a great job. Finally, that's why you are where you are . . . because you just kept going up. You need to understand something. You two are some of the best people in the world at what you do."

Then, with awe and a slight falter in his voice, Murphy states: "That was probably one of the best compliments I ever got in my life." It was another of the three Gifford power-complements Murphy received, the first coming at the Christmas party encounter with Jack years earlier.

However, it was at that thank you dinner meeting, says Murphy, that he and Neil realized that Gifford "actually had been a bigger influence in our careers and direction than maybe we knew." Clearly, he says, "Though Jack could be harsh to his staff, he had a huge heart and just did the right thing for people when it really mattered." The dinner provided a nice sense of closure for them, says Murphy. Despite leaving under challenging circumstances, Gifford had "come to terms with separating from Maxim … and he wasn't bitter. He never said a bad word about his treatment. It was really about us … how we were doing."

Murphy and Neil's final meeting with Gifford, and their epiphanies, provide evidence of the legacy of impact left by Jack, the founders, staff, and the analog company called Maxim. The company they built deeply impacted both people and the wider society, through team interaction, mentoring, prolific ingenuity, and clear vision of the future. Yes, the company grew to produce over $2-billion in revenues and employ 10,000 people in the early 2000s. In addition, its record-breaking string of thousands of products and competitor-busting growth made waves in the tech world and created "a legend." Industry insiders referred to Maxim as an "execution machine."

And, as Beck stated, Maxim's number one position as a mixed-signal chip creator placed it ahead of its competition. During Maxim's early era, the company rose to the top by taking a countercultural approach. "It grew during a time in which the consensus in the tech world was that analog was dead," states Murphy. "Now the analog industry's probably a $60-billion industry. It's enormous. It's one of the biggest subsegments of the whole chip industry, which is $400-billion. Analog turned out to be the most profitable segment of the chip industry during that heyday of Maxim."

According to a 2006 business-wire article:

"Mr. Gifford has successfully taken Maxim from a small private operation of eight founding employees to an international leader in chip development with a market cap of nearly $10-billion and over two thirds of its revenues coming from outside the United States. Along the way, Mr. Gifford was named CEO of the year by Electronic Business Magazine in 2001 and America's Best Semiconductor Industry CEO by Institutional Investor Magazine in 2005."[1]

Yes, it's a phenomenal growth story, springing from the founding team's amazing foresight, declares Murphy.

That foresight inspired an exuberant corporate confidence, leading Gifford, during the economic downturn of the mid-1990s, to make a seeming illogically bold claim. "Quite frankly, we are the economy," he announced, during a CNBC interview on *Squawk Box*, according to Murphy, when explaining his lack of concern about the economic recession. Jack then noted that in the foreseeable future, semiconductor technology, biotech, and software would become the main engine of the economy. Though media pundits were astonished by Gifford's statement, he was right.

The Maxim story is not only one of business impact, but also one about a team that cared for people and society. "A guy like Jack, a charismatic figure leading that story, that group, I think is a big deal," says Georges. "I think people need heroes, and in my mind he was a hero. Most heroes are flawed, but that's part of what makes them believable." Clearly, he says, Gifford "had a core set of values that were just really good. Do the right thing, treat people well, create long-term employment opportunities . . . live by the golden rule." Those values bred great loyalty throughout Maxim.

Notably, when a company sometimes runs more like a family, staff expectations can be unusual. For instance, says Fullagar, when the company lawyer went on a Sahara camel trek, "Jack insisted that he have a satellite phone with him, so he could talk to him every day" while he was away. On another occasion, Fullagar says, his wife, who oversaw marketing and communications at Maxim, found herself feeding coins to a "rusty old communist phone" in Czechoslovakia in a futile attempt to call back to her company department.

Despite Gifford's high expectations of staff, his and Maxim's greatest legacy was the investment in its people. The company highly valued the development of people and took great pains to encourage their success in career, personal life, and finances. Murphy describes Gifford as a "tremendous coach and a role model" to the staff of Maxim:

> *"Quite frankly, if I had not worked underneath him for those first 12 years, I would not have been equipped to be the CEO of Marvell. There's no way . . . seeing what great leadership looks like on a day-in and day-out basis . . . how you make really important decisions, how you treat people. I learned everything from him on that."*

Georges also describes the significant difference Gifford made in his life:

> *"Jack was a guy that challenged you, frustrated you, argued with you, and he was like a dad to me in a lot of ways. I learned so much from him about how to manage. I learned how not to manage too. Jack constantly pushed you, challenged you. A little side note, he passed away the same day that my dad passed away, and the same day that I was attending the funeral of one of my good friends' dads. It was just not a good day. He was really a father figure to me."*

Paradoxically, though tough as nails, as a father figure, Gifford had an aversion to firing or letting people leave. Once Maxim had invested years into people, notes Hagopian, if people wanted to leave or had personal problems, Gifford would give them a leave of absence and then encourage them to return. At times, he would find former employees who were dissatisfied at another company and bring them back on staff.

"We had one case where the guy got offered a great job in another company and a promotion. Jack got me to spend two hours on the phone with him convincing him not to go to this startup . . . I tried to give him the pluses and minuses of staying and going to a startup. We finally ended up keeping him. That's just part of Jack's philosophy. Don't lose any good people."

For Gifford, a beach in Hawaii was as good a place as any to recruit. Hagopian recalls sunning himself on the beach in 1996 when Jack coincidentally spotted him, walked up, and greeted him like a best friend. At the time, Hagopian had been off the Maxim board for seven years. "It was like I had just seen him the day before. Maxim's top management and board members were holding a planning meeting in Hawaii. He asked me if I would speak to the group about the history of Maxim. The next day he asked me to come back on the board." After considering the offer for a couple of weeks, he says, "I agreed to do it. I was honored. I was in the right place in my life."

Besides his legacy of corporate achievement and investment in people, Gifford left a legacy of personal achievement and impact. Yes, he is known for his "CEO of the year" and "America's Best Semiconductor Industry CEO" recognitions.[2] However, it's his charitable extra-corporate activities, which made a great difference in thousands of lives, that not everyone knew about. Gifford "supported several college baseball programs: Stanford, California, Santa Clara University, San Jose State University, and UCLA.

At UCLA he funded and oversaw the construction of the Jack and Rhodine Gifford Hitting Facility, a 10,500-square-foot (980 m²) practice facility at Jackie Robinson Stadium."[3] He also supported youth baseball and tennis camps in Hawaii.

In 2010, San Jose State and Santa Clara Universities began hosting an annual Jack Gifford Memorial Tournament. In what Gifford considers a highlight of his career, in 1990, he was elected to the UCLA Baseball Hall of Fame, along with other esteemed inductees, Jackie Robinson and Dr. Bobby Brown. Then, in 2004, he was named "oldest player ever to participate in the National Baseball Congress World Series."[4]

Gifford's former baseball head coach at UCLA, Gary Adams, says, "I never played with a more confident or competitive player . . . He was the kind of player you wanted most on your team—committed to excellence, hard work and whatever was best for the team. I never met a man who loved baseball more than Jack—not just watching it being played; I mean actually getting out there on the field and playing it.[5]

One of Gifford's and Maxim's greatest legacies has come through continued wider impact by its founders and those trained within the high-stakes crucible at the semiconductor's headquarters. Several Maxim employees have gone on to lead other companies and found ventures of their own.

For instance, as I previously mentioned, in 2016, Murphy went on to become CEO of Silicon Valley based semiconductor solutions company, Marvell Technology Group. He worked for Gifford for 12 years, plus another 10 years under my leadership. Before assuming his VP position, at the young age of 33, Jack and other founders went to bat for him, and the board was eventually swayed. "Jack was willing to bet on me at a very young age in a huge job where the average age is probably 55," says Murphy. His extensive experience throughout the company, from running a BU to overseeing worldwide sales as a VP, under the tutelage of the founders, prepared him for his present high-level position.

Then there's Sparkman, today CEO of Spin Memory in Fremont, CA. This MRAM company is presently in the middle of raising its Series B round of $52-million in funding, with hopes of bringing Magnetic Memory into the mainstream. He, too, considers Maxim and Jack's training to have been essential in his continued corporate entrepreneurial success: "I do consider Jack my mentor and strive every day to live up to his expectations."

Like Murphy and Sparkman, I owe my excellent training and current CEO role at Maxim to Jack and the challenging Maxim environment. Somehow, Jack saw leadership potential and groomed that in me for 20 years.

Maxim alumni have also gone on to make impacts both inside and outside of the corporate world. After retiring from Maxim, early founder, Fullagar, became involved in two post-retirement legacy projects. The first endeavor, he says, originated in Africa:

"In 2007, my wife and I did a safari in Kruger Park, South Africa. Little did we know that this would turn into a five-year venture in an African village. On the last day of the safari, our guide, Alweet, asked if we would like to see more lions and elephants, or visit his village and meet his family. Of course, we opted for the latter!

After we returned home, my wife started thinking about what she had seen, most notably a school with no books or library. Most of the jobs are hospitality-related in the nearby game parks and require a knowledge of English, but the local language is Shangaan. We felt that a library of English language books would help the kids, and maybe also the adults, to improve their English skills and open up more employment opportunities ... We purchased a prime piece of real estate next to the school, (buying land in a tribal village, where the chief took his 30 percent 'commission,' was an adventure in itself!) designed and built a 1,200 square foot building, and collected and cataloged 7,000

English-language books. Maxim generously paid shipping costs for the
books, shelving and tables . . . The library continues to be a great success.
We also built a much-needed day-care center. We could not have done it
without the support of many friends who donated generously, some of
whom also traveled to Boxahuku as volunteers."

Most recently, from 2011 to 2017, Fullagar became a consultant and scientific advisory board member for a startup called Genia, founded by Roger Chen, who used to work in his group at Maxim. Fullagar tells the story of how he became involved:

"One day in 2008 I ran into Roger at Radio Shack. He took me to his
garage (in true Silicon Valley startup fashion) where he showed me
his prototype DNA sequencing circuit. A year later he founded Genia,
in conjunction with Stefan Roever, Pratima Rao, and Randy Davis
(both Randy and Pratima were Maxim alumni) with the goal of using
semiconductor-based biological nanopore sequencing to enable a $100
genome . . . A number of other ex-Maximites joined the team, and it
was fun working with old friends. After successfully demonstrating
proof of concept for the semiconductor-based sequencing concept, the
company was acquired by Roche in 2014."

Other founders, like Hood, retired to a more relaxed life of travel, fishing, gardening, and grandchildren. He says, "I felt like I accomplished enough in my life to be satisfied and leave feeling like I won. I won professionally and financially. It was just hard to leave the people. That was the hardest part, leaving some really good people that worked for me."

Like Gifford, some founders—Fred Beck, Dave Bingham, Lee Evans, and (near-founder) Ziya Boyacigiller—have passed away since their days at

Maxim, leaving this planet richer for their contributions. They each impacted lives and revolutionized the chip industry.

These men, along with Jack and other founders, established a distinct culture. Besides the lessons of the Maxim founding and growth journey previously discussed, Georges and Sparkman highlight some cultural keys that particularly stand out to them. Sparkman remembers the effectiveness of Gifford's "management by chaos" method and has made use of it himself at times. Georges says he learned from Jack's example of making "early gut level decisions." Sometimes, he says, you need to make split second decisions. "You can't wait for analysis paralysis" to set in. He also learned to "hire people smarter than you" by seeking both a cultural and technical fit. "The culture has to be preserved or the character of your company changes," explains Georges. He also highlights the Maxim emphasis on genuinely caring about people and taking interest in society, as evidenced in both Gifford's and the company's constant generosity and charitable actions.

Murphy describes an incident that deeply impacted him and demonstrated the corporate "caring for people" culture. It came in the form of the final of three compliments from Gifford he still vividly remembers today. He received a Gifford Christmas card in 2008, just a month before Jack died.

"I remember my wife and I were on our family room floor. It was like 10 at night. We were sitting on the floor wrapping gifts and opening Christmas cards from friends and family. Then she says, 'Oh, hey, we got one from the Giffords, and she flings it over to me, spinning across the floor. I pick it up . . . this beautiful photo [of] him and all his grandkids and extended family. Open it up and . . . there was actually writing in *the* red pen: "Dear Matt, I am very proud of you. Others didn't believe but I always did. Jack."

Murphy says that he carried this lesson of caring and many other Maxim lessons into his role as CEO at Marvell. Today, he notes, when making vital decisions, in the back of his mind he is asking himself, "What would Jack do?"

Leaving Maxim was very difficult, he says. "I was Tunç's number two guy. I was running a lot of the company. I thought I would be CEO of Maxim one day. It was tough to leave . . . I didn't want to let him down. He had been my boss for 10 years, but at the same time he's doing a great job there." However, the milestone events that took him to his new company helped convince him to move.

Looking back on the interview that led to his big move to Marvell, says Murphy, he vividly recalls an interaction that followed the many questions about his experience and Maxim training. The chairman of the board, Rick Hill, turned to him and said, "You come from a really good culture." It was then, says Murphy, that he again sensed "a silent hand behind the scenes," the hand of Jack, still helping him in some way. That Maxim cultural legacy seemed to follow, infuse, and propel Murphy throughout his career. In turn, like the thousands of people positively affected by the analog semiconductor company and the people who molded it, he seeks to continue the legacy of impact. "Now, being CEO, I'm telling you . . . I look at all the young people coming up, and I want them to be successful. And, I probably end up doing things to move them along even if they never see it."

Today, Maxim and the legacy of its founders live on. And, under my watch, with the many gifted members of the Maxim family who carry that DNA, we look forward to a new season of impacting the tech world through transformational ingenuity. But even more, we look forward to touching the lives of many thousands more people for the better, in America and beyond. We hope you have gleaned some treasures in these pages that will allow you to do the same.

APPENDIX

Maxim Founders Bios (Ch. 11)

Here are the background bio stories of the dozen Maxim pioneers and founders (with badge number, role, and notes), bios that in 1988 that convinced investors to fund the company:

#1 - Jack Gifford (President and CEO): As Director of Analog Products at Fairchild Semiconductor, Jack developed and implemented the industry's first analog business concept. He founded Advanced Micro Devices and rose to become the President/CEO of Intersil Corporation before starting Maxim Integrated. Although an engineer by education, he is first a businessman, who has observed the problems of the IC industry in consistently supplying a quality part with on-time delivery at a fair price.

#2 - Dave Fullagar (Vice President, Research & Development): While at Fairchild Semiconductor in the late 1960s, Dave designed one of the most successful analog products of all time, the μA741 operational amplifier, which is still the industry standard. He later joined a fledgling semiconductor company as their first analog design manager and was responsible for many of the products that helped establish the company as an analog leader with sales of $100-million. Dave rose to Vice President of Research and Development with responsibility for all new product development and Computer Aided Design, before coming on board in a similar capacity at Maxim.

#3 - Fred Beck (Vice President, Sales & Marketing): For over sixteen years, Fred held executive management positions with both Hamilton-Avnet and Schweber Electronics, playing a major role in shaping distribution as it is known today. In addition, he served as President, Director and CEO of a linear integrated circuit manufacturer, and as Senior Vice President, Worldwide Sales and Marketing, for a major semiconductor company.

#4 - Lee Evans (Senior Scientist): As well as being a founder of Siliconix and Intech, Lee is a renowned pioneer in CMOS analog products. He developed the first single chip DVM circuit, the first 4-1/2 digit A/D Converter in CMOS, the first monolithic CMOS chopper stabilized amplifier, and the first monolithic 16 bit A/D converter. Not surprisingly, he was named General Electric's "Scientist of the Year" in 1982. And now he's coming up with more firsts for Maxim.

#5 - Dave Bingham (Senior Scientist): Dave, a pathfinder in early CMOS analog circuits, introduced the first CMOS power supply circuits, as well as the first counter and timer products. He also invented the first monolithic CMOS amplifiers with auto-zeroing for negligible input offset errors. In partnership with Lee Evans, he developed the first single chip digital voltmeter IC, which dominates 90 percent of the marketplace today. Dave deservedly received the "Designer of the Year" award from *Electronics Magazine* and was named, along with Lee Evans, General Electric's "Scientist of the Year" in 1982.

#6 - Dick Wilenken (Senior Scientist): The acknowledged "father" of CMOS monolithic analog switches and multiplexers, Dick single-handedly developed the most successful complete product line in the industry. He can take credit as well for the first monolithic CMOS switch to replace hybrids and the first CMOS video analog switch. He also conceived of the "virtual ground" switch concept, which has since become an industry standard.

#7 - Roger Fuller (Senior Scientist): Designed numerous successful timer and counter products. As well as being a skilled circuit designer, Roger is also an expert in Computer Aided Design (CAD) and simulation software.

#8 - Steve Combs (Vice President, Operations): During a decade of distinguished work in the areas of technology research/development and engineering management, Steve developed innovative CMOS integrated circuit technologies for Hewlett Packard, designed and built major wafer manufacturing facilities, and managed a multi-division effort of 100 scientists in a 1μ VSLI process development for General Electric. Dr. Combs has published more than a dozen papers on IC technology and received several awards for his contributions.

#9 – Rich Hood (Director, Test Engineering): Directed Intersil's test engineering department, where he managed a multi-million-dollar equipment budget and ran test operations in both the US and overseas. Rich was also responsible for the development of wafer sort and final test programs for hundreds of Intersil's analog products.

#10 – Sam Ochi (Senior Scientist): While Director of R&D at Teledyne Semiconductor, Sam and his team developed 4 proprietary and 12 second-source products, including several of Intersil's more popular designs. Prior to Teledyne, he worked at National Semiconductor and AMD where he specialized in A/D and D/A converters.

#11 – Jean Taylor (Senior Layout Designer): As a former school teacher, Jean was trained in the art of mask design by Dick Wilenken during his tenure at Intersil's Northern California design center in Yreka. She was responsible for the layout of dozens of Wilenken's pioneering analog switch products.

#12 – Bev Fuller (Senior Layout Designer): As one of Intersil's most highly regarded mask designers, Bev worked on many of the circuits that made Intersil famous as an innovator in analog CMOS. Her work provides the vital link between the electrical design and the database from which the manufacturing masks are made.

Maxim Acquisition Timeline[1] (Ch. 21)

- 1990: Purchased first wafer fabrication (fab) facility [Saratoga Semiconductor] in Sunnyvale, California.
- 1994: Acquired Tektronix Semiconductor Division in Beaverton, Oregon, giving Maxim high-speed bipolar processes for wireless RF and fiber-optic products.
- 1997: Purchased an additional wafer fab from IC Works in San Jose, California, to increase fab capacity.
- 2001: Acquired Dallas Semiconductor in Dallas, Texas, to gain expertise in digital and mixed-signal CMOS design, as well as an additional wafer fab.
- 2003: Purchased submicrometer CMOS fab from Philips in San Antonio, Texas, to ramp up capacity and support processes down to the 0.25-micrometer level.
- 2007: Purchased 0.18-micrometer fab from Atmel in Irving, Texas, approximately doubling fab capacity.[8]
- 2007: Acquired Vitesse Semiconductor's Storage Products Division in Colorado Springs, Colorado, adding Serial ATA (SATA), Serial Attached SCSI (SAS), and enclosure-management products to Maxim's product portfolio.
- 2008: Acquired Mobilygen in Santa Clara, California, to add H.264 video-compression technology to its portfolio.

- 2009: Acquired Innova Card, headquartered in La Ciotat, France, for the financial transaction terminal semiconductor market.
- 2009: Acquired two product lines from Zilog, Inc. Maxim purchased the Secure Transactions product line, featuring the Zatara family and the hardware portion of Zilog's Wireless Control product line, commonly found in universal remote controls.
- 2010: Acquired privately held Teridian Semiconductor Corporation for approximately $315-million in cash. Teridian was a fabless semiconductor company located in Irvine, California, supplying systems on a chip (SoC) for the smart meter market.
- 2010: Maxim acquired the technology and employees of Trinity Convergence Limited, a software company based in Cambridge, U.K. Trinity was part of the ecosystem to bring Skype video conferencing to the LCD TV market.
- 2010: Maxim acquired Phyworks, a supplier of optical transceiver chips for the broadband communications market.
- 2011: Maxim acquired SensorDynamics, a semiconductor company that develops proprietary sensor and microelectromechanical systems.
- 2012: Maxim acquired Genasic Design Systems Ltd., a fabless RF chip company that makes chips for LTE applications.
- 2013: Maxim acquired Volterra Semiconductor.
- 2018: Maxim acquired Icron Technologies.

[1] Wikipedia, "Maxim Integrated," https://en.wikipedia.org/wiki/Maxim_Integrated; accessed 12/5/2017.

[8] Wikipedia, "Maxim Integrated," https://en.wikipedia.org/wiki/Maxim_Integrated; accessed 12/5/2017.

Maxim Milestone Timeline (Ch. 23)

1983 – Maxim founded: and located at first Sunnyvale, California, HQ in old bank building

1984 – First products sold (in Germany, then Japan, then USA)

1985 – Office opened in Pangbourne, UK

1986 – MAX610: first proprietary product wins EDN Innovation of the Year

    – Maxim passes $10-million annual sales

    – MAX232: first integrated, 5V-only powered RS-232 transceiver milestone product

1987 – MAX690: First full-function microprocessor supervisor milestone product

1988 – HQ Office opened in Sunnyvale, California in the "Boy Scout Building"

    – Maxim's **Initial Public Offering** on NASDAQ market (February 29)

    – Maxim passes **$20-million** annual sales

1990 – Maxim acquires First Wafer Fab (in Sunnyvale, CA)

    – Maxim passes **$50-million** annual sales

    – MAX252: first isolated RS-232 solution in one package

1991 – Maxim GMbH Opened in Munich, Bavaria (Germany)

    – MAX900: comparator with best speed/power ratio

1992 – Office opened in Voisins le Bretonneux, France

    – MAX406: lowest power CMOS Op Amp

    – Maxim Japan (Tokyo) becomes wholly owned Maxim subsidiary

1993 – Office opened in Taipei, Taiwan

    – Maxim passes **$100-million** annual sales

    – MAX782: First complete notebook computer supply milestone product

    – DS80C320: high-speed, low-power microcontroller, a finalist for *Innovation of the Year* by *EDN Magazine* (a milestone product)

1994 – Design center opened in Colorado Springs, CO

    – Maxim acquires Tektronix Semiconductor Division in Beaverton, Oregon, including wafer fab and high-speed wafer process technologies

    – MAX3213: First 1μA supply current RS-232 IC with auto shutdown

1995 – Office opened in Seoul, Korea

    – Office opened in Singapore

    – UK main office moves to Theale

    – Maxim team established in Hong Kong

    – Design center opened in Tucson, Arizona

    – Design center opened in Chelmsford, MA

– Design center opened in Austin, TX

– Maxim passes **$250-million** annual sales

– MAX3260: First complete, 5V-Powered, 1 Gbps fiber-optic chipset

– MAX471: current-sense amplifier, a finalist for *Innovation of the Year* in *EDN Magazine*

1996 – Office opened in Osaka, Japan

– MAX1647: first SMBus smart battery charger

– MAX3238: autoShutdown/AutoWakeup RS-232 transceiver named *Innovation of the Year* by *EDN Magazine*

– Maxim's Charlie Allen and Dave Bingham named *Innovators of the Year* by *EDN Magazine*

– Office opened in Beijing, China

1997 – Office opened in Agrate Brianza, Milan, Italy

– Office opened in Sollentuna, Sweden

– MPOC testing facility opened in Cavite, Philippines

– X3 wafer fab acquired in San Jose, CA

1998 – Design Center opened in Phoenix, AZ

– Maxim's Hans Haagerats and Tad Yamaguchi named *Innovators of the Year* by *EDN Magazine*

– MAX2640: SiGe wireless chip named finalist for *Innovation of the Year* by *EDN Magazine*

– Maxim passes **$500-million** annual sales

1999 – Design center opened in Hanover, Germany

– Design center opened in Swindon, UK

– Design center opened in San Diego, CA

– Design center opened in Melbourne, FL

– MAX108: best 1.5Gsps sampling 8-bit analog-to-digital converter

– Richard Wilenken named a finalist for *Innovator of the Year* by *EDN Magazine*

2000 – MIPT test facility opened in Bangkok, Thailand

– Design center opened in Newbury/Andover, UK

– Design center opened in Milan, Italy

– Design center opened in Irvine, CA

– Office opened in Hillsboro, OR

– Design center opened in Fort Collins, CO

– Products introduced surpass 1,800

– Maxim passes **$1-billion** annual sales

– Office opened in Glattbrugg, Switzerland

2001 – Design center opened in Kawasaki, Japan

– Design center opened in Greensboro, North Carolina

– Design center opened in Raleigh, North Carolina

– Maxim acquires Dallas Semiconductor

– DS1077L: all silicon oscillator named *Product of the Year* by *analogZONE*

– DS20770: battery monitor/charger, a finalist for *Innovation of the Year* in *EDN Magazine*

– *Electronic Business Magazine* names Maxim's Jack Gifford CEO of the Year

– Design center opened in Champaign, IL

2002 – Design center opened in Catania, Sicily

– Design center opened in Bangalore, India

– MAX4410: directdrive stereo headphone driver named *Product of the Year* by *analogZone*

– DS80C400: network microcontroller, a finalist for *Innovation of the Year* in *EDN Magazine*

2003 – Office opened in Shanghai, China

– New wafer fab acquired in San Antonio, TX

– MAX2055: digitally controlled, variable-gain differential ADC driver/amp named *Product of the Year* by *analogZone*

– Maxim Yankees amateur baseball team win *Best in the West Invitational Tournament*

2004 – Maxim UK main office moves to Winnersh

– Maxim achieves TS16949 quality certification for automotive suppliers

– Nine Maxim products finalists for *Industry Awards*

– MAX1211: 65Msps, 12-bit, IF sampling ADC named *Top Product* by *Microwaves and RF Magazine*

– Maxim Yankees finish 13th in *Baseball Congress World Series*

– Relocated MIPT test facility opened in Chonburi, Thailand

2005 – Office opened in Shenzhen, China

– Design center opened in Istanbul, Turkey

– Design center opened in Brighton, MI

– Maxim joins the *Fortune 1000*

– QA support center opened in Japan

– Employees reach 8,000 worldwide

– Maxim products win four (and are finalists in five more) industry awards

– Design center opened in Gieres (Grenoble), France

– Design center opened in Cranston, RI

– Maxim Korea Daegu office established

2006 – Maxim Korea design center established in Seoul

– Sales team established in Bangalore, India

– Assembly facility opened in Batangas, Philippines

– MAX2711: loose cell NiMH charger wins *EDAW-NEC Power-Supply Product Award*

– MAX5547: dual, 10-bit, current-sink output DAC named *EE Times Ultimate Product Finalist*

– Design center opened in Westfield, IN

– Design center opened in Hartland, WI

2007 – Tunç Doluca becomes new President and CEO

– Maxim team established in Wuhan, China

– Maxim team established in Qingdao, China

– Maxim entered joint operating agreement with Seiko-Epson of a wafer fab in Sakata, Japan

– Design center Opened in Dresden, Germany

– Design center Opened in Delft, Holland

– DS3600: secure battery-backup controller named *Product of the Year* by *Electronic Products Magazine*

– MAX9508/MAX9512: video filters named *Product of the Year* by *analogZone*

– New wafer fab acquired in Irving, TX

– Maxim passes **$2-billion** annual sales
– Maxim team established in Chengdu, China
– Design center opened in Graz, Austria

ENDNOTES

Introduction

[1,2] Adam Lashinsky, "The Valley's Best Chipmaker May be Poised for a Fall... and That's the Good News. Here's One to Keep on Your Radar Screen," *Fortune*, (April 30, 2001), http://archive.fortune.com/magazines/fortune/fortune_archive/2001/04/30/301974/index.htm; accessed 12/05/2017.

[3] Rob Walker, "Interview with Jack Gifford," Silicon Genesis: An Oral History of Semiconductor Technology, (July 17, 2002), http://silicongenesis.stanford.edu/transcripts/gifford.htm; accessed 11/14/2017.

Chapter 1

[1] Dorris Kilbane, "Jack Gifford: Baseball's Loss was the World's Gain," [1]*Electronic Design*, (Dec. 6, 2009), http://www.electronicdesign.com/analog/jack-gifford-baseball-s-loss-was-world-s-gain; accessed 11/14/2017.

[2-5] Rob Walker, "Interview with Jack Gifford," *Silicon Genesis: An Oral History of Semiconductor Technology*, (July 17, 2002), http://silicongenesis.stanford.edu/transcripts/gifford.htm; accessed 11/14/2017.

Chapter 2

[1-3,13-15,17-23,31-32] Rob Walker, "Interview with Jack Gifford," *Silicon Genesis: An Oral History of Semiconductor Technology*, (July 17, 2002), http://silicongenesis.stanford.edu/transcripts/gifford.htm; accessed 11/14/2017.

[4-8] Wikipedia, "Traitorous Eight," https://en.wikipedia.org/wiki/Traitorous_eight; accessed 12/5/2017.

[9-12,16,35-38,40] Todd Nelson, "Maxim – Before it all Started," *Analog Footsteps*, (May 16, 2014), https://analogfootsteps.blogspot.com/2014/05/maxim-before-it-all-started.html; accessed 12/5/2017.

[24-30,33-34] Wikipedia, "Bob Widlar," https://en.wikipedia.org/wiki/Bob_Widlar; accessed 12/5/2017.

[39] Norman Doyle, "Fairchild Oral History Panel: Linear Integrated Circuit Products," Fairchild@50 (Panel Session #6) (Oct. 5, 2007), http://archive.computerhistory.org/resources/text/Oral_History/Fairchild_at_50/102658281.05.01.acc.pdf; pg. 4, accessed 12/5/2017.

Chapter 3

[1,3-10] Rob Walker, "Interview with Jack Gifford," *Silicon Genesis: An Oral History of Semiconductor Technology*, (July 17, 2002), http://silicongenesis.stanford.edu/transcripts/gifford.htm; accessed 11/14/2017.

[2] Staff, "Wild West Tales From John East, CEO of Actel For 22 Years," (November 22, 2010), https://www.electronicsweekly.com/blogs/mannerisms/yarns/wild-west-tales-from-john-east-2010-11/; accessed 12/06/2017.

[11-15] Wikipedia, "Traitorous Eight," https://en.wikipedia.org/wiki/Traitorous_eight; accessed 12/5/2017.

Chapter 4

[1] Rob Walker, "Interview with Jack Gifford," *Silicon Genesis: An Oral History of Semiconductor Technology*, (July 17, 2002), http://silicongenesis.stanford.edu/transcripts/gifford.htm; accessed 11/14/2017.

[2-4] Mark Simon, "Profile / Jerry Sanders / Silicon Valley's tough guy," *SFGate*, (October 4, 2001), http://www.sfgate.com/bayarea/article/PROFILE-Jerry-Sanders-Silicon-Valleys-tough-2873326.php; accessed 12/9/2017.

[5-15] Rob Walker, "Interview with Jack Gifford," *Silicon Genesis: An Oral History of Semiconductor Technology*, (July 17, 2002), http://silicongenesis.stanford.edu/transcripts/gifford.htm; accessed 11/14/2017.

Chapter 5

[1-7] Rob Walker, "Interview with Jack Gifford," *Silicon Genesis: An Oral History of Semiconductor Technology*, (July 17, 2002), http://silicongenesis.stanford.edu/transcripts/gifford.htm; accessed 12/26/2017.

[8] Wikipedia, "Jack Gifford," https://en.wikipedia.org/wiki/Jack_Gifford; accessed 12/5/2017.

Chapter 6

[1,4-12,16,17] Rob Walker, "Interview with Jack Gifford," *Silicon Genesis: An Oral History of Semiconductor Technology*, (July 17, 2002), http://silicongenesis.stanford.edu/transcripts/gifford.htm; accessed 12/26/2017.

[2] Paul Rako, "Voices: Dave Fullagar, analog-IC designer and entrepreneur," *DN Network*, (Nov. 20, 2007), http://www.edn.com/electronics-news/4326905/Voices-Dave-Fullagar-analog-IC-designer-and-entrepreneur; accessed 12/26/2017.

[3] Todd Nelson, "Maxim – Before it all Started," *Analog Footsteps*, (May 16, 2014), https://analogfootsteps.blogspot.com/2014/05/maxim-before-it-all-started.html; accessed 12/26/2017.

[13-15] Interview by David Laws, "Life and Times in the Semi-Conductor Industry," *Computer History Museum*,

(Sept. 9th, 2014), Mountain View, CA, http://www.computerhistory.org/collections/oralhistories/video/36/; accessed 12/26/2017.

Chapter 7

[1,16] Rob Georges, Interview at Maxim Integrated, San Jose, CA, 2017.

[2-17] Rob Walker, "Interview with Jack Gifford," *Silicon Genesis: An Oral History of Semiconductor Technology*, (July 17, 2002), http://silicongenesis.stanford.edu/transcripts/gifford.htm; accessed 12/26/2017.

Chapter 8

[1-2] Rob Walker, "Interview with Jack Gifford," *Silicon Genesis: An Oral History of Semiconductor Technology*, (July 17, 2002), http://silicongenesis.stanford.edu/transcripts/gifford.htm; accessed 12/26/2017.

[3] Todd Nelson, "Maxim – Before it all Started," *Analog Footsteps*, (May 16, 2014), https://analogfootsteps.blogspot.com/2014/05/maxim-before-it-all-started.html; accessed 12/26/2017.

Chapter 9

[1] Eric S. Hintz, "Historic Silicon Valley Bar and Restaurant Review," *Lemelson Center*

for the Study of Invention and Innovation, (September 9, 2013), http://invention.si.edu/historic-silicon-valley-bar-and-restaurant-review; accessed 2/19/2018.

[2] Todd Nelson, "Maxim – Before it all Started," *Analog Footsteps*, (May 16, 2014), https://analogfootsteps.blogspot.com/2014/05/maxim-before-it-all-started.html;   accessed 12/5/2017.

Chapter 18

[1] Wikipedia, "Black Monday," https://en.wikipedia.org/wiki/Black_Monday_(1987); accessed 12/5/2017.

[2] Funding Universe, "Maxim Integrated Products, Inc. History," http://www.fundinguniverse.com/company-histories/maxim-integrated-products-inc-history/; accessed 9/24/2018.

[3] Wikipedia, "Volcanic Ash," https://en.wikipedia.org/wiki/Volcanic_ash; accessed 9/24/2018.

[4] Alaska Volcano Observatory, "Redoubt Reported Activity," https://avo.alaska.edu/volcanoes/activity.php?volcname= Redoubt&page=impact&eruptionid=442;   accessed 9/24/2018.

[5] Pratima Rao, "The Book of Jack," (1997).

Chapter 19

[1-2] Pratima Rao, "The Book of Jack," (1997).

Chapter 21

[1] Alan Lewis and Dan McKone, "So Many M&A Deals Fail Because Companies Overlook This Simple Strategy," Harvard Business Review, (May 10, 2016), https://hbr.org/2016/05/so-many-ma-deals-fail-because-companies-overlook-this-simple-strategy; accessed 5/25/2018.

[2] Maxim Integrated, "Acquiring Fabs to Control Our Own Business," Maxim Insider 25th year anniversary issue, (2,008).

Chapter 23

[1] Pratima Rao, "The Book of Jack," (1997).

[2] The Wall Street Transcript, Maxim Integrated Products Inc. (MXIM),   Vol.   CIV Number 9, (May 29, 1989).

Chapter 24

[1] Todd Nelson, "Maxim – Before it all Started," *Analog Footsteps*, (May 16, 2014), https://analogfootsteps.blogspot.com/2014/05/maxim-before-it-all-started.html; accessed 12/5/2017.

Chapter 27

[1] Business Wire, "Maxim Integrated Products Founder John F. Gifford Retires as Chairman and CEO for Health Reasons." (Dec. 19, 2006), https://www.businesswire.com/news/home/20061219006021/en/Maxim-Integrated-Products-Founder-John-F.-Gifford; accessed 9/26/2018.

[2] Los Angeles Times, "John F. (Jack) Gifford," http://www.legacy.com/obituaries/latimes/obituary.aspx?n=john-f-gifford-jack&pid=122966540; accessed 9/26/2018.

[3] Mark Schwanhausser, "SEC files backdating charges against ex-Maxim execs," San Jose Mercury News, (Dec. 4, 2007), https://www.mercurynews.com/2007/12/04/sec-files-backdating-charges-against-ex-maxim-execs/; accessed 9/26/2018.

[4] Ed Medlin, "Maxim Reaches Agreement in Principle to Settle Class Action Stock Option Litigation," Maxim Integrated, (May 5, 2010), https://www.sec.gov/Archives/edgar/data/743316/000144530510000431/maximq310revisedeprex992.htm; accessed 9/26/2018.

Chapter 29

[1-2] Business Wire, "Maxim Integrated Products Founder John F. Gifford Retires as Chairman and CEO for Health Reasons." (Dec. 19, 2006), https://www.businesswire.com/news/home/20061219006021/en/Maxim-Integrated-Products-Founder-John-F.-Gifford; accessed 9/26/2018.

[3] Wikipedia, "Jack Gifford," https://en.wikipedia.org/wiki/Jack_Gifford#cite_note-11; accessed 12/5/2017.

[4] Wikipedia, "Jack Gifford," https://en.wikipedia.org/wiki/Jack_Gifford; accessed 12/5/2017.

[5] Los Angeles Times, "John F. (Jack) Gifford," http://www.legacy.com/obituaries/latimes/obituary.aspx?n=john-f-gifford-jack&pid=122966540; accessed 9/26/2018.

Lightning Source UK Ltd.
Milton Keynes UK
UKHW020037090321
379992UK00004B/267/J